Finding Private Venture Capital for Your Firm

Finding Private Venture Capital for Your Firm: A Complete Guide

ROBERT J. GASTON

WILEY

JOHN WILEY & SONS

New York • Chichester • Brisbane • Toronto • Singapore

658.152
G 256

Copyright © 1989 by John Wiley & Sons, Inc.

All rights reserved. Published simultaneously in Canada.

Reproduction or translation of any part of this work
beyond that permitted by Section 107 or 108 of the
1976 United States Copyright Act without the permission
of the copyright owner is unlawful. Requests for
permission or further information should be addressed to
the Permissions Department, John Wiley & Sons, Inc.

This publication is designed to provide accurate and
authoritative information in regard to the subject
matter covered. It is sold with the understanding that
the publisher is not engaged in rendering legal, accounting,
or other professional service. If legal advice or other
expert assistance is required, the services of a competent
professional person should be sought. *From a Declaration
of Principles jointly adopted by a Committee of the
American Bar Association and a Committee of Publishers.*

Library of Congress Cataloging in Publication Data

Gaston, Robert J.
  Finding private venture capital for your firm: A complete guide/Robert J. Gaston.
    p. cm.
  Bibliography: p.
  ISBN 0-471-61008-9
  1. Venture capital. I. Title.
  HG4963.G37   1989
  658.1′5224—dc19   88-15519
                                                              CIP

Printed in the United States of America

10 9 8 7 6 5 4 3 2 1

To
JDB, BLB, RWG, and JRG
but most of all to
CLG

≡ ACKNOWLEDGMENTS ≡

During more than two decades of professional life I have learned from more people than I can possibly name. Those I would like to acknowledge personally have been instrumental in one way or another in bringing this book to life. My very able research associate, Sharon E. Bell, has contributed materially through the past five years toward the underlying database, as has my expert statistical consultant, Rachel Craig. Thomas A. Gray ably leads the staff at the U.S. Small Business Administration's Office of Economic Research. He and others, including Frank Swain, Chief Council for Advocacy, Charles Ou, Bruce Phillips, and Bill Whiston, had the faith, foresight, and endurance to see the underlying program through its five-year duration. Their support and that of the entire SBA staff were absolutely vital. Bruce Herrick of Washington and Lee University has been a friend, colleague, mentor, and sometimes conscience to me since I was his student at UCLA, where they know what markets are all about. Professor Ron Shrieves of the Finance Department of the University of Tennessee first suggested the idea of publishing in book form. Many others have assisted and encouraged me from the start. Clearly none can be cited without including Ed Miller, Mel Koons, Vice-President of the Tennessee Innovation Center, and Dr. Hugh Granade, Chief of Economic Development for the Tennessee Valley Authority. William Wetzel and C. Seymour of the University of New Hampshire provided inspiration. Most of all, CLG was there from first to last.

The Wiley staff has been outstanding in its aid in transforming a terse technical report into a practical tool for both Angels and entrepreneurs. Special thanks to my editor, Mike Hamilton, and to Marilyn Dibbs, his administrative assistant.

Thanks is not enough for the hundreds of business Angels who responded to an obscure, burdensome questionnaire and who forever will remain anonymous, as I promised.

Technical Note: The draft manuscript was written in pencil on yellow pads. It was translated by a bilingual artist into English on an IBM PC-XT using WordPerfect software.

CONTENTS

Finding Private Venture Capital for Your Firm

═ INTRODUCTION ═

The difficulty of finding risk capital is the number one barrier preventing good business ideas from becoming profitable enterprises, because most entrepreneurs do not qualify for traditional funding. Many sound business ideas are too risky for commercial bankers, most entrepreneurs can only dream of a public stock offering, and start-up firms usually can't offer the extremely high payoffs required by professional venture capitalists. Lack of outside cash backing causes too many good business plans to gather dust or become lost to someone else. Yet nearly 600,000 new businesses are launched each year. Of these, only 2100 are financed by professional venture capitalists, who reject 99 percent of all deals they see. Thousands of entrepreneurs get their "go ahead" cash directly from private investors whom I call "business Angels."

Business Angels are the most important but least understood suppliers of risk capital to new and growing firms. They're important because they are the largest suppliers of outside risk capital, and they're misunderstood because they are diverse, dispersed, and elusive. Precisely what is a business Angel? Simply put, Angels are private individuals who supply risk capital dollars directly (without paid middlemen) to new or growing small businesses. They are also known as informal investors, "check writers," and "money men," as well as by many other terms. For simplicity, this book refers to them as *Angels*.

Finding Angels is not easy, because they have a passion for privacy and are deliberately anonymous. Without help the search for an Angel can be an expensive, time-consuming, hit-or-miss affair. The search is studded with pitfalls and dead ends that often result in failure and frustration. Until now, entrepreneurs have had to learn for themselves, the hard way. Doing it the hard way is no longer necessary, however, because this book provides the first comprehensive guide to the investment preferences and behavior of Angels. It is the only source of systematic and authentic

data based on the real investment experience of over 400 Angels throughout the United States. It's only a bit of an exaggeration to say that you
will learn almost everything here about Angels except their names and
telephone numbers.

Hundreds of books have been written about public stock markets and
venture capital firms, but until now there has been no comprehensive
source of information on how the informal (Angel) market works. In the
past the Angel market segment has been a greatly underestimated, virtually invisible, do-it-yourself affair. Yet all of us have heard "war stories"
of how the fabulous wealth and business success achieved by some local
entrepreneur was started with a direct Angel investment. In fact, the pre-
eminent entrepreneur of the twentieth century, Henry Ford, was launched
into auto manufacturing by a total of $41,500 invested by five Angels.
Ford's Angels earned $145 million on that investment between 1903
and 1919!

Angels are a diverse and dispersed population of individuals, most
of whom are successful entrepreneurs themselves. They invest both their
dollars and their experience to ensure success for their chosen entrepreneurs. They finance new and growing firms that usually do not qualify
for other sources of capital. Most importantly, it is sound business deals
and not Angels that are in short supply. Forget most of the financial
"folklore" you have heard about Angels; much of it is simply not true.

In the chapters that follow, I describe for the first time the real-world
market experience of actual Angels, successful entrepreneurs, and the
deals they make together. I present facts, not theory—success probabilities, not "blue sky" hypotheses. In other words, the focus of this book
is on how Angel capital markets actually operate. These pages are designed to extract practical financial guidelines from the complex behavior
of Angels as they have actually gone about the work of financing new
and growing small firms. The key theme that runs throughout this volume
is that the financial behavior and experience of Angels are widely diverse,
accommodating many different types of winning combinations of Angels,
entrepreneurs, and deals.

This is not a technical book for sophisticated investors or entrepreneurs. Instead, it is intended as an introduction only. Despite the abundance of facts that appear here, understanding them does not require great
experience in business finance or any other special skills. The operation of the Angel financial market can be understood in the same way
that most card games are understood: Learn the rules and play the odds
to win. I will explain the Angel capital market rules as they are really
played and reveal the odds for the hand you hold. The objective seems
simple enough, but a book like this has never been offered before, despite
the fact that thousands of people play the informal investment "game"

every day. Everyone in that sense is a beginner and will benefit from what is presented here.

I use both text description and data to clarify how Angel financial markets work, because the numbers do not "speak for *themselves*." Those readers who are looking for sophisticated data analysis and advanced finance theory will be disappointed. But those who desire new insight into the largest of all risk capital markets will be richly rewarded. Even business veterans with extensive experience at raising or investing capital will gain new insights and better understanding of their own performance by comparison to that of their peers, as profiled in this book. The simple format used to present market odds (behavior) and a glossary of basic terms are evidence of the book's elementary approach to this important capital market.

While the message here is straightforward and the approach is as uncomplicated as possible, the reader will find the contents practical and useful. The information, most of which has never before been published, provides the necessary foundation for relationships between entrepreneurs and investors, who often end up "living together" for 4 to 10 years or more. What you can gain here is a basis for self-appraisal that underscores the strengths of your business plans and also their weaknesses. With new understanding gained from these pages, you will have the tools to rethink your business plans and strategy and adjust them where possible to increase the odds of winning the capital dollars you need. By revising your financial strategy to maximize your chances of success, you acquire more realistic expectations, and success becomes more likely and will come faster and at less cost.

ANGEL CAPITAL MARKETS

The Angel market segment, like any market, is composed of suppliers (Angels) and demanders (entrepreneurs) who engage in transactions (investment deals). The objective is to show how each of these elements responds to a variety of specific financial circumstances. Angel markets differ from the public and venture capital firm markets in clear and important ways, including:

- Balkanization (local markets only)
- Surplus capital dollars
- Casual or no organization
- Private people and private deals (nondisclosure)
- Leading supplier of external risk capital
- One-source financing (equity and loans in one place)

These differences are briefly explained in the following subsections.

Balkanization (Local Markets Only)

The formal, organized capital markets (public offerings and professional venture capitalists) operate on a national and international scale based in well-known financial centers such as New York, London, and Tokyo. Informal (Angel) markets are local; rarely do Angels invest farther than 150 miles from home. Fortunately for entrepreneurs, Angels live virtually everywhere. Wherever self-made, successful business owners live is where you find Angels. The single best predictor of where Angels can be found is the size of the local population; the typical ratio is 1 Angel for every 250 adults. Therefore, in a city of 250,000 adults there are about 1000 Angels, give or take a few. If the city size doubles, so does the number of Angels in the local market.

Surplus Capital Dollars

Contrary to every notion you might have about how scarce risk capital is, Angels can't find enough good deals! The conventional wisdom says there is a small business capital shortage, but it just isn't so. The majority of Angels say they want to invest more than opportunity has allowed. The dollar surplus averages out at 35 percent for each and every Angel (although some don't want to invest more). The so-called shortage is not lack of available capital but the inability of entrepreneurs and Angels to find each other and come to terms.

Casual or No Organization

In contrast to the situation in formal capital markets, there are no paid middlemen in the informal market. Nobody has figured out exactly how to do it. But some new ideas are being tried. (See, for example, the section on computerized matching services in Chapter 5.) Presently, entrepreneurs hunting dollars must operate on a do-it-yourself basis. This hit-or-miss system has been dictated by the fact that both Angels and entrepreneurs are searching around in the dark for each other, almost as if they are playing a giant game of hide-and-seek with everyone blindfolded. If there is any system at all, it exists as a loose network of Angels and their personal friends and associates. Worse yet, this "old-boy" system seems to operate only on the supply side of the informal market (among Angels) and then only to circulate some general information about the availability of a few deals they happen to stumble on. One of the major assets of this book is that it provides systematic knowledge about how the Angel market operates and how that information system can be more easily penetrated and made to work for your success.

Private People, Private Deals

Angels are elusive and secretive and operate as individuals. This is unlike the situation in formal markets, where public disclosure of big deals handled by large organizations is routine. Most informal investment deals are composed of 3 to 5 individual Angels—rarely more than 10. While a few local Angels may be linked into loose information networks, they act as individuals when they commit their personal wealth. The deals that result are not often heard about except via rumor or personal anecdote.

Leading Supplier of External Risk Capital

An Angel typically commits $37,500 equity to each investment. But there are so many Angels that their commitments add up to over $32 billion in equity financing each year. This makes Angels the single largest supplier of external equity capital to new and growing small businesses in the United States. By contrast, professional venture capitalists supply only about $3 to $8 billion per year, and small business public stock issues are not even in the same league. Moreover, Angels are virtually the only source of external risk capital outside of the major financial centers of the United States.

One-Source Financing

Almost 9 out of 10 Angels provide personal loans or personally guaranteed loans to entrepreneurs over and above their equity dollar commitment. Angel loans boost their total dollar commitment by 57 percent over equity alone. Industry practice discourages loans from professional venture capitalists, and government regulations divide public markets into separate sources for equity (stocks) and loans (bonds). At present, commercial banks lend working capital (but not if it's risky), and legally they can't advance equity funds. Angels do it all. Since Angel loans are usually more "friendly and patient" than those from outside lenders, they take on much of the riskiness of ownership funds and become "near equity" dollars.

Other market differences exist, too. Some investments are attractive to business Angels but unattractive to others, especially venture capital firms. Individual business Angels tend to invest in riskier, early stage situations (start-up and early growth). They invest smaller amounts (usually $25,000 to $50,000 in any one deal) less frequently (approximately one deal every 18 months). Angels typically participate with friends and business associates to finance larger transactions. They tend to have more patient exit horizons (larger holding periods) than professional venture capitalists. Thus, Angels can accommodate companies with limited prospects for a public stock offering or merger with a larger firm. Finally, Angel investment decisions are often influenced by nonfinancial rewards, so-called "hot buttons." These hot-button motives include creating local jobs, developing humanitarian technology, supporting female and minority entrepreneurs, and assisting young entrepreneurs to build successful ventures.

Angel investments and markets clearly differ from other market segments, but they all share a strong concern for the quality of management and the policy of rewards equal to the risks taken. Despite their low profile, Angels represent the most potent and underused pool of risk capital available. Just how big, we see next.

MARKET SCALE

Some eye-opening facts lie behind the preceding Angel market outline. Each year, a pool of about 720,000 U.S. Angels makes some 490,000 investments in 87,000 entrepreneurs. The total dollars of risk capital that change hands add up to almost $56 billion annually, of which about $32 billion is equity and $24 billion appears as loans/guarantees. Depending on the level of market activity, the $56 billion yearly total may range upward to $82 billion or as low as $32 billion. Further, Angels wanted to but were unable to invest some $20 billion more (35 percent) than they did. Consequently, the total sum of available risk capital each year tops $76 billion. Professional venture capital markets are small by comparison. They invest less than one-tenth as many dollars and assist only one-fortieth as many entrepreneurs.

ANGEL MARKET PROFILES

The Angel market segments described above are summarized throughout this book by market profiles. The first three profiles describe Angels, entrepreneurs, and their deals. Market Profile 1-1 on page 16 is a composite of the 20 key Angel traits that are most common in the market; the second profile, on page 29, presents the 10 most likely characteristics of successful entrepreneurs and their firms; and Profile 3-1, on page 43, lists 10 basic elements that commonly structure the actual deals between Angels and entrepreneurs. Taken together, these first three market profiles (1-1, 2-1, and 3-1) are the basis of later chapters whose comparative profiles include all three segments (Angel, entrepreneur, and deal) and are keyed to specific business circumstances, such as amount of cash needed (Chapter 6); industry—retail, manufacturing, and so on (Chapter 9); geographical location (Chapter 10); business growth stage (Chapter 8); voting control issues (Chapter 6); and different Angel types (Chapter 4).

Each of the 40 items in the basic market profile represents either a large share of Angel market behavior or at least its median. The median value is presented when large majorities don't exist because it represents the most practical center of gravity of market experience. More precisely, the median divides all experience into two equal parts; half the experience is higher than the median and half is smaller. The mean value or common average is not often used because it is overly influenced by extremely high or low values and thus is distorted by the unusual experience of only a few Angels. To illustrate this point, the median amount of equity dollars invested by one Angel in one firm is $37,500, but the average (or mean value) is $67,800. This great difference exists because some Angels made single investments as large as $800,000. From the viewpoint of the entrepreneur, the probability of encountering the median, $37,500, is greater than that of obtaining the distorted value of $67,800.

Market profiles by themselves can be misleading because they cover up the rich underlying diversity of actual experience. The text discussion accompanying each profile provides the necessary look behind the profile composite, giving needed detail and drawing the reader's attention to key points. In brief, beware of using the market profiles without a good feel for the diversity of experience explained in the text. In addition, the numbers representing market behavior are often not exact. This means that you should not attach much importance to "small" numerical differences. Small means about 4 percentage points, plus or minus. For example, 72 percent of the Angels in the Los Angeles market are satisfied with the performance of their entrepreneurs, as are 75 percent in the New York market. Since these numbers are within 8 percentage points of each other, they should not be considered "different" from each other. However, if the percentages were 61 and 75, respectively, they would be considered different levels of satisfaction.

The reader may notice changes of perspective or point of view within a single chapter. Because the focus in most chapters is on how the market and its three main elements interact, the book examines the market separately and jointly through the perspective of Angels, entrepreneurs, and the deals they make. To emphasize one at the expense of the other two would lead to an overly simplistic, distorted view of what really happens. Real markets are complex, and, like the elephant analyzed by the blind men, is not a rope, wall, or log, as would seem to be true from a "blind" or single perspective.

DATA ORIGINS

The market profiles and accompanying discussion are based on a series of comprehensive surveys of the actual investment experience of 435 active Angels* who reported their experience in making almost 900 investments valued at about $60 million during the five-year period ending in 1987. The Angels surveyed were not just any we could find but were carefully screened and identified through a scientific probability sample of 240,000 U.S. business enterprises. The five-year survey research program was supported in part by the Office of Economic Research of the U.S. Small Business Administration, and additional work is still in progress.

All data have both strengths and limitations, and this book's portrait of the business Angel financial market is no exception. Its major strength is that it is the first comprehensive and factual description of real-world Angels' investment experience based upon careful scientific data collection. Some of the most important data limits are worth noting. The experience summarized here is not the last word but only the first on the subject; much more needs to be discovered and made known. Generally, the text offers few explanations of *why* things happen. At this stage of our knowledge it is a major advance just to describe what is actually taking place, without attempting to explain why. Another limitation is that the descriptions given here are static—they are fixed snapshots of a continuing process. Consequently, the evidence provided is only a glimpse of an intricate, ongoing process whose fundamental nature is dynamic. Descriptions of Angel investment experience are not reinforced with elaborate personal anecdotes, because the survey facts permit advancing beyond "war stories." Moreover, the promise of absolute confidentiality I gave to the cooperating Angels forbids revealing any individual details. Finally, market behavior is human behavior and therefore very complex. In summarizing that behavior, there is always a risk that it can become overly simplistic.

PREVIEW OF CHAPTERS

The market profiles of Angels, entrepreneurs, and their deals are the prime topic of the first three chapters. Each of these basic profile subparts is introduced, explained, and examined in a separate chapter, beginning with Angels in Chapter 1, continuing with successful entrepreneurs in Chapter 2, and finishing with the structure of investment deals in Chapter 3. After the profile subparts are established, they are used as a basis for comparison in most subsequent chapters.

*Robert J. Gaston and S. E. Bell, *The Informal Supply of Capital*. Final report on contract SBA-2024-AER-87, U.S. Small Business Administration Office of Economic Research, by the Applied Economics Group, Inc., Knoxville, Tenn. 1988. Statements and conclusions herein are those of the authors and not necessarily the views of the U.S. government or the Small Business Administration.

Portrait of an Angel (Chapter 1)

There is no stereotypical Angel, but there is a nationwide composite of Angels' leading characteristics. This U.S. Composite Angel is the beginning point for our understanding of Angel market behavior. The composite portrait is made of 20 key characteristics, each of which is defined, interpreted, and dissected into its diverse component pieces. The 20 characteristics, taken collectively, form the baseline for comparison with specialized market profiles in later chapters.

Successful Entrepreneurs (Chapter 2)

The second part of the basic market profile, which deals with successful entrepreneurs, is developed in Chapter 2. These entrepreneurs have actually obtained financing from one or more Angels. This chapter characterizes that success by introducing, describing, and analyzing their 10-point composite profile. This profile becomes the reference point for later comparisons with important market segments. Chapter 2 addresses the main characteristics of successful entrepreneurs/firms, including:

- Psychological biography
- Company size (employment, sales)
- Firm's life-cycle stage
- Distance (miles) from investors
- Total equity dollars received
- Loans from Angels
- Number of Angel investors
- Industry

Real Deals in the Real World (Chapter 3)

The third and final part of the market profile is introduced in Chapter 3, which illustrates the principal elements commonly included in the investment deals between Angels and entrepreneurs. The structure of actual investment deals is highlighted by a 10-point profile, using the U.S. Composite Deal as the beginning example. Each deal element and its major variants are explained and interpreted. Major deal elements include:

- Voting control
- Return on investment (ROI)
- Risk expectations
- Equity pricing
- Cash-out provisions
- Loans and guarantees
- Buy-back features

With the conclusion of Chapter 3, the three separate market profile subparts are rejoined into a single market profile in many subsequent chapters, beginning with Chapter 4. These later chapters contain a series of specially constructed profiles that reveal important market differences.

The Cast of Angels (Chapter 4)

In Chapter 1, the U.S. Composite Angel is described in detail. In Chapter 4, I present a series of 10 special types of Angels who differ in ways that are important for the investment process. Each subtype is compared to the U.S. Composite, and the important differences are highlighted and discussed. The 10 types of Angels are:

- Devils—Angels who gain control of the company
- Godfathers—Successful, semiretired, consultants/mentors
- Peers—Active business owners helping new entrepreneurs, with a vested interest in the market, industry, or individual entrepreneur
- Cousin Randy—A family-only investor
- Dr. Kildare—Professionals such as MDs, CPAs, lawyers, and others
- Corporate Achievers—Business professionals with some success in a large corporate organization but who want to be more entrepreneurial and in top-management roles
- Daddy Warbucks—The one-third minority of Angels who are as rich as all Angels are commonly—and incorrectly—believed to be
- High-Tech Angels—Investors who invest only in firms manufacturing high-technology products
- The Stockholder—An Angel who does not participate in the firm's operations
- Very Hungry Angels—Angels who want to invest over 100 percent more than deal flow permits

Where to Look and What to Say (Chapter 5)

Chapter 5 gives the facts on Angels' geographical limits, how their decisions are affected by the information channel they use, exactly what information Angels find most useful, how Angels who say ''yes'' often can be spotted, and why serious deals are sometimes killed.

I discuss the main channels of communication used (and not used) by Angels, along with the most important types of information they rely on to make their investment decisions. Market profiles are examined for both the direct approach (by entrepreneurs) and the indirect approach (through the Angels' friends and associates). Emphasis is placed on how the market profiles and market behavior change from one information channel to another and on the importance of the information content.

What is it exactly that Angels want to know? This chapter reveals the seven pieces of information that are key to an investment decision and their relative importance in Angels' judgments. Many seriously considered deals are killed (about one-third fail), and the reasons are many. I present the nine leading reasons, along with Angels' evaluation of their relative importance.

Some Angels are one-shot investors, and others invest more often. The frequency of saying "yes" to investment proposals varies over a wide range from only once in a lifetime to several times a year. The focus is to distinguish "high-probability Angels" from their "seldom-invest" colleagues. The market profiles and the accompanying discussion illuminate how to identify high-potential Angels and how they are likely to respond.

Pricing the Deal: Issues of Investment Size, Risk, Control, and Return (Chapter 6)

A central issue in any investment transaction is the Angel's return on investment, ROI. This is determined by equity price, ownership share, risk assessments, and other factors. As Chapter 6 demonstrates, there is a wide range of Angel behavior on each of these critical "pricing issues." The capital needs of entrepreneurs do not come in neat, uniform packages (nor do business Angels); the objective of the chapter is to examine market differences as revealed by answers to the following questions:

- How does investment equity size change market performance and equity pricing factors?

- How do market profiles change as Angel risk perceptions change?

- How do rising ROI expectations actually change Angels' investment behavior?

- How does voting control vary with risk and ROI, and how does the market vary with different degrees of voting control at stake?

Super Angel-Entrepreneur Matchups and Others (Chapter 7)

Some combinations of Angels and entrepreneurs are outstandingly successful, and others are not. Achieving the right combination does not ensure a firm's success, but the wrong matchup can spell disaster. Chapter 7 focuses primarily on the positive side of matchups, where business success has greatly exceeded initial expectations. This chapter dissects the market profiles of very successful Angels, entrepreneurs, and their deals. The down side—that is, very unsuccessful combinations—is explored in a section titled "The Odd Couples." Finally, under the heading "Mixed Couples," we see what happens when Angels and professional venture capitalists invest in the same firm.

When to Look for Angels (Chapter 8)

When entrepreneurs need external capital, their firm will likely occupy one of four growth or life-cycle stages. Chapter 8 highlights Angels who have definitive experiences among these growth stages, which influence what he or she looks for in an investment, and how subsequent deals are structured.

Angels Who Already Like Your Business (Chapter 9)

Firms exist in specific industries (e.g., manufacturing, retail, services, etc.), and Angels have definite industry preferences. The consequence of Angels' industry preferences is that each industry has its own market profile. Success in attracting Angels to retail trade is not necessarily useful if your industry happens to be manufacturing. Chapter 9 presents and explains the market profiles for seven major industry groups.

Angels Where You Live (Chapter 10)

Angels keep their money close to home, and their characteristics and those of sucessful entrepreneurs and investment deals change from one metropolitan area to another. Houston investors and entrepreneurs want the facts for their market; they don't want to be misled by market patterns in Boston, San Francisco, or some mythical composite of U.S. cities. Chapter 10 reveals the local market conditions for 26 major metropolitan and surrounding areas.

Devils, Dead Ends, and Deal Breakers (Chapter 11)

In Chapters 1 through 10, emphasis is on the positive—or "what you should do or look for"—aspects of successful Angel financing. That principle is reversed in Chapter 11. Knowing when to be cautious and what situations to avoid increases the probability of success. For example, some investors want to get control of the firm from the entrepreneur. These investors are often considered business "Devils" rather than Angels. Entrepreneurs should know how Devils operate and what to look for to increase their chances of avoiding them. The chapter highlights a series of specific investment scenarios that often lead to trouble, including the most common trouble spots, blind alleys, and effective ways to sidetrack investment deals. Accompanying each "down side" example is a reciprocal, success-oriented example. Some of the featured scenarios are:

- Business Devils—Investors who get voting control of the firm away from the entrepreneurs
- High Flyers—Angels who want only the super-high payoff
- Impatient Angels—Angels who demand quick payoff via a fast exit

- Green Angels—Investors without any personal entrepreneurial experience
- Nickel-and-Dime Angels—Those who make very small investments only
- Corporate Achievers—Frustrated middle managers who "jump ship" by buying into a small firm and who often take over
- Kiss of Death—Investment situations that, while not always absolutely fatal, are unlikely to succeed

Custom Market Profiles (Chapter 12)

The concluding chapter presents five specific examples of entrepreneurs/firms that need first-stage external financing. Each example "walks" the reader through the process of assembling a customized market profile that targets the probable Angels and their unwritten investment rules. The structure of the most likely deal is also defined. Each case is tailored to a set of six specific business circumstances, including:

- City location
- Firm's industry
- Capital size needed
- Firm's growth stage
- Maximum ROI
- Maximum voting control

The cases are set up so that the reader can easily substitute his or her own case to produce a customized Angel market strategy that is destined for success.

1

PORTRAIT OF AN ANGEL

Medieval theologians were never able to decide how many Angels could stand on the head of a pin because their Angels were spiritual and heavenly. Business Angels, while not exactly heavenly, have fulfilled the dreams of many entrepreneurs. Business Angels are the supply side of the informal capital market. They are one of three market parts, the others being entrepreneurs (demanders) and deals (transactions between Angels and entrepreneurs). Understanding the informal market requires an awareness of each of its parts. This is the first of three chapters that together present, define, and interpret the dimensions of the Angel market profile, a summary of the most frequent (probable) characteristics of the informal capital market. Specifically, this chapter presents the profile of the U.S. Composite Angel. This is no simple task, since Angels are both varied and complex. Each profile element is defined and interpreted, and the diversity of Angels' underlying experience is examined.

To begin our exploration of how Angels operate, let us examine the U.S. Composite Angel profile. This profile is a useful fiction—too general to be used for specific planning purposes, but accurate in outlining the most common characteristics of the 435 Angels surveyed. With this prototypical profile we can begin to develop practical answers to some important questions:

- How will I know a real Angel when I meet one?
- How active are Angels?
- What is their investment capacity?
- What are Angels' investment targets?

The U.S. Composite Angel is nothing more than the "center of gravity" of the characteristics of Angels all over the United States. This "fictional" profile is used to introduce terms, concepts, and interpretations of what

Angels are all about. It also can serve to familiarize the reader with the formal appearance of Angel profiles, so they will be easily recognized and understood when they are encountered in later chapters. The U.S. Composite Angel is the baseline standard of reference. This baseline will be used to highlight important differences that exist among the Angel market segments—differences that can make or break specific business plans.

U.S. COMPOSITE ANGEL

Despite their prevalence, Angels do not generally resemble the average person, except that both have wide-ranging experience and behavior. Generalizing from the experience of individuals as diverse as Angels can be hazardous if it leads to overemphasis on misleading "averages." The risk is acceptable if the wealth of individual experience points to some common and useful patterns. Those patterns are shown in Profile 1-1. Like any summary, the profile should be approached with caution. It is important to understand both the composite profile and the wide variety of Angel experience behind it. The theme that repeatedly emerges from Angels' investment behavior is clear: Neither Angels nor their capital comes in neat, uniform packages.

Profile 1-1 is made up of 20 composite Angel characteristics organized into four parts. The first seven items are essentially a biographical summary of the Angels' personal attributes. The second six entries are related to their degree of market activity. The third set shows their total (portfolio) investment commitment. Lastly, the profile shows Angels' investment objectives.

What kind of portrait does the U.S. Composite profile reflect? The average investor is a business owner with personal entrepreneurial experience. He is a 47-year-old white male with a college degree in business or engineering. He has substantial income of about $90,000 per year, but he is *not* a millionaire. The median net worth of the typical Angel is $750,000. The investor's business associates and personal friends are equally ranked as the most frequent and reliable sources of information about investment opportunities. He accepts only 3 out of every 10 investment opportunities that he investigates. Rejection of a proposed deal most often occurs because the projected growth rate was insufficient. Over the 3-year period covered by the survey, the typical Angel added 2 investments, 1 every 18 months or so, to his average portfolio size of 3.5 firms. In any given investment he participates along with 2 other individuals as coinvestors. These investments are "arm's-length" deals; only 1 in 10 investments is made in a family-owned firm.

PROFILE 1-1. U.S. Angel (Composite)

- Business owner/manager is principal occupation (69%)
- Has personal entrepreneurial experience (83%)
- 47 years old*
- White male (84%)
- College degree (72%) in business (44%) or engineering (19%)
- $90,000 annual income*
- $750,000 net worth*

- Friends and associates are primary information source
- Accepts 3 out of 10 investment opportunities*
- Rejects deals mostly due to insufficient growth potential
- Invests about every 18 months* and has 3.5 firms in portfolio
- Satisfied with past investments (72%)
- Two other coinvestors* per deal

- $131,000 informal equity invested in portfolio*
- $75,000 more via loans/guarantees to portfolio firms*

- Prefers investing in service or finance, insurance, and real estate firms (35%)
- Minimum ROI target is 22% per year
- Active as a consultant, board member, or employee (81%)
- Does not seek voting control (85%)
- Wants to invest 35% more than oppoortunity permits

---

*Median value—half higher, half lower.

The U.S. Composite Angel has invested a total of $206,000 in his informal portfolio, of which $131,000 (64%) is equity and another $75,000 (36% percent) represents his personal loans or loan guarantees. By a margin of over three to one, these investments have met or exceeded the Angel's expectations.

Angel investment targets favor a minimum annual rate of return (ROI) of 22 percent from a start-up firm in the service or finance, insurance, and real estate industries. Most often he invests within 50 miles of his home or office. The informal investor usually contributes time and experience in addition to money. He becomes actively involved in company operations, usually as a consultant but frequently as a board member or employee. Angels' investment objectives usually do not include gaining control of the firm. A majority of Angels have not been able to invest as much as desired. On average, investors say they would have invested about 35% more than they did, if given sufficient opportunity.

The composite profile raises almost as many questions as it answers. Some of them will be answered here or in later chapters, but not all can be answered. Important information is still missing. For example, knowledge about why Angels are motivated to invest the way they do is not available. Important information about many other factors could not be collected, so that at best we have a limited picture. The profile is a static snapshot of a dynamic human process that does not stand still; no matter how complete or detailed our view, it is still frozen in time. Even the "facts" aren't really facts because they are based on a sample of all Angels. The percentage numbers presented here are not precise enough to be significant within a range of plus or minus four percentage points. In other words, there may be no important difference between numbers that are eight or fewer percentage points apart. With these caveats in mind, let's look at the meaning and variety of Angel behavior behind the composite profile.

Angels' Personal Characteristics

Occupation. One of the fastest ways of identifying anyone is by occupation. If you know their occupation, you have narrowed the search area greatly. Finance folklore says that raising capital from individuals means you have to make the rounds of doctors and lawyers, because that's where the money is. Well, another myth can now be forgotten. Angels, by a large majority, are business owners or managers. Not only are Composite Angels businesspeople helping other businesspeople, but they are also experienced entrepreneurs (83 percent). However, not all Angels fall into the business owner category. The percentages of Angels from each occupation group are:

- Business owner   44%
- Business manager/administrator   25%
- Science and engineering professionals   5%
- Physicians, lawyers, CPAs, and other professionals   8%
- All other occupations   18%

The evidence is clear: Look for Angels inside the business community. (Physicians, lawyers, and other professionals outside the business community are a small but important source of risk capital, and their special characteristics are presented in Chapter 4 under the heading "Dr. Kildare.")

Age. Angels are generally about 20 years older than the entrepreneurs they finance (see Chapter 2). Nevertheless, they are in the prime age group, with half of them under 47 years old and half older. Few Angels are under 35 years old or over 65, but they are very active between 35 and 55 years old. This clearly suggests that Angels are businesspeople who have already achieved success and are turning to help others capture some too. It is not at all farfetched to speculate that reliving earlier achievements and triumphs may be a major motive for some Angels. The probabilities of finding an Angel by age group are:

- Under 35 years old   11%
- 35–44   33%
- 45–54   31%
- 55–64   19%
- Over 65   6%

Gender/Ethnic Group.   The majority of Angels are white males. This group represents over 8 out of 10 active Angels (84%). The percentages of Angels belonging to each gender/ethnic group are:

- White males   84%
- White females   5%
- Minority males   11%
- Minority females   0.3%

(Note that in this and all other such tables in this book, the total percentage range may be from 99 to 101. This tolerance range reflects rounding.)

Education.   Surviving the market test is a hard ordeal, and Angels have prepared themselves beforehand. They are a highly educated group; 7 out of 10 have completed a college degree (72%). Moreover, 1 in 4 has earned a graduate degree (28%). This is especially notable since their age cohort reached college age in the late 1950s and early 1960s when college education was not as common as it has since become. I don't know how many Angels are financially "self-made," but of those who are, few did it without first achieving a far-above-average education. The percentages of Angels belonging to each education group are:

- High school or less   12%
- Some college   16%
- Bachelor's degree   44%
- Graduate degree   28%

What is the content of the education Angels have had? In large part their degree fields reflect their occupations. The single most common college degree is from a business school; business school graduates outnumber the second-place engineers by two to one. Together these two groups make up almost two-thirds of all Angels with degrees. The percentages of Angels by degree field are:

- Business   44%
- Engineering   19%
- Natural sciences   7%
- Law and medicine   10%
- All others   20%

Family Income.   Angels receive high incomes: $90,000 per year (median). Not many have very high incomes, which is consistent with the shortage of millionaires. The percentages of Angels by family income group are:

• Under $40,000   10%
• $40,000–$99,999   54%
• $100,000–$199,999   23%
• $200,000 or more   13%

Wealth.   In considering the typical Angel's net worth, another myth evaporates because Angels are not often millionaires. "Daddy Warbucks" is not where all the money is. Angel median wealth is $750,000, and two out of three Angels have a net worth of less than a million dollars—that's where the money is. Nevertheless, extremely wealthy Angels are a substantial minority, and their special market behavior characteristics are presented in Chapter 4 under the heading "Daddy Warbucks." The proportion of Angels in each wealth (net worth) class is:

• Under $500,000   39%
• $500,000–$999,999   24%
• $1,000,000 or more   37%

Angel Market Activity

The activity of Angels in the informal capital market is characterized by six entries in Profile 1-1. These items include Angels' sources of investment information, their deal acceptance rate and their reasons for deal rejection, how frequently they fund a new entrepreneur, the size of Angel coinvestor groups, and their degree of satisfaction with their informal investments.

Angels' Information Sources.   How do Angels find out about investment opportunities? Which sources do they use most often and which do they think are most reliable? We asked our 435 Angels just these questions, and their answers were clear. Personal friends and business associates are about equally ranked as the most frequent sources of information about investment opportunity. Second in importance was information received directly from entrepreneurs themselves. Channels such as investment bankers, business brokers, and others were ranked as "seldom a source." Besides being asked about the frequency with which they consulted various sources, Angels were also queried about the reliability of their information sources. Their actual experience with reliability is the same as that reported for frequency: first, friends and business associates; second, directly from entrepreneurs—all others run a poor third. (The term associates rather than business associates is used in the profiles throughout the book because of space considerations; the business connection is always intended.)

Angels use the sources they find most reliable, and the message to entrepreneurs is, Approach Angels through their friends and associates, but don't hesitate to contact them directly. Investment information channels are so vital that they are examined in detail in Chapter 5.

Deal Acceptance Rate.   What is the raw probability that any proposal to any Angel will be funded? It's not high, but it's much higher than it would be with professional venture capitalists. Angels reported that they had received almost 4000 proposals from entrepreneurs over a 36-month period preceding the survey. Out of this total they seriously considered about one-third of them (1350) and actually invested in 896. Thus the typical Angel learned of 9 investment opportunities (1 every 4 months), seriously considered 3 of them, and invested in 2. Compared to the 1-in-100 acceptance rate of venture capital professionals, Angels appear absolutely generous! It is interesting to note that almost one-fourth of the survey Angels have acceptance rates in the range of 60 to 100 percent. The market profiles of these "high-frequency" Angels are presented in Chapter 5, under the heading "Angels Who Say 'Yes' Often." The diversity surrounding these composite facts is shown by the percentage of Angels who fall into each acceptance-rate class:

- Accept 0–19%   21%
- 20–39%   38%
- 40–59%   19%
- 60–79%   9%
- 80–100%   13%

The flip side of the deal-acceptance coin is, of course, rejection. Angels were asked why they commonly rejected investment proposals, and their answers are shown next.

Deal Rejection Reasons.   There are literally dozens of reasons why an entrepreneur's investment proposal might be rejected after serious consideration. The most frequent deal killer is a business plan that does not promise enough potential market growth to satisfy the Angel. The top four rejection reasons ranked by their importance to Angels are:

1. Inadequate growth potential
2. Inadequate personal knowledge of the firm, its principals, and key personnel
3. Management's lack of experience or talent
4. Unrealistic proposed value of firm's equity

The ranking of rejection reasons gives an interesting picture of where entrepreneurs are weakest in their proposals and business plans. Angels place prime importance on revenue growth, entrepreneurial and key personnel talent, and realistic equity pricing. Entrepreneurs would do well to consider what Angels are saying here and carefully read Chapter 5, in which the topics of decision information content and rejection reasons are developed in detail.

Investment Frequency. The median investor financed 2 entrepreneurs in the 36 months preceding the survey. This is an annual rate of 0.68 investment or about 1 every 18 months. However, there is wide dispersion of Angels' investment frequency. The percentages of Angels in relation to their number of investments in the 36-month-survey period are:

- 1 investment   42%
- 2   34%
- 3   15%
- 4   5%
- 5 or more   4%

Despite the fact that the largest single group of Angels made only one investment, the majority have made two or more, and one-fourth have financed three or more entrepreneurs. With the above information plus the mean investment holding period we can determine the average size of a composite Angel's total informal portfolio. Angels' investments turn over about once every five years; consequently, this means that their average portfolio contains three and a half investments at any one point in time. In other words, Angels are not beginners or novices with one venture to their credit. Instead, they are seasoned veterans with an average holding of between three and four informal investments apiece.

Coinvestors. Angels prefer company. Only 1 in 12 Angels is a loner. Typically they band together to share information, accumulate the needed capital funds, and spread the risk. The reported size of coinvestor groups ranges from 0 to over 50. The percentages of Angels relative to the number of their coinvestors per deal are:

- 0   9%
- 1   21%
- 2   22%
- 3   14%
- 4   9%
- 5 or more   26%

Entrepreneurs seeking Angel financing should plan to find and land more than just one or two Angels. The solo or "lone wolf" investor is an unlikely case.

Angel Satisfaction with Portfolio Performance.   One-third of investors nationwide (34 percent) say that their past informal investments have performed above expected levels, compared to 29 percent who reported below expected performance. Slightly more than one investor in three says performance is about equal to expectations. The overwhelming majority—71.5 percent—feel that their experience with informal investment is as expected or better. These results may be overly optimistic, though, since the investors' experience is based on a time period of continuous economic recovery and growth (1982–1987). If an episode of stagnation or decline in the economy had been included in the survey period, the degree of investor satisfaction may have been less bullish. The percentages of Angels for each level of satisfaction are:

- Well above expectations   14%
- Above expectations   20%
- Equal to expectations   37%
- Below expectations   17%
- Well below expectations   11%

These survey responses about satisfaction demonstrate that Angels as a group are not being sold "blue sky" business plans. Given the risk and uncertainty of small businesses, they seem to be pretty adept at picking out winners. Only time will really tell, though, since final outcomes are not yet known. Chapter 7, "Super Angel-Entrepreneur Matchups (and Others)," closely examines the full set of characteristics for both super-successful deals and very unsuccessful ones.

Informal Portfolios

Angels' investment commitment is defined by the size of their existing informal portfolios. Their total commitment of risk capital is typically $206,000. This total is composed of equity dollars (ownership share) and debt dollars (Angels' personal loans and loan guarantees). Profile 1-1 reveals that the median Angel has $131,000 informal equity invested, with an additional $75,000 in loans and guarantees. The details surrounding these commitments are examined next.

Equity Dollars.   Angels' portfolios contain an average of 3.5 informal investments. Their investment per deal is $37,500, for a portfolio total of $131,000. Wide diversity surrounds this center of gravity, as demonstrated by the percentage of Angels in each total portfolio equity size class:

- Under $35,000   21%
- $35,000–$84,999   22%
- $85,000–$174,999   21%
- $175,000–$349,999   14%

- $350,000–$875,000   15%
- Over $875,000   8%

Notice that Angels' commitments are fairly uniform across a wide range of equity dollar investments until they reach the very highest class, over $875,000. In other words, the probability of locating an Angel does not greatly decline with the size of equity needed until you begin to approach $1 million, which is almost exactly the point at which professional venture capital firms first become interested.

Angel Loans/Guarantees.   An Angel's financial contribution extends beyond direct equity funds and includes substantial amounts of loans and loan guarantees. (The terms *loan* and *loan guarantee* have their usual, everyday meanings here.) It includes the total value of personal loans by the Angels to the firms in their portfolios and any loans from traditional lenders personally guaranteed by the Angels. These funds are considered "friendly and patient" loans by comparison to those from traditional lenders. Because Angels are generally more tolerant and understanding toward a debtor who is also an investment partner, these loans often become liable to the same risks as equity dollars. Thus, Angel loans are considered "near equity" capital.

Angels reported the frequency and amount of their loans/guarantees, and almost 9 out of 10 investors (86 percent) have made 1 or more, with a portfolio median value of $75,000. This friendly and patient debt increases the total informal capital available to the firm by 57 percent. The percentage of Angels in each size class of total portfolio loans/guarantees is:

- None   14%
- Under $50,000   32%
- $50,000–$99,999   23%
- $100,000–$500,000   24%
- Over $500,000   7%

How do these equity and loan amounts break down on a per-deal or per-entrepreneur basis? Briefly (and anticipating these topics in chapters 2 and 3), the amount of equity per deal and per entrepreneur is $37,500 and $112,500, respectively. Loans and guarantees per deal are $21,400 and $64,200 per entrepreneur. These add up to a total dollar commitment by the composite Angel of $58,900 per deal and $177,000 per entrepreneur.

Investment Goals

Angels were asked to spell out where they target their investments regarding industry preference, firm's growth stage, voting control, investing more dollars, and their own day-to-day participation in firm operations. The replies were surprising.

Industry Preferences.   Angels nationwide do *not* hyperventilate over the opportunity to invest in high-technology manufacturing firms. High-tech preference is outranked by service firms and by finance, insurance, and real estate (FIRE) firms, as well as retail trade. Entrepreneurs will find willing ears for proposals in almost any industry. When all types of manufacturing firms are added up, they rank as the leading target among Angels, but not by a majority. Scoring lowest are investment proposals in transportation, communication, public utilities, and natural resources/mining ventures. Angel interests are clearly well diversified across the whole range of industries. The proportion of Angels who have a strong interest in each of 10 major industry groups is:

- Natural resources/mining   11%
- Construction   21%
- Manufacturing—high-technology products   23%
- Manufacturing—industrial products   17%
- Manufacturing—consumer products   18%
- Transportation, communication, and utilities   9%
- Wholesale trade   19%
- Retail trade   24%
- Finance/insurance/real estate   39%
- Service   38%

(The total percent is well over 100 since Angels could indicate more than one preference.)

Firm's Growth Stage.   Most firms grow through a series of development stages that vary in their appeal to Angels. No universal agreement exists on how best to characterize the various stages of growth, but the set of stages that Angels responded to is:

- Start-ups: Business ventures in the idea stage or in the process of being organized. There may be no formal financing at this point. Equity funds may be provided to entrepreneurs developing a new product, process, or other marketable concept.

- Infant firms: Firms that may be losing money but that have the potential for attractive profits in one to three years. Often they are about a year old.

- Young firms: Firms still establishing a track record, expecting to enter a period of rapid and profitable growth, and generally less than five years old.

- Established firms: Small, profitable firms that are growing too fast to finance their growth from retained earnings.

Angel preferences among growth stages appear to have no overriding favorite in any one stage except start-ups. This avowed preference stands in contrast to where Angel dollars are *actually* invested, which is heavily dominated by start-up and infant firms. (See Chapter 2.) The percentages of Angels with a strong interest in investing in the various growth stages are:

- Start-up stage   48%
- Infant stage   32%
- Young stage   27%
- Established stage   30%

(Again, the percentages of figures do not add up to 100 percent because some Angels indicated preferences for more than one growth stage.)

Minimum ROI Targets.   Angels were asked what minimum rate of return they targeted for their informal portfolio investments. Their response is surprisingly low. The median is 22 percent annual ROI. This clearly suggests that in most deals high investor payoffs are not required. The percentages of Angels by minimum level of portfolio ROI are:

- Under 10% minimum ROI   3%
- 10–14%   13%
- 15–19%   20%
- 20–24%   28%
- 25–29%   17%
- 30% or more   20%

Investor Participation in Firm Operations.   Once informal financing is in place, what role do Angels take or plan to take in the firm's operations? An Angel's money arrives with the Angel actively attached. That is to say, he or she usually assumes an active role in day-to-day operations. Less than one Angel in five (17 percent) limits himself or herself to the traditionally passive role of a mere stockholder. The remaining four out of five investors divide their participation about equally between "as needed" consulting, board membership, and employment. Moreover, almost one investor in five is or becomes a full-time employee. The percentages of Angels by type of participation are:

- None, other than reviewing periodic
  reports and attending stockholders'
  meetings   17%
- Being a member of the board of directors   15%
- Providing consulting help as needed   29%
- Working part time with the firm   22%
- Working full time with the firm   17%

Angels' involvement can be a two-edged sword. It is not clear whether participation is a plus or a minus. Some entrepreneurs may see it as little more than meddling, while others will be pleased to get experienced advice and help wherever they can.

Voting Power Goals.   Control of the firm is always a critical and touchy issue when outside investors are approached. Apart from absolute control, even the size of a minority position will be the subject of intense negotiation. For the entrepreneur, knowing what the investor's goals are beforehand can be a major advantage. A full profile of actual voting power is provided in Chapter 6. Here the focus is on Angels' objectives *before* going into negotiations. The bad news is that one in seven Angels (15 percent) admits to wanting majority control. The good news is that 85 percent of Angels expect to obtain a minority position. The percentages of Angels seeking various degrees of voting power are:

- Under 25%   35%
- 25–49%   34%
- 50%   16%
- Over 50%   15%

Appearances can be deceiving. Despite the fact that 15 percent of the surveyed Angels admit to wanting control, in reality they get it more often (27 percent of the time). Wresting control from entrepreneurs is not what an "Angel" is all about. (In fact, power-hungry investors are called business devils, and their characteristics are described in Chapter 11.)

Angels Want to Invest More.   The literature of small business finance is peppered with the notion that risky start-up capital is especially scarce and in short supply. Not so, says our composite Angel! Another myth bites the dust. A majority of Angels cannot find enough deals meeting their requirements! They want to see more proposals and invest more dollars with entrepreneurs. Over half (54 percent) of all Angels said they would have invested more if they had had sufficient opportunity. How much more? When averaged over all Angels, they want to invest 35 percent more than they were able to. For just those who wanted to invest more, the average surplus was 51 percent more than they actually invested. The percentages of Angels for each level of added investment desired are:

- None   47%
- Up to 100% more   38%
- Over 100% more   16%

SUMMARY OF KEY POINTS

Up to this point we have seen both the composite profile and the diversity of the U.S. Angel. They are only the first of three parts that form the full market profile. The remaining two parts are developed in chapters 2 and 3. It may be useful to review the themes that have been interwoven in the discussion so far:

- Despite the attractive precision of the composite Angel profile, it is the diversity around each profile entry that tells the full story.

- Facts presented here are neither complete nor carved in stone; what we see is a single frame cut from a moving picture.

- The Angel you find is likely to be a well-educated white male who is a successful businessman between 45 and 55 years old. He is likely to have started his own company and earns a high income but is not a millionaire (yet).

- Angels know what they're doing; they are veteran investors with a portfolio of past investments that meets or exceeds expectations.

- You will most probably find Angels through their personal friends and associates, although the direct approach by entrepreneurs is the second most likely channel.

- Angels reject 7 out of 10 proposals, mostly because market growth potential is inadequate or because critical information pieces are too vague.

- Both equity and loan dollars are supplied by Angels, who may also provide consulting and advice based on their experience.

- Successful entrepreneurs will probably need more than one Angel to finance capital needs.

- The vast majority of Angels say that they are not looking for voting control.

- Angels want to invest more than opportunity has allowed—you will be doing them a favor by approaching them with a solid business plan that merits their involvement in your success!

2

SUCCESSFUL
ENTREPRENEURS

This chapter is the second of three chapters that collectively introduce, define, and explain the three-part Angel market profile. The market profile outlines the most probable success characteristics of Angels, who supply start-up and growth capital; entrepreneurs, who seek risk capital; and deals, the investment transactions between them. This chapter focuses on the entrepreneur.

The one common experience shared by the entrepreneurs profiled here is that they're all winners. Each has successfully attracted risk capital dollars from one or more Angels. In a very real sense, almost any entrepreneur can be a winner because the investment goals and behavior of Angels are so diversified. Virtually any sound business plan (and many that aren't) can find Angel backing. Despite this chapter's deliberate focus on the profiles of successful entrepreneurs, the theme of diversity will be sounded again and again. Winning entrepreneurs are complex and possess a wide array of different but successful characteristics. Just as a "typical" Angel does not really exist, neither is there a "typical" successful entrepreneur. There are, however, some qualities of entrepreneurs that are most attractive to Angels. These qualities are spotlighted in Profile 2-1. The discussion accompanying the profile details the range of success that surrounds each profile line item. These details of success provide needed balance and emphasis for the picture that emerges from Profile 2-1. What is the picture that emerges?

Entrepreneurs who are most often successful in the United States are white males, 25 to 35 years of age, who obtain risk capital for new, small manufacturing firms. Their success is typically crowned by $177,000 in equity and debt capital provided by a group of three Angels, all of whom live within an hour's drive. Equity dollars account for about $112,000 of the total risk capital invested, and the rest comes as Angel loans or loan guarantees. These entrepreneurs have not slighted their paperwork;

PROFILE 2-1. Successful Entrepreneurs and Their Firms
(U.S. Composite)

- Entrepreneurs obtain $176,700 in total Angel financing* ($112,500 equity and an additional $64,200 in loans/guarantees*)
- Three private individuals (Angels) form coinvestor group*
- Entrepreneur is a white male, age 25–35   (79%)
- He is a talented, highly motivated, time-conscious believer that hard work brings achievement and success
- Firms have zero to nine employees at time of investment   (74%)
- Firms are at start-up or infant stage of growth   (69%)
- Top five industries attracting Angel dollars are:

  - Manufacturing (all sectors)   (26%)
  - Service   (17%)
  - Finance, insurance, and real estate   (17%)
  - Retail trade   (14%)
  - Construction   (10%)

- Entrepreneur is 50 miles or less from Angels' homes or offices   (72%)
- Entrepreneur has a comprehensive business plan   (61%)
- Entrepreneur has a detailed marketing and financing plan   (% unknown)

---

*Median value—half higher, half lower.

a majority have prepared comprehensive business plans that include specialized marketing and financing details. On the personal level, successful entrepreneurs have styles and personality traits that clearly say that time is precious in their lives, they believe in the "American Dream," and they are convinced that hard work can achieve success. They have extraordinary drive and the maturity to control and direct it to effectively implement practical solutions to real market opportunities. Successful entrepreneurs are single-minded and rarely distracted from their business goals. They find joy in the little accomplishments they make along the entrepreneurial way.

Don't worry if this thumbnail summary does not describe you exactly. For every item in the picture there are numerous exceptions, as explained later in this chapter. Remember, there is no shortage of Angels, but there is a shortage of sound business plans and effective entrepreneurs.

The total number of actual and potential entrepreneurs today is not known, but the U.S. pool of 720,000 Angels provides needed capital to 87,000 entrepreneurs and their firms each year. This is over 40 times the number receiving dollars from the highly touted professional venture capitalists. In total, Angels supply some $54 billion dollars of risk capital each year to successful entrepreneurs. All this implies that successful entrepreneurs represent about one in every six U.S. corporations. That is, out of every six corporations, one currently has an Angel-investor on board. Angel dollars typically arrive and leave in the short period of four to five years. This turnover rate means that almost all entrepreneurs who hope to survive and grow will need Angels at one growth stage or another.

Profile 2-1 represents the U.S. Composite Entrepreneur. Later chapters present profiles that reveal similar details for particular cities, industries, capital size needs, business growth stages, and other special cases. Here, the U.S. Composite is the vehicle for introducing important concepts and their interpretations. The Composite will serve as a baseline standard of comparison and will be a constant reference in later chapters. Remember, the U.S. Composite Entrepreneur is a collection of dissimilar individuals who have followed many different paths to their common experience of success with Angel financing. It is the underlying diversity and not the composite that is most important to your success. In this chapter, the key to entrepreneurial success is explored for each of the following questions:

- How much capital is invested?
- What personal characteristics are shared by winning entrepreneurs?
- What types of entrepreneurs and firms attract Angel financing?
- Where do entrepreneurs find Angels?
- What information about entrepreneurs is important to Angels?

The single most common path to Angel dollars is presented in Profile 2-1, which represents the collective experience of almost 900 recent investments in entrepreneurs. Each of the profile line items is either a large majority or a median value. The median value separates entrepreneurs' experience into equal halves: Half of all actual experience is larger than the median and half is smaller. Reported percentages that differ by less than eight percentage points may not actually be different because of sampling error. The reader is again cautioned that U.S. Composite data in this chapter are often too general to fit specific business plans. Information in later chapters is better suited for planning purposes.

THE BOTTOM LINE: ANGELS AND DOLLARS

The lead item in Profile 2-1 is the payoff; dollars invested by Angels. Entrepreneurs obtain a median of $176,700 in Angel financing, a total usually composed of both equity dollars and loans or loan guarantees supplied by a group of three Angels. The odds of entrepreneur success for different amounts of Angel risk capital are:

- Under $125,000   41%
- $125,000–$249,999   16%

- $250,000–$500,000   12%
- Over $500,000   31%

The breakdown of this total investment into equity and debt components is summarized next.

Equity Dollars

The typical amount of equity is $112,500, which represents a wide spread of actual deals. Angels report total equity dollar funding for a single firm that ranges from under $500 to a high of $2.5 million. The percentages of entrepreneurs receiving varying amounts of equity are shown below:

- Under $30,000   21%
- $30,000–$74,999   22%
- $75,000–$149,999   15%
- $150,000–$299,999   12%
- $300,000–$750,000   23%
- Over $750,000   7%

It is clear that Angels' response to the capital needs of entrepreneurs is diverse and that neither Angels nor capital funding needs come in uniform packages. Accommodation is possible for almost any start-up or growth financing requirement.

Angel Loans

Angels rarely stop with just equity dollars. Almost 90 percent of them provide additional risk capital by making personal loans to the entrepreneur and/or by personally guaranteeing loans from banks and other sources that the firm could not qualify for otherwise. Angel loans generally total $64,000 per firm. These loans are often called "near equity" dollars, since Angels are likely to be more patient toward the firm than outside lenders are. Because of this, Angels take greater risks than conventional lenders, and Angel loans consequently take on many of the risks of equity dollars. The diversity of Angel loan experience is just as broad as that for equity dollars, ranging from as little as $700 up to $600,000 per firm—all *in addition to* equity dollars. The percentages of successful entrepreneurs receiving different sizes of loans/guarantees are shown below:

- None   14%
- Under $40,000   32%
- $40,000–$84,999   23%
- $85,000–$425,000   24%
- Over $425,000   7%

Bands of Angels

The composite U.S. Entrepreneur receives funding from a group of 3
Angels. The size of the group formed to finance an entrepreneur usually
depends on the amount of risk capital needed and thus varies widely.
Reported sizes of coinvestor groups range from only 1 Angel to as many
as 50. Below are the percentages of investments made by different sizes
of Angel groups:

- 1 Angel   9%
- 2–3   42%
- 4–5   23%
- Over 5   26%

Next, we turn to some of the personal characteristics of the successful
entrepreneur.

PERSONAL CHARACTERISTICS OF
SUCCESSFUL ENTREPRENEURS

In a financial world too often influenced by first impressions, even
cautious Angels take note of the entrepreneur's superficial characteristics.
Only later, if he or she has made that initial cut, will the entrepreneur's
internal or substantive character become of interest. We will examine both.
The research of some authorities sheds valuable light on the qualities
successful entrepreneurs share. One such expert is A. David Silver, a
highly accomplished entrepreneur himself as well as one of today's most
widely known professional venture capitalists. Silver surveyed and in-
terviewed over 400 entrepreneurs who have generated capital gains for
themselves of over $5 million each. He summarizes their characteristics
in the form of advice to new venture capitalists in his book *Venture
Capital: The Complete Guide for Investors.** Silver advises investors on
how to conduct entrepreneur audits during the investigative process
called "due diligence." In effect, we can eavesdrop as this experienced
professional counsels fledgling investors on how to pick winners. Entrepreneurs' external or superficial characteristics are presented first, followed by their internal or psychological profile.

External Characteristics

The great majority of successful entrepreneurs are white males between
the ages of 25 and 35 years old. The age range should come as no surprise,

*A. David Silver, *Venture Capital: The Complete Guide for Investors* (New York: Wiley, 1985),
pp. 102–8, 153–74. Also see A. David Silver, *The Entrepreneurial Life: How To Go for It
and Get It* (New York: Wiley, 1983).

because this age cohort is also in its most energetic life-cycle stage. Despite the fact that most entrepreneurs are white males, there are many very successful entrepreneurs who are women or members of minority groups. The demographics of successful entrepreneurs are:

- White males   79%
- White females   10%
- Racial/ethnic minorities   11%

Time is precious to Silver's entrepreneurs, as reflected by their frequent adoption of simple, easy-to-care for fashions. Often they are bearded (little or no time spent shaving), wear no extra jewelry, and prefer loafer-style footwear and similar items. They are often physically thin but in excellent health and do not display excesses in eating, drinking, or smoking. Silver's entrepreneur sample contained no bachelors (never married); one in three is still married to a first spouse, and two in three have been divorced (and may or may not be remarried). (Remember, these are observations and not recommendations!) Successful entrepreneurs speak fluently, quickly, and convincingly; they are quick-witted and often modest, says Silver. They vote "liberal" 80 percent of the time. Eight out of 10 drive foreign cars requiring minimum maintenance, and most live in urban areas.

Internal/Substantive Characteristics of Success

Silver's advice to investors is to dig into the background of potential entrepreneurs for two main features: (1) Where does their *drive* or motivation come from, and (2) do they have the psychological *means* to pull it off? Successful entrepreneurs must have both the drive to succeed and the mental discipline to direct, control, and channel that drive.

Silver describes a constellation of attitudinal and background factors (such as childhood environment and even guilt feelings!) that experience and interviews have convinced him are related to an entrepreneur's drive and ability to succeed. Most of these factors are not items that would even be mentioned in a business plan, so the interested Angel may attempt to get information about them by asking questions that may seem unrelated to the business objective.

For example, when Angels ask the seemingly simple question "What did your parents do?" or "What kind of a home did you grow up in?" you should know the implications. Most often, according to Silver's survey, successful entrepreneurs come from middle-class homes rather than from backgrounds of wealth, professionalism, or poverty. (A sense of being deprived as a child, however, either psychologically or economically, seems to be a plus factor no matter what the entrepreneur's background, perhaps inspiring an "I'll-show-them" attitude that spurs the adult to extra efforts.) Obviously you cannot go back and change your background even if you wanted to (and adding "deprivation" would appeal only to masochists), but being aware of Angels' perceptions about the importance of "roots" may help you answer innocent-seeming questions in a way that furthers your cause and presents your personal history to best advantage.

The successful entrepreneurs that Angels are looking for seem to embody "middle-class values" such as the belief that through hard work anyone has the chance to achieve success, which is measured by most of Silver's respondents as material rewards and the satisfaction of the work itself. Answering questions in terms that suggest belief in the "work ethic" and "the American dream" may help assure a potential investor of your drive to succeed.

Interestingly, Silver's survey seems to indicate that successful entrepreneurs often turn seeming "negatives" into drives that have positive results. Three out of four of Silver's male respondents, for example, report having a dominant mother and often an absent or nonsupportive father. For female entrepreneurs it is frequently the reverse. The "plus side" of these circumstances may be early maturity, a practical sense of purpose, and an appreciation of careful contingency planning in the absence of a parental "safety net."

Many of Silver's respondents reported that they had a sense of guilt that drove them to or resulted from their choice of the entrepreneurial lifestyle. They may feel they have disappointed parents by not following in their professional footsteps, for example, or that their choice is not seen as "respectable" by important people in their lives, such as siblings or (ex)spouses. Entrepreneurial guilt can produce great energy to succeed. Next, we look at some of the psychological characteristics providing the ability for entrepreneurs to focus and direct that energy.

Winning entrepreneurs often have a combination of dissatisfaction with the world as it exists, the insight to formulate a practical solution, and the energy to implement the solution. Moreover, successful entrepreneurs have the ability to focus intently on one subject for as long as success requires. Having a sense of dissatisfaction does not mean, however, that the successful entrepreneur is an unhappy person. Winning takes all the energy one can muster. Unhappiness and especially bitterness drain energy and deflect from positive success. Silver's entrepreneurs laugh frequently and easily find joy in small victories along the way.

Experienced investors look for entrepreneurs with creativity, which Silver discusses in terms of problem-formulating. This factor can be made apparent in a thoroughly documented business plan. Silver advises Angels to test for honesty by doublechecking what entrepreneurs tell them. They want references who are both friendly and hostile (or at least less than friendly.) It should not surprise you that they call former coworkers, supervisors, and subordinates; confirm educational claims and credit references; and check out key elements of your business plan.

Silver even advises the readers of his book to seek evidence of a "courage" factor. Entrepreneurs cannot conceive of failure and do almost anything to ensure success. If you hear the question, "How do you intend to achieve your 'hockey stick'?" you are probably dealing with an Angel who has taken the mentor's advice and who is hoping for an answer that shows your "gutsiness" and determination to go on with your enterprise with or without Angel support.*

For the best chance of success, you will answer an Angel's probing questions fluently and with confidence. Practicing answers to possible queries may make you more at ease, although responses that sound "rehearsed" will not be impressive. Successful entrepreneurs are excellent speakers. They are persuasive and convince the inquiring Angel that they have the personal background and attitude that lead to success.

Silver's words are not carved in stone. Each Angel may add to the list of desirable characteristics or change its emphasis. Nevertheless, Silver has distilled years of personal experience in selecting successful entrepreneurs combined with interviews from over 400 successful entrepreneurs. His advice is a good place to start.

SUCCESSFUL ENTREPRENEURS' FIRMS

Not all firms needing capital appeal equally to all Angels. The most frequent Angel choice is a small, young manufacturing firm (Profile 2-1). In this section we look at how Angels actually allocate their dollars among the full variety of firm sizes, growth stages, and industries.

Size of Firm

Angels put almost 6 of every 10 dollars in very small firms with less than 4 employees and sales of under $150,000 per year. Almost 100 percent are smaller than 50 employees. The percentages of Angel investments for each class of employment and sales revenue are:

- Under 4 employees and $150,000 sales   57%
- 4–9 employees and $250,000   17%
- 10–19 employees and $500,000   14%
- Over 20 employees and $1,000,000   12%

The strong Angel preference for small size is consistent with their expressed desire for the young, start-up, and infant-stage firms examined next.

*For a very detailed exemplary answer to this question, see page 106 of Silver's book *Venture Capital*.

Firms' Growth Stages

Most firms grow through a series of four development stages (defined in Chapter 1, page 24) that vary in their appeal to Angels. All four stages involve economic growth, and all attract Angels. Chapter 8 gives a specialized market profile for each stage, but for now a brief look at their relative success with Angels is appropriate. Nationwide, Angels are most often attracted to pure start-ups, but their investments are spread among all stages. The shares of actual Angel financing for each growth stage are:

- Start-up firms   56%
- Infant firms   13%
- Young firms   11%
- Established firms   20%

Young firms under 18 months old stand the best chance of attracting Angel financing. The probability of Angel funding decreases as the firm's age goes up, until it reaches the established firm stage, where popularity again rises.

Industry Rankings

A wide diversity of interests is also apparent in the rankings of Angels' preferences for specific industries. Contrary to financial folklore, Angels are not programmed to throw money at high-tech manufacturing firms. While all types of manufacturing firms are the single largest target of Angel dollars, the subcategory of technology-based manufacturing receives only 10 percent of Angels' investments. The percentages of actual investments by major industry groups are:

- Natural resources/mining   5%
- Construction   10%
- Manufacturing–high technology   10%
- Manufacturing–industrial products   9%
- Manufacturing–consumer products   6%
- Transportation, communication, and public utilities   2%
- Wholesale trade   6%
- Retail trade   14%
- Finance/insurance/real estate   17%
- Services   17%
- All other   4%

Notice that no single industry group has been able to attract more than about one in five Angels.

WHERE TO LOOK FOR ANGELS

Geographical Patterns

Angels exist everywhere people do. The single best guide to their location is the local population size (see Chapter 10, "Angels Where You
Live"). It is not necessary to travel to distant and expensive financial
centers for needed capital, because it's right in your home town. This
fact is clearly underscored by Profile 2-1, which shows that 7 out of 10
Angels invest in entrepreneurs within 50 miles of their home or office.
Since Angels are "homebodies," entrepreneurs' success falls off rapidly
as the physical distance grows between the entrepreneur and investor.
The percentages of entrepreneurs' success by distance from the Angel's
home or office are:

- Within 10 miles   41%
- 11–50 miles   31%
- 51–150 miles   10%
- Other distances   11%
- No mileage limit   7%

The entrepreneur seeking low-cost capital would do well to remember
the reply given by the noted bank robber Willie "The Actor" Sutton to
the question of why he robbed banks. Sutton replied, "That's where the
money is." Equally focused entrepreneurs will seek out Angels close to
home because "that's where the money is."

Communication Channels

Successful entrepreneurs reach Angels most easily through the information source that Angels listen to: personal friends and business associates
(Profile 1-1). This topic is detailed in Chapter 5. Suffice it to point out
here that the single most frequent and reliable channel for making your
business opportunity known to an Angel is indirectly through his personal friends and business associates. This does not mean bankers,
accountants, lawyers, business brokers, or government officials, unless
they are also the Angel's personal friend or associate. The direct approach
by entrepreneurs themselves is the second most successful contact
method. Channels not often successful include investment bankers,
venture capital professionals, investment/business brokers, and government economic development agencies. Among these low-probability
channels, the government agency connection is often a sure deal killer.
Angels want no association with public bureaucrats and politically
motivated deals.

WHAT TO SAY TO AN ANGEL

What is it that Angels want in the way of information from an entrepreneur in addition to the clues to personal drive discussed earlier? Chapter 5 examines this topic in detail, but first and foremost is a comprehensive business plan.* Winning entrepreneurs place heavy emphasis on two specialized business-plan components: the marketing plan and the financing plan. Comprehensive business plans of successful entrepreneurs emphasize the following topics, in rank order:

1. Clear description of proposed financing from start to finish
2. Complete marketing strategy and tactics
3. Summary statement of purpose and goals
4. Complete and factual history of the firm and its key personnel

Angels I surveyed expressed a need for both personal and financial information. They report that many entrepreneurs fail to adequately communicate:

• Skills and talent capability of the entrepreneur and other key personnel
• Sufficient *personal* knowledge about both the entrepreneur and key personnel
• Business sales projections to satisfy Angels' growth targets
• The reasonableness of equity pricing

Lack of communication in these areas can kill a deal that might have been highly successful for both the Angel and the entrepreneur.

SUMMARY OF KEY POINTS

This chapter presents the U.S. Composite Entrepreneur as a base case. It is the second of three interrelated chapters that develop the concepts and details of the three-part market profile. The intention of the profile of successful entrepreneurs is to concentrate attention on the meaning and interpretation of the base case facts.

Out of this chapter emerge some general themes about successful entrepreneurs and some lessons for success:

• Angel diversity and accommodation allow almost any type of entrepreneur to succeed. Don't be discouraged if you don't fit the composite profile. It is entrepreneurs, not Angels, who are in short supply.
• The U.S. Composite Profile is not specific enough for realistic planning. See later chapters for special business circumstances.

*There are many sources on writing a business plan. Two especially good ones are A. David Silver, *Up Front Financing: The Entrepreneur's Guide* (New York: Wiley, 1982) and Harold McLaughlin, *The Fundamentals of the Business Plan: A Step by Step Approach* (New York: Wiley, 1985).

- Angels will want many details of your personal life and background.
- Not all characteristics of successful entrepreneurs can be adopted by others. But be aware and be prepared.
- The success profile is not complete or "carved in stone." Much remains unknown.

More specific advice for the entrepreneur is:

- Look close to home for Angel dollars.
- Find Angels through their friends and business associates or by contacting them directly.
- Prepare a complete and comprehensive written business plan.
- Emphasize marketing, sales growth, finance, key people, and equity valuation in the business plan. Don't be evasive or vague when communicating with Angels.
- Be realistic in appraising the merits of the deal; Angels certainly will be.
- Be aware of profile odds and use them to advantage. Reexamine plan elements that have low Angel probabilities and correct them if possible. Emphasize high-hit probability characteristics.
- Expect success; there is an Angel for every sound deal.

3

REAL DEALS
IN THE REAL WORLD

Angels and entrepreneurs agree on terms and conditions almost half a million times each year, and for simplicity I call these transactions *deals*. No two deals are exactly alike, yet most share a common set of core elements and conditions. This chapter summarizes these core elements into a composite profile, describes and interprets them, and then looks behind the profile to expose some important differences in how real deals are made. In practice, deals are often surrounded by any number of additional side agreements that take into consideration the special needs and circumstances of individual transactions, but the sheer number of these special side deals precludes a full discussion of them here. The composite profile presented in this chapter depicts only the main features of the most likely deal structure.

Chapter 1 profiled and dissected the composite Angel, while Chapter 2 did the same for successful entrepreneurs. This chapter finishes the development of the three-part market profile by examining the common structure of the deals made by Angels and entrepreneurs. Because it is a continuation of the work of chapters 1 and 2, it can be misleading if read out of context. Many important details and qualifications explained earlier are not repeated here.

Agreements between Angels and entrepreneurs are fundamentally one-on-one transactions, despite the fact that it commonly takes three to five Angels to supply the entrepreneur's full capital needs. This does not mean that Angels make deals in isolation from each other—quite the contrary. The one Angel–one entrepreneur deal perspective simply reflects the fact that regardless of how the details are arrived at, ultimately it is the individual Angel who personally commits a part of his or her wealth. A deal is the investment transaction between the entrepreneur and one Angel, even though several Angels usually are involved in a complete financing.

The one factor all the deals reported in this chapter have in common is that they are real; they actually happened. This single common bond reinforces the continuing theme that diversity rules the market. A typical deal does not exist any more than a typical Angel or entrepreneur does. It is the most likely or common traits gleaned from almost 900 real deals that are highlighted in the composite.

The composite deal profile, however useful, is not complete because it is a static picture of a fluid process. Neither the profile nor its underlying facts tell us *how* Angels and entrepreneurs reach their agreements; the profile reflects only the most likely final resting point of a complex set of human interactions. Nowhere can we see a full picture of the rich fabric of offer and counteroffer that leads to the composite deal. We cannot see where Angels and entrepreneurs begin their bargaining or any of the details of the dynamic process of reaching mutually acceptable terms and conditions. Because negotiations rarely leave permanent "tracks" or records, when the truck and barter of negotiations finish, all that is left to see are the facts summarized in the composite profile.

What picture emerges from the composite? When the sample of almost 900 reported deals is summarized, its pattern represents the hundreds of thousands of informal deals actually occurring each year. That pattern begins with the amount of money changing hands. The median deal transfers a total of $58,900 from the Angel to the firm; of this sum, $37,500 is equity dollars (64 percent), with $21,400 more in loans/guarantees (36 percent). In return the Angel receives a minority business share, usually between 20 and 40 percent. Based on the investment size and ownership share, Angels expect to receive between 20 and 26 percent annual ROI. Part of this expected return compensates for the Angels' belief that the typical risk (odds) they face runs about 30 percent likelihood of substantial capital loss. The deal is formalized by the use of either common stock or a partnership equity interest as the investment instrument. The investment agreement also embodies the Angels' expectation of holding the investment from 4 to 10 years before liquidation. Resale to the entrepreneur or other existing coinvestors is the usual liquidation method. The Angel is or becomes an employee of the firm in one deal out of three. As precise as this general pattern may appear, it is an oversimplification unless we also examine the range of actual events that accompanies each of the common characteristics.

ELEMENTS OF THE COMPOSITE DEAL

The remainder of this chapter examines the full array of the deal elements which include:

- Total dollars invested
- Equity dollars
- Loans/guarantee dollars
- Voting power (ownership share)
- Risk of investment loss
- Return on investment (ROI)
- Investment instruments
- Investment holding periods
- Liquidation (cash-out) methods
- Angels as employees

It cannot be repeated too often that the U.S. Composite Deal appearing in Profile 3-1 is based on real people and their actual investment experience in the day-to-day reality of business start-up and growth. As helpful as the composite may be, it is not specific enough for most planning purposes; also, it needs added perspective. Ironically, both of these shortcomings stem from the profile's two main advantages: First, it's a point of departure, and, second, it's a baseline reference. The shortcomings are quickly remedied. Perspective is added in this chapter from the underlying range of experience for each profile line item. Planning usefulness is covered in subsequent chapters, which describe how deals are tailored to account for specific market circumstances. For now, the U.S. Composite Deal allows us to see key concepts and their meaning while at the same time establishes a baseline standard for later reference.

Dollars at Risk

Topping the list of deal elements in Profile 3-1 is a key consideration: How much money is invested? The median U.S. Angel puts up $37,500 in equity funds (with an average of $67,800), and in addition there is another $21,400 committed in the form of the Angel's personal loans and/or loan guarantees, for a total of $58,900. Individual Angels report investing as little as $250 in equity up to as much as $800,000 per deal. Deals cover a wide range of investment sizes, reinforcing the notion that there is an Angel for virtually any capital amount needed. The percentages of deals reported for each class of equity dollars per Angel are:

- Less than $10,000   21%
- $10,000–$24,999   22%
- $25,000–$49,999   21%
- $50,000–$99,999   14%
- $100,000–$250,000   14%
- Over $250,000   8%

Angels' funding does not stop at providing equity dollars; almost 9 out of 10 add more capital to the deal in the form of personal loans and loan guarantees. Typically these "friendly and patient" loans range just as widely as equity dollars. The percentages of deals for each class of Angel loans/guarantee size are:

- None   14%
- Under $15,000   32%
- $15,000–$29,999   23%
- $30,000–$150,000   24%
- Over $150,000   7%

PROFILE 3-1. Investment Deal Structure (U.S. Composite)

- $37,500 in equity per investor* ($67,800 average)
- $21,400 in loans/guarantees per investment* ($65,000 average)
- Minority voting power to Angel in 73% of deals, with a median Angel equity share of 37%
- 30% risk of substantial capital loss expected by Angel
- 25% rate of return per year anticipated by Angel* (27% average)
- Common stock or partner equity instruments used in 79% of all deals
- Liquidation (cash-out) plans appear in 78% of deals
- Investment holding period (cash-out horizon) of 4 years anticipated* (5.1 years average)
- Resale of equity back to entrepreneur or other "insiders" specified in 50% of all deals
- Investor becomes active in firm as an employee (39%), consultant (29%), or board member (15%)

---

*Median value—half higher, half lower.

Voting Power (Ownership Share)

The reverse side of the investment dollar is the amount of ownership share/voting power that the entrepreneur gives up in exchange. Voting power and company control are almost always a key issue when equity dollars change hands. The clear message of Profile 3-1 is that Angels usually accept a minority equity position. Amost three-fourths of all deals transfer 50 percent or less ownership to the Angel. Conversely, in only one in four deals did the entrepreneur lose absolute control of the firm to the Angel (Devil?). The percentages of deals and the amount of control gained by the Angel are:

- Under 25% control   41%
- 25–49%   15%
- 50%   17%
- 51% or more   27%

How closely does the investment dollar size influence the amount of control passing to the Angel? The correlation is undoubtedly high. The dollar control trade off is further examined in Chapter 6.

How Much Risk Do Angels See?

Financial folklore emphasizes the riskiness of investing in new and growing small businesses, and Angels agree that substantial risk exists. While there is no common agreement on how best to define and measure expected risk, one useful method was applied to the Angels in my survey. Instead of trying to measure the risk of each unique deal, I asked Angels how often they expected a major capital loss from a portfolio of any 10 informal deals they select. Their typical response was clear: "It's high." Angels generally believe that 3 of 10 deals will go sour, meaning they expect a capital loss of 50% or more despite their best due diligence efforts. Some "doom and gloom" Angels anticipate over 5 "loser" deals out of 10. Yet a substantial number of Angels see no more than 20 percent risk. Because the Angels surveyed are reporting the probable losers out of hypothetical deals they pick, risk perception could be interpreted as an expression of a lack of self-confidence in picking winners. However, given the Angels' overall success in business and investments, this interpretation seems hollow. It's more realistic to hypothesize that the degree of risk seen by the sample of business veterans reflects their evaluation of market conditions they can neither foresee nor control. The percentages of Angels reporting each level of expected risk are:

- 0–2 losers   37%
- 3 losers   16%
- 4–5 losers   23%
- Over 5 losers   24%

Again, Chapter 6 explores the impact of risk expectations on equity pricing and Angels' anticipated ROI.

Expected ROI

The annual return that Angels realistically anticipate on their investments is influenced by specific deal circumstances. These circumstances include the price of equity, the size of ownership share at stake, risk of loss, ROI available on alternative deals, projected business growth, and others. When all factors are evaluated, the U.S. Composite Angel accepts a median ROI of 25 percent per year. Some high ROIs raise the average (mean) to 27 percent. The percentages of Angels buying into a deal at each ROI level are:

- Under 20% ROI   41%
- 20–29%   34%
- 30–50%   12%
- Over 50%   13%

Again, the lesson is clear: A super-high ROI is not often necessary to reach deals with Angels. This may be especially true if you can find any of their so-called "hot buttons." A hot button is the Angels' nonmoney reward. These include their personal interest in the entrepreneur, market, or product or perhaps their sense of "community" because an investment brings more jobs or economic growth or gratification that there is a humanitarian product involved (for example, new medical technology).

From the viewpoint of the entrepreneur, the minimum cost of informal capital is the smallest ROI that an Angel demands. Angels report a typical willingness to accept a 22 percent *minimum* ROI (Chapter 1). Comparing this minimum to the actual ROI suggests that entrepreneurs are skillful enough to bargain Angels up close to their maximum equity prices.

Investment Instrument

Angels and entrepreneurs strongly favor easy, direct equity instruments. Eight out of 10 deals involve only ordinary common stock or a simple partnership equity interest. Deal makers seem especially wary of convertible preferred stock and combinations involving debt instruments (for example, notes with warrants or convertible debenture bonds). The array of investment instruments and the percentages of deals using each are:

- Common stock   40%
- Partnership equity interest   39%
- Notes with warrants   9%
- Convertible preferred stock   2%
- Convertible debentures   2%
- Other or combinations   7%

Sometimes numbers do speak for themselves. Here they're saying, "Stay away from complicated instruments; keep it simple."

Exit Plans (Deal Liquidation)

Angels have a strong taste for capital gains income. Over 8 in 10 (82 percent) prefer at least half of their investment earnings as capital gains. This is true even though the 1986 income tax reforms changed the status of capital gains income. In order to realize their equity gains, investors must sell. Thus, cash-out agreements are a part of over three-fourths of all deals. The most common exit plans specify both the liquidation horizon (holding period) and who has the first option to buy out the Angel. Generally deals are designed to liquidate themselves after a holding period of about four years (average of five and one-tenth years). Patient Angels are not difficult to find; almost half of all Angels anticipate a holding period of five years or more (or indefinitely). The percentages of deals by anticipated holding periods are:

- 3 years or less   21%
- 3–5 years   31%
- 6–9 years   29%
- 10 or more years   6%
- Not important   13%

The wide mix of expected exit dates again shows the willingness of Angels to accommodate diverse business needs.

Investment deals with Angels usually include a provision specifying who has the first buy-out option. Only one in five deals makes no stipulation on how the equity is to be sold. A strong majority of exit provisions (64 percent) favor giving "insiders" the right of first refusal. Most often either the entrepreneurs or existing coinvestors have first option. Less than one in five deals anticipates sale of equity primarily to an "outsider." Potential equity buyers are listed here along with their frequency as the prime source of Angels' cash out:

- Company/entrepreneur   44%
- Inside investor   20%
- Merge (sell) with another company 9%
- Institutional investor   1%
- Public offering   9%
- Other or multiple   17%

Angels as Employees

Angels come firmly attached to their money. Profile 3-1 reveals that two out of five deals involve Angels as employees. Some Angels are employees before the deal is cut, and some become employees later. Unfortunately, we don't have a clear picture of the relationship of Angels to the firm prior to the deal. The employment relationship, whatever its timing, is composed of a majority of part-time Angel-employees (56 percent) and a minority (44 percent) of full-time employees. Even if Angels are not employees, they are unlikely to be passive investors. Only 17 percent of Angels become stockholders in the traditional sense. The rest, 83 percent, become active in the firm's operation either as employees, consultants, or board members.

FITTING THE ENTREPRENEUR TO THE ANGEL

It is not true that "all money is green." The deal elements of liquidation and participation combine with others to give clear notice to Angels and entrepreneurs alike: Select each other carefully. The combination of the length of Angel holding periods and the likelihood of their active involvement in the firm says that selecting an Angel goes far beyond mere money. Entrepreneurs and Angels are going to "live together" daily for the next 5 to 10 years! Under these circumstances, some money is "greener" than others. An analogy with mariage is not too farfetched, and unfortunately, giving advice on how best to select the "right" partner is probably as useful: De gustibus non est disputandum (figuratively speaking, "There is no accounting for taste"). Nevertheless, later chapters detail characteristics of Angels, entrepreneurs, and their successful combinations. The pitfalls and dead ends (Chapter 11) in particular provide some useful warnings.

SUMMARY OF KEY POINTS

This chapter completes the third and final part of the Angel market profile by presenting the U.S. Composite Deal. The point of view adopted is that of one Angel dealing with one entrepreneur. The composite is intended to familiarize the reader with deal profiles and serve as a baseline for later comparisons. It is not a profile to be used for planning purposes. Later chapters present profiles that are designed to apply to specific market circumstances. The common core of informal deals suggests some important ideas:

- The variety of actual deal structures is flexible enough to fit almost any set of busines needs.
- The amount of capital you can obtain depends on how much you need, but don't expect it all from one Angel.
- Both equity and loans can be obtained from your Angel (one-source financing).
- Angels will usually accept a minority position, but it's not small.
- Angels anticipate substantial risk, so uncertainty of outcome does not necessarily mean you cannot find start-up financing.
- Few Angel deals use complex investment instruments. Keep it simple.
- Anticipate a written repurchase or cash-out agreement with your Angels. Plan an exit time and method.
- Select each other carefully, because you will "live together" actively in the firm for 5 to 10 years.

The picture of informal deals presented here is the first word, not the last word. The limitations of the profile—especially its incompleteness and static character—are important considerations.

4

THE CAST OF ANGELS

The U.S. Composite Angel presented in Chapter 1 is a conglomerate of Angel subtypes that differ in ways that are important to entrepreneurs and investment deals. In this chapter the composite Angel is subdivided into 10 of its most important individual categories. A complete market profile is provided for each Angel subtype, but the text discussion focuses primarily on the characteristics that set the subtype apart from the U.S. Composite. The subtypes include:

- Business Devils
- The Godfather
- Peers
- Cousin Randy
- Dr. Kildare
- Corporate Achievers
- Daddy Warbucks
- High-Tech Angels
- The Stockholder
- Very Hungry Angels

This is the first chapter that presents a complete market profile, which incorporates the market characteristics of Angels, entrepreneurs, and deals in essentially the same format as they were introduced individually in chapters 1 through 3. The market profile line items should therefore look familiar. The first part of the complete market profile displays on the left-hand side 20 characteristics of the Angel subtype. The right-hand column repeats the baseline U.S. Composite as a convenient reference for comparison. The second part of the profile shows the market characteristics of successful entrepreneurs corresponding to the market profile subtype and their baseline U.S. Composite references. High-probability deal structures make up the third part of the profile, in the same format as the other elements. The most important differences between the specialized profiles and the U.S. Composite are marked with a plus (+) sign on all market profiles in the remainder of this book.

BUSINESS DEVILS

An investor who obtains absolute majority control (51 percent or more of the voting equity) from the entrepreneur is classified as a business "Devil." Out of the 896 investments reported, 222 (27 percent) transferred majority control to the investor. The concept of Devils is only introduced here because they are treated as a major topic in Chapter 11, "Devils, Dead Ends, and Deal Breakers." The range of voting control is treated as a separate major topic in Chapter 6.

THE GODFATHER

Venture capital veterans frequently describe a type of Angel who has been successful in business, is often semiretired, and who wants to stay active in business by being a mentor to a younger entrepreneur. In their role of mentor these Angels often consult or work part time for the entrepreneur's firm. An Angel who fits this general description I call the "Godfather." The folklore description of a Godfather is not very precise when it comes to actually identifying one. At first I operationally defined Godfathers as Angels over 60 years old, with a net worth of $1,000,000 or more and income exceeding $100,000, whose principal occupation was business owner (but not manager), and who had personal entrepreneurial experience. The problem with this set of characteristics is that there are not enough Angels fitting it for a reliable profile. Fewer than five percent of all Angels matched this initial definition. Consequently the Godfather definition was broadened to include Angels who are 50 years of age or older, with a net worth of over $750,000 and income over $90,000, and who have personal business experience. From this definition, one in four Angels qualifies as a Godfather. As it turns out, their typical age, wealth, and incomes are well above the minimum definitions, as shown in Profile 4-1.

Godfathers as a group differ from other Angels because they are wealthy people with high incomes who are relatively older and more experienced and who find investment opportunities through business associates. Their equity investment size is average, but they loan or guarantee large amounts of risk capital. Godfathers require a comprehensive business plan more frequently than other Angels do and rarely seek majority control. Their participation in the firm's operations does not often involve full-time employment. Above all, they are extraordinarily successful with their investments.

MARKET PROFILE 4-1.   The Godfather

ANGELS	U.S. Composite

+ • Business owner/manager is principal occupation (100%)   (70%)
   • Has personal entrepreneurial experience (83%)   (83%)
+ • 59 years old*   (47 years)
+ • White male (92%)   (84%)
   • College degree (74%)   (72%)
+ • $150,000 annual family income*   ($90,000)
+ • $1,000,000 net worth*   ($750,000)
+ • Associates are the primary information channel   (Friends and associates)
   • Accepts 3 of 10 investment opportunities*   (3)
+ • Rejects deals mostly due to lack of personal knowledge   (Growth potential)
   • Invests about every 18 months and has 3.5 firms
     in portfolio*   (18) (3.5)
+ • Satisfied with past investments (83%)   (72%)
   • Three other coinvestors*   (Two)
   • $131,000 equity invested in informal portfolio*   ($131,000)
+ • $300,000 more via loans/guarantees to portfolio firms*   ($75,000)
   • Prefers investing in FIRE firms (33%)   (Service/FIRE)
   • Minimum ROI target for informal portfolio (22%)*   (22%)
   • Active as a consultant, board member, or employee (80%)   (81%)
+ • Does not seek voting control (98%)   (85%)
   • Wants to invest 37% more than opportunity permitted   (35%)

SUCCESSFUL ENTREPRENEURS/FIRMS

   • $493,000 total Angel financing* (equity and loans)   ($176,700)
   • $150,000 in equity and $343,000 more in
     loans/guarantees*   ($112,500) ($64,200)
+ • Four private individuals supply funding*   (Three)
   • Entrepreneur is a white male, age 25–35 (83%)   (79%)
   • Zero to nine employees at time of investment (69%)   (74%)
   • Start-up or infant stage of firm growth (74%)   (69%)
+ • FIRE firms are most frequently financed (19%)   (17% in service)
   • 50 miles or less from investor's home or office (66%)   (72%)
+ • Has a comprehensive business plan (70%)   (61%)
   • Has detailed marketing and financing plans

HIGH-PROBABILITY DEAL STRUCTURE

   • $37,500 in equity per investor*   ($37,500)
+ • $86,000 in loans/guarantees by Angel*   ($21,400)
   • 30% voting power transferred to investor   (37%)
   • Majority control to Angel in 20% of investments   (27%)
   • 30% capital risk seen by Angel*   (30%)
   • 25% expected annual ROI (28% average)   (25%) (27%)
   • Common stock or partner equity instrument (84%)   (79%)
   • Four-year liquidation horizon*   (Four years)
+ • Liquidation buyback by insiders planned (36%)   (50%)
   • Investor is or becomes an employee in 36% of investments   (39%)

---

*Median value—half higher, half lower.   + Differs importantly from U.S. Composite.

Profile 4-1, like the others in this chapter, is a complete market profile that includes entrepreneur and deal elements, although only the Angels' characteristics will be emphasized.

Real Differences Between Godfathers and the Composite Angel

Market Profile 4-1 can only hint broadly at the real differences that exist between Godfathers and the U.S. Composite Angel because the profiled Godfathers are also composites of diverse market experience. The objective now is to look behind the composite Godfathers at the real range of their actual characteristics.

All Godfathers are business owners, and they are 10 years older than other Angels (both facts are influenced by the Godfather definition). Apparently even Godfathers retire—there are relatively few of them investing after the age of 65 years. The percent of Godfathers in each age bracket is:

- Under 50 years   0%
- 50–54   40%
- 55–64   45%
- 65 or more   15%

The vast majority of Godfathers are males whose median income is $150,000 per year and who have a net worth in excess of $1 million. Considering their age, they are an extremely well-educated group with 74 percent college graduates. The percent of Godfathers by income class is:

- Under $60,000   0%
- $60,000–$99,999   34%
- $100,000–$199,999   33%
- $200,000 or more   33%

The percentages of Godfathers by net worth are:

- Under $750,000   0%
- $750,000–$1,000,000   28%
- Over $1,000,000   72%

Godfathers are more likely to be reached by an entrepreneur through the Godfathers' business associates than through their friends, although friends are a close second. The direct approach by the entrepreneur is the third-most-likely way that Godfathers learn of investment opportunities. The percent of Godfathers who favor or rely on each source of investment opportunity information is:

- Business associates   35%
- Friends   32%
- Entrepreneurs   12%
- Bankers/Brokers   9%
- Other and combinations 12%

Because of the closer personal relationship between Godfathers and their entrepreneurs, Godfathers want a thorough personal knowledge of the potential entrepreneur prior to investment. As can be expected, lack of this personal knowledge is the leading deal killer. The top five reasons for Godfathers' rejection of deals, in rank order, are:

1. Inadequate personal information about the entrepreneurs/key personnel
2. Inadequate growth potential
3. Management's lack of necessary talent
4. Overpriced equity
5. Insufficient overall information

It is noteworthy that three of the five top reasons deal with not having enough information or the wrong answers to concerns about the entrepreneur. While this personal relationship to the entrepreneur is important to Godfathers, they do not neglect or downplay the economic considerations of growth potential and equity pricing. Godfathers are also sticklers when it comes to getting comprehensive business plans prior to investing— 70 percent of the successful entrepreneurs provide them.

A Godfather investment does not involve an unusually large equity dollar amount, but the amount of loans/guarantees is larger than usual. Godfathers lend/guarantee a median of $300,000 to their informal portfolio firms compared to only $75,000 for all Angels. Godfathers do not lend any more frequently overall than other Angels, but they lend/ guarantee much more frequently in the $100,000 and over range. The percentages of Godfathers by size of loans/guarantees are:

- None   16%
- Under $50,000   21%
- $50,000–$99,999   12%
- $100,000–$500,000   32%
- Over $500,000   19%

Godfathers do not target majority control as an investment objective; almost all say that it's not an objective, compared to 85 percent of all Angels. In the end, it is results that really count both for Godfathers and their entrepreneurs. By that measure Godfathers have one of the highest success levels of all Angel types. Godfathers are satisfied with their investments' performance in 83 percent of cases, compared to 73 percent for all Angels. The biggest satisfaction difference is for performance that exceeds expectations. Godfathers rate 47 percent of their investments as performing better than expected, while all Angels assign this level of success to only 34 percent of their investment experience. The percentages of Godfathers by level of investment performance are:

- Well above expected performance   20%
- Above expected   27%
- About equal to expected   36%

- Below expected   11%
- Well below expected   6%

Key Points about Godfathers

- Godfathers, representing about one in four Angels, are older, wealthier, more experienced, and more successful with their chosen entrepreneurs than other Angels.

- Godfathers reject potential entrepreneurs more often because of lack of personal knowledge about the entrepreneur or key personnel than for any other reason.

- The investment brings to the entrepreneur not only the valuable experience of the Godfather but also over twice as much risk capital as usual, especially in the form of loans/guarantees.

- Comprehensive business plans prior to investment are the standard for Godfather financings.

- Godfather-entrepreneur combos are rated by the Godfather as "successful" in 83 percent of all cases—one of the highest satisfaction rates of all Angel groups.

PEERS

Peers are one of the largest, if not the single largest, subtype of business Angel. Peers are Angels who are themselves entrepreneurs, currently are business owners/managers, and who invest within 50 miles of their home or business—in other words, local entrepreneurs helping local entrepreneurs. Over one in three Angels is a Peer. Peers often become Angels because they have a vested interest in a local market, product, or the potential entrepreneur. The problem with Peers as an Angels subtype is that they represent such a large proportion of all Angels that their characteristics do not differ greatly from the composite Angel. Apart from the differences due to their definition, this group shows only five distinct traits. Relatively speaking, Peers are younger, more sensitive to the entrepreneur's management talent, less likely to seek majority control, more insistent on a comprehensive business plan, and more patient about eventual liquidation of the investment than is usual for all Angels. The full complement of Peer characteristics is presented in Market Profile 4-2.

Real Differences Between Peers and the Composite Angel

Profile 4-2 presents a Peer composite, which still obscures some of the real differences that exist between Peers and the U.S. Composite Angel. The objective again is to look behind the composite Peer at the real range of Peers' actual characteristics.

MARKET PROFILE 4-2. Peers

ANGELS   U.S. Composite

+ • Business owner/manager is principal occupation   (100%)   (68%)
+ • Has personal entrepreneurial experience   (100%)   (83%)
+ • 39 years old*   (47 years)
  • White male   (86%)   (84%)
  • College degree   (70%)   (72%)
  • $90,000 annual family income*   ($90,000)
  • $750,000 net worth*   ($750,000)
  • Friends and associates are the primary   (Friends and
    information channel   associates)
  • Accepts 3 of 10 investment opportunities*   (3)
+ • Rejects deals mostly due to management's lack of talent   (Growth potential)
  • Invests about every 18 months and has 3.5 firms
    in portfolio*   (18) (3.5)
  • Satisfied with past investments   (77%)   (72%)
  • Two other coinvestors*   (Two)
  • $131,000 equity invested in informal portfolio*   ($131,000)
  • $75,000 more via loans/guarantees to portfolio firms*   ($75,000)
  • Prefers investing in service firms   (44%)   (Service/FIRE)
  • Minimum ROI target for informal portfolio   (22%)*   (22%)
  • Active as a consultant, board member, or employee   (88%)   (81%)
+ • Does not seek voting control   (94%)   (85%)
  • Wants to invest 33% more than opportunity permitted   (35%)

SUCCESSFUL ENTREPRENEURS/FIRMS

  • $176,700 total Angel financing* (equity and loans)   ($176,700)
  • $112,500 in equity and $64,200 more in loans/guarantees*   ($112,500) ($64,200)
  • Three private individuals supply funding*   (Three)
  • Entrepreneur is a white male, age 25–35 (78%)   (79%)
  • Zero to nine employees at time of investment (79%)   (74%)
  • Start-up or infant stage of firm growth (71%)   (69%)
  • Service firms are most frequently financed (22%)   (17% in service)
+ • 50 miles or less from investor's home or office (100%)   (72%)
+ • Has a comprehensive business plan (73%)   (61%)
  • Has detailed marketing and financing plans

HIGH-PROBABILITY DEAL STRUCTURE

  • $37,500 in equity per investor*   ($37,500)
  • $21,400 in loans/guarantees by Angel*   ($21,400)
  • 36% voting power transferred to investor   (37%)
  • Majority control to Angel in 29% of investments   (27%)
  • 30% capital risk seen by Angel*   (30%)
  • 25% expected annual ROI (25% average)   (25%) (27%)
  • Common stock or partner equity instrument (79%)   (79%)
+ • Liquidation horizon of seven and a half years*   (Four years)
  • Liquidation buyback by insiders planned (51%)   (50%)
  • Investor is or becomes an employee in 47% of investments   (39%)

---

*Median value—half higher, half lower.   + = Differs importantly from U.S. Composite.

By definition, Peers are 100 percent business owners/managers with personal entrepreneurial experience. As a group they are younger than might be expected. The typical Peer is 39 years old (still about 10 years older than the typical entrepreneur), compared to the composite Angel at 47 years of age. The percentage of Peers in each age class is:

- Under 35 years old   15%
- 35–44 years   38%
- 45–54 years   25%
- 55–64 years   18%
- 65 or older   4%

As active business owners and entrepreneurs themselves, Peers are naturally sensitive to the potential entrepreneur's management talent for achieving success. This sensitivity is reflected by Peers rejecting seriously considered deals more often for the lack of entrepreneur's managerial talent than for any other reason. Peers do not ignore economic values in their decision making, but two of the top three deal killers put clear emphasis on the personal character of the entrepreneur. Out of nine specific reasons for rejecting deals, Peers rank the top four as:

1. Entrepreneurs' lack of sufficient management talent to ensure success
2. Inadequate growth potential
3. Inadequate personal knowledge about the entrepreneurs/key personnel
4. Overpriced equity

Information is key to successful results for Peer investments. Peers have uncommonly high requirements for comprehensive business plans prior to investing. Seven out of 10 successful entrepreneurs provide these plans to Peers in contrast to 6 out of 10 for all Angels.

Peers as Angels are both patient and nonaggressive. They seek majority control as an investment objective only 6 percent of the time, compared to the composite's 15 percent. However, events turn out differently; Peers actually gain control in 28 percent of their investments. When the discussion turns to voting share, listen very carefully to what Peers have to say—they mean it. The percentages of Peers by the amount of voting power actually achieved are:

- Under 25% voting share   31%
- 25–49%   18%
- 50%   22%
- 51% or more   28%

Once Peers are interested in an investment, they can be very patient awaiting its eventual liquidation and payoff. They expect a holding period of seven and a half years, compared to four years for all Angels. The percentages of Peers by length of investing holding period are:

- Under 3 years   18%
- 3–5 years   27%

- 6–10 years   32%
- Over 10 years or unimportant   23%

Key Points about Peers

- Peers are the most common subtype of Angel and account for one in three nationwide.

- They are clearly characterized as entrepreneurs and business owners who invest close to home (within 50 miles or less)—they are young, experienced entrepreneurs themselves helping new, less-experienced entrepreneurs.

- Because of their prevalence they share almost all the characteristics common to all Angels *except:* The number one deal killer is lack of management talent in the potential entrepreneur; peers do not often seek majority control, but usually get it when they do look for it; and peers are more patient than usual in waiting for an investment's eventual payoff.

COUSIN RANDY

The Angel who invests only in family business is called "Cousin Randy" for short. Finance folklore might call this Angel something like "Aunt Agnes" or "Uncle Moe," but like much conventional wisdom, it's misleading. In fact, Angels who invest only in family firms are young males with a median age of 39 years who have substantial amounts of personal entrepreneurial experience and are business owners themselves—not exactly the Aunt Agnes image. In a practical sense the profile of the Cousin Randy subtype is not very useful simply because they invest only in family businesses and display no interest in other deals. However, they do constitute a large and distinct Angel subtype, and for that reason alone they are important. Besides, there may be one in your family.

The most significant fact about Cousin Randy deals is that they are not "at arm's length" because of family ties and the special knowledge that exists within the family. As a consequence, Cousin Randy's market profile resembles no other and differs from the U.S. Composite on almost every characteristic. A glance at Cousin Randy's characteristics in Profile 4-3 will quickly confirm that they're very different. Because family-only investors are not available to most entrepreneurs, I will not go into the usual detail of how they differ from the U.S. Composite. Instead, I will review them with a brief summary.

Overview of Cousin Randy

The typical Cousin Randy is a 39-year-old male who classifies his occupation as a business owner or, more likely, as a business manager. He has entrepreneurial experience before making the family business investment. His education is lower than most Angels, and so is his income,

MARKET PROFILE 4-3. Cousin Randy

ANGELS   U.S. Composite

- • Business owner/manager is principal occupation   (79%)   (85%)
- • Has personal entrepreneurial experience   (80%)   (83%)
- + • 39 years old*   (47 years)
- • White male   (82%)   (84%)
- + • College degree   (62%)   (72%)
- + • $70,000 annual family income*   ($90,000)
- • $750,000 net worth*   ($750,000)
- + • Family members are the primary information   (Friends and associates)
  channel
- + • Accepts 5 of 10 investment opportunities*   (3)
- + • Rejects deals mostly due to overpriced equity   (Growth potential)
- + • Invests about every 36 months and has 1.0 firm
  in portfolio*   (18) (3.5)
- + • Satisfied with past investments   (85%)   (72%)
- + • One other coinvestor*   (Two)
- + • $37,500 equity invested in informal portfolio*   ($131,000)
- + • $25,000 more via loans/guarantees to portfolio firms*   ($75,000)
- • Prefers investing in FIRE firms   (38%)   (Service/FIRE)
- + • Minimum ROI target for informal portfolio   (17%)*   (22%)
- + • Active as a consultant, board member, or
  employee   (92%)   (81%)
- • Does not seek voting control   (89%)   (85%)
- • Wants to invest 32% more than opportunity permitted   (35%)

SUCCESSFUL ENTREPRENEURS/FIRMS

- + • $125,000 total Angel financing* (equity and loans)   ($176,700)
- + • $75,000 in equity and $50,000 more in loans/guarantees* ($112,500) ($64,200)
- + • Two private individuals supply funding*   (Three)
- • Entrepreneur is a white male, age 25–35   (82%)   (79%)
- + • Zero to nine employees at time of investment   (83%)   (74%)
- • Start-up or infant stage of firm growth   (69%)   (69%)
- + • Retail firms are most frequently financed   (30%)   (17% in service)
- • 50 miles or less from investor's home or office   (73%)   (72%)
- + • Has a comprehensive business plan   (73%)   (61%)
- • Has detailed marketing and financing plans

HIGH-PROBABILITY DEAL STRUCTURE

- • $37,500 in equity per investor*   ($37,500)
- • $25,000 in loans/guarantees by Angel*   ($21,400)
- • 41% voting power transferred to investor   (37%)
- • Majority control to Angel in 30% of investments   (27%)
- + • 40% capital risk seen by Angel*   (30%)
- + • 10% expected annual ROI (21% average)   (25%) (27%)
- • Common stock or partner equity instrument   (76%)   (79%)
- • Four-year liquidation horizon*   (Four years)
- + • Liquidation buyback by insiders planned   (61%)   (50%)
- + • Investor is or becomes an employee in 61% of investments   (39%)

*Median value—half higher, half lower.   + = Differs importantly from U.S. Composite.

although net worth is average. Naturally the investment opportunity was discovered through family channels, but when he rejects family deals it is most often because of overpriced equity. Cousin Randy has only one family investment in his informal portfolio. In total, Cousin Randy has $37,500 in equity committed to his family investment and another $25,000 in loans, for a total commitment of $62,500—about average by market standards. His preferred investment target is a firm in the finance, insurance, and real estate industry (FIRE), despite the fact that his family investment is actually made in a retailing firm. By composite standards Randy's minimum target ROI is a modest 17 percent, well below the 22 percent norm. In actuality, he goes into the family deal expecting an average ROI of 21 percent. Cousin Randy becomes active with the family firm in 9 cases out of 10, usually as an employee (61 percent of the time). Randy neither seeks nor gains majority control, but he says he would have invested more if opportunity had permitted.

The family entrepreneur who succeeds in winning Cousin Randy's financial support is a young male representing a very small retail trade firm. Cousin Randy and one other Angel put up a total of about $125,000 in the firm, only 70 percent of the normal capital size. This undercapitalization reflects the unusually small number of participating investors and not less capital per Angel. Despite the fact that the Angel and entrepreneur are relatives, there is no slack cut when a business plan is involved. On the contrary, the successful family entrepreneur provides a comprehensive business plan to family members more frequently than is usual for "arm's length" deals.

The deals made between relatives have some strange aspects. Cousin Randy sees the investment as more risky than usual but accepts an ROI that is below market standards. The amount of equity dollars and loans invested by Cousin Randy is about average. Despite a family relationship, Cousin Randy expects to liquidate his investment over the usual four-year period, but he is much more inclined than usual to cash out by reselling his equity to other insiders.

Key Points about Cousin Randy

- Family-only investors represent about 1 in 10 Angels but are outside the market for all entrepreneurs except family members.
- The family relationship between Angel and investor results in a market profile that differs from the composite for almost all characteristics.
- Contrary to common wisdom, the typical family Angel is not an Aunt Agnes type but is a young, experienced male who accepts a minority position, becomes active in the firm, and expects a lower-than-usual rate of return on the investment.
- Deals are usually made with very small retail firms with better-than-usual documentation (i.e., a comprehensive business plan).

• Cousin Randy, perhaps because of low ROI expectations, is more than typically satisfied with the performance of the investment.

DR. KILDARE

The title "Dr. Kildare" refers to Angels who are in the "traditional" professions: medicine, law, and others, excluding science and engineering. The Dr. Kildare group of Angels represents what many people believe to be the "typical" Angel, but this is a misconception. Dr. Kildare does represent, however, a large and important Angel subgroup that accounts for about 1 of every 10 Angels (9 percent) and their deals. Thus Dr. Kildare represents some 65,000 Angels out of the total pool of 720,000. The composite characteristics are shown in Market Profile 4-4.

As a subtype of Angel Dr. Kildare is very different from the Composite Angel; out of 40 comparisons Profile 4-4 shows differences on 13 points. These differences add up to a picture of an Angel that includes fewer white males and much higher education levels than the U.S. Composite. Dr. Kildares are Angels who rely on friends and not business associates for investment opportunity information. They are relatively inactive in the daily operations of their firms. They seek absolute control less often than usual and want to invest considerably more than usual if opportunity permits. For whatever reasons, Dr. Kildares are much less satisfied with the performance of their informal portfolios than any other Angel subgroup.

Entrepreneurs who are successful in obtaining a Dr. Kildare investment are absolutely unremarkable; that is, they fit the market composite exactly. The deals made between Dr. Kildare and the successful entrepreneur yield the good doctor less than the usual percent of voting control. The ROI expectation formed by Dr. Kildare at deal time is well below market standards, and the use of simple equity instruments occurs far more frequently than usual. The planned liquidation of Dr. Kildare's equity favors existing insiders less often than the composite deal.

Real Differences Between Dr. Kildare and the Composite Angel

The Dr. Kildare shown in Profile 4-4 is a composite of diverse experience that only hints at the real differences that exist between Dr. Kildare and the U.S. Composite Angel. It is important to look behind the composite Dr. Kildare at the diversity of the actual characteristics.

Almost half the Angel characteristics common to the composite Angel do not apply to Dr. Kildare. Apart from occupational differences, Dr. Kildare is poorly equipped when it comes to entrepreneurial experience; less than 6 out of 10 Dr. Kildares have any previous entrepreneurial experience, compared to 8 out of 10 composite Angels. This may explain in part why Dr. Kildare accepts a low ROI and is less happy with investment performance. Dr. Kildare is composed of a much higher proportion

---

MARKET PROFILE 4-4. Dr. Kildare

ANGELS   U.S. **Composite**

+ • Business owner/manager is principal occupation   (0%)   (85%)
+ • Has personal entrepreneurial experience   (58%)   (83%)
  • 49 years old*   (47 years)
+ • White male   (68%)   (84%)
+ • College degree   (94%)   (72%)
  • $90,000 annual family income*   ($90,000)
  • $750,000 net worth*   ($750,000)
+ • Friends are the primary information channel   (Friends and associates)
  • Accepts 3 of 10 investment opportunities*   (3)
  • Rejects deals mostly due to inadequate growth
    potential   (Growth potential)
  • Invests about every 18 months and has 3.5 firms
    in portfolio*   (18) (3.5)
+ • Satisfied with past investments   (61%)   (72%)
  • Two other coinvestors*   (Two)
  • $131,000 equity invested in informal portfolio*   ($131,000)
  • $75,000 more via loans/guarantees to portfolio firms*   ($75,000)
  • Prefers investing in FIRE firms   (45%)   (Service/FIRE)
  • Minimum ROI target for informal portfolio (22%)*   (22%)
+ • Active as a consultant, board member, or employee (72%)   (81%)
+ • Does not seek voting control   (94%)   (85%)
+ • Wants to invest 53% more than opportunity permitted   (35%)

SUCCESSFUL ENTREPRENEURS/FIRMS

  • $176,700 total Angel financing* (equity and loans)   ($176,700)
  • $112,500 in equity and $64,200 more in loans/
    guarantees*   ($112,500) ($64,200)
  • Three private individuals supply funding*   (Three)
  • Entrepreneur is a white male, age 25–35   (79%)   (79%)
  • Zero to nine employees at time of investment   (73%)   (74%)
  • Start-up or infant stage of firm growth   (70%)   (69%)
  • Service firms are most frequently financed (25%)   (17% in service)
  • 50 miles or less from investor's home or office   (68%)   (72%)
  • Has a comprehensive business plan   (57%)   (61%)
  • Has detailed marketing and financing plans

HIGH-PROBABILITY DEAL STRUCTURE

  • $37,500 in equity per investor*   ($37,500)
  • $21,400 in loans/guarantees by Angel*   ($21,400)
+ • 28% voting power transferred to investor   (37%)
+ • Majority control to Angel in 14% of investments   (27%)
  • 30% capital risk seen by Angel*   (30%)
+ • 10% expected annual ROI (24% average)   (25%) (27%)
+ • Common stock or partner equity instrument   (94%)   (79%)
  • Four-year liquidation horizon*   (Four years)
+ • Liquidation buyback by insiders planned   (41%)   (50%)
  • Investor is or becomes an employee in 33% of investments   (39%)

---

*Median value—half higher, half lower.   + = Differs importantly from U.S. Composite.

of minority and female members than the norm. The biggest difference is in the percentage of white females; they account for only 5 percent of the U.S. Composite Angel but almost three times more among Dr. Kildares. Minority males increase their participation rate from 11 to 18 percent. The probabilities of a Dr. Kildare Angel by demographic group are:

- White male   68%
- White female   14%
- Minority male   18%
- Minority female   0%

It should come as no surprise that the education level of Dr. Kildare Angels is exceedingly high, because most professions legally require college degrees and usually advanced degrees. Dr. Kildares are 94 percent college graduates, versus 72 percent in the market composite.

Investment information sources consist mostly of Dr. Kildare's friends. Friends are frequently used by 42 percent of "professional" Angels but only by 30 percent of the composite. The use of business associates by Dr. Kildare and the composite is about equal. It is not known whether the information source difference is because of preference or opportunity, but it is clear that friends are more frequently used by Dr. Kildare, and not that business associates are used less.

Once they invest, Dr. Kildares are not active in the firm's operations. Full-time employment for Dr. Kildare is rare and is replaced by more frequent participation as a traditional stockholder. The percentages of Dr. Kildares' activity in the firm are:

- Traditional stockholder   27%
- Board of directors   11%
- Consulting as needed   27%
- Part-time employment   29%
- Full-time employment   5%
- Other   0%

Consistent with the lower level of firm participation, Dr. Kildare seeks voting control less frequently than usual. Of all Angels, 15 percent have the objective of majority control, but only 6 percent of Dr. Kildares are thus inclined.

When businesspeople gather "even for merriment and diversion," the conversation invariably turns to investment "war stories," which almost always include a tale about the physician who invested and was "burned." There is an element of truth to this generic tale. When it comes to investment performance, Dr. Kildare is not very successful. He or she has the lowest rate of performance satisfaction of any identifiable Angel subgroup. Ony 61 percent of the Dr. Kildare Angels are satisfied, compared to the market norm of 72 percent. The biggest difference lies in the group who experiences below-expected investment performance. For Dr. Kildare it is 26 percent, but it is only 17 percent for the composite. Both groups

of Angels record the same when it comes to performance about equal
to expectation. This says that when surprises arrive they aren't good ones
for Dr. Kildare, while for all Angels surprises are about equally divided
between good and bad. The percentages of Dr. Kildare Angels by level
of satisfaction with investment performance are:

- Well above expected performance   10%
- Above expected   16%
- Equal to expected   36%
- Below expected   26%
- Well below expected   13%

Despite investing the usual amounts, Dr. Kildare ends up with only 28
percent of ownership, compared to 37 percent for the U.S. Composite Deal.
Moreover, Dr. Kildare obtains majority control in only 14 percent of deals,
consistent with the investor's objectives but well below average for all
Angels. The percent of each level of Dr. Kildare ownership is:

- Under 25% ownership   50%
- 25–49%   25%
- 50%   11%
- Over 50%   14%

Dr. Kildares' share of ownership carries a smaller-than-usual expected
rate of return. They have a median expected ROI of 10 percent and a mean
average of 24 percent, compared to 25 and 27 percent, respectively, for
all Angels. The percentages of Kildare deals by expected ROI are:

- Under 20% ROI   61%
- 20–29%   22%
- 30–39%   0%
- 40–49%   4%
- 50–99%   9%
- 100% or more   4%

This lower ROI expectation is not matched by lower risk as might be expected. Dr. Kildare's risk expectation is as high as that of any given Angel.
Perhaps this too reflects a relative lack of business experience.

    Dr. Kildares like simple equity documentation better than most; 94
percent of all their deals involve only simple common stock or a partnership equity interest. When it comes to investment liquidation, Dr. Kildares
often make no plans at all or plan to resell their interest to the firm. The
apparent lack of plans to resell to insiders mostly reflects no plans at
all and more emphasis on eventual public stock offerings. The percentages of Dr. Kildare deals by type of cash-out method are:

- None   32%
- Resell to company   26%
- Resell to coinvestors   16%
- Sell or merge with another firm   10%

- Public offering   11%
- Other and combinations   4%

Key Points about Dr. Kildare

- Dr. Kildare represents Angels whose occupations include the traditional professions of medicine, law, accounting, and others but not science or engineering.

- Dr. Kildare as a subgroup of Angels represents about 1 out of 10 Angels in the market, far less than is commonly believed.

- Dr. Kildare Angels are clearly distinct from other Angels in ways that are both expected and unexpected. Perhaps one of the most unexpected results of isolating their type of Angel comes in the form of how they are *not* different when we would expect them to be. They are quite average when it comes to income levels, wealth, number of deals and frequency of investing, dollars invested both total and per deal, characteristics of successful entrepreneurs, and rejection reasons.

- What sets Dr. Kildares apart from other Angels are their: low percentage of white males; lack of business and entrepreneurial experience; reliance on friends for information; high price paid for equity (low percent of ownership per dollar invested); low participation in firm operations; low ROI; low success rate (satisfaction level); and, somewhat incredibly, the extraordinarily high desire to invest in more of the same!

CORPORATE ACHIEVERS

Professional venture capitalists often identify a subtype of Angel who is a business executive with some degree of success in large corporate organizations but who wants to be more entrepreneurial in a top management slot. Even though they are easily identified, they are few in number, accounting for about 13 percent of all Angels. Nevertheless, they are a clearly distinct type that differs substantially from the U.S. Composite. I introduce Corporate Achievers here only for the sake of completeness. As a group, their behavior might be more aptly named "Corporate Claim Jumpers" since they appear to be frustrated middle-level corporate managers who want to run the show and in the process of a career change often take control of a small business from the entrepreneur. Because entrepreneurs frequently lose control to Corporate Achievers, I have placed the profile and discussion of them in Chapter 11, "Devils, Dead Ends, and Deal Breakers," where they fit nicely.

DADDY WARBUCKS

In the comic strip "Little Orphan Annie," the character of "Daddy Warbucks" is a benevolent business tycoon. I use the name in a more limited sense here to refer to any Angels who have a net worth of $1 million or more—whether they are benevolent remains to be seen. Millionaires merit an Angel class of their own because folklore claims that Angels are *usually* millionaires or people of substantial means. In reality, very wealthy Angels represent only one-third of all Angels. As a large minority with money, Daddy Warbucks Angels are important, just not all important. They make 39 percent of all deals, but they provide a disproportionately large share (68 percent) of all risk capital. In other words, when they invest it's big!

What does Daddy Warbucks look and behave like? As shown in Profile 4-5, Daddy is male, owns his own business more often than usual, and uses business associates more than friends to learn of investment opportunity. He insists on comprehensive business plans prior to investing in his favorite industry: finance, insurance, and real estate (FIRE).

The equity dollars Daddy Warbucks commits per deal are no more than average, but he does provide four times the usual amount of loans/guarantees. His interest in majority control is lower than that of the U.S. Composite, and he is successful in his investments.

Real Differences Between Daddy Warbucks and the Composite Angel

Profile 4-5 gives us a composite millionaire picture that obscures diverse market experience. The objective now is to look behind the composite Daddy Warbucks at the distinguishing characteristics.

Like his comic strip namesake, Daddy Warbucks is a wealthy, self-made, male business owner who is about as well educated as other Angels. The percentages of Daddy Warbucks by occupation group are:

- Business owners/managers   78%
- Salespeople   3%
- Science and engineering professionals   1%
- Other professionals   5%
- Other   13%

Daddy Warbucks relies more on business associates than on friends for information about investment opportunity, although friends are a close second source. The direct approach by entrepreneurs is the third-most-likely information source but is the channel less than half as frequently as business associates or friends. The percentages of source of investment information for Daddy Warbucks are:

- Business associates   37%
- Friends   32%
- Entrepreneurs   15%
- Bankers/brokers   8%
- Others   8%

MARKET PROFILE 4-5. Daddy Warbucks

ANGELS	U.S. Composite
+ • Business owner/manager is principal occupation (78%)	(69%)
• Has personal entrepreneurial experience (85%)	(83%)
• 49 years old*	(47 yrs.)
+ • White male (96%)	(84%)
• College degree (76%)	(72%)
+ • $150,000 annual family income*	($90,000)
+ • $1,000,000 net worth* or more	($750,000)
+ • Associates are the primary information channel	(Friends and associates)
• Accepts 3 of 10 investment opportunities*	(3)
• Rejects deals mostly due to inadequate growth potential	(Growth potential)
• Invests about every 18 months and has 3.5 firms in portfolio*	(18) (3.5)
+ • Satisfied with past investments (82%)	(72%)
• Three other coinvestors*	(Two)
• $131,000 equity invested in informal portfolio*	($131,000)
+ • $300,000 more via loans/guarantees to portfolio firms*	($75,000)
• Prefers investing in FIRE firms (41%)	(Service/FIRE)
• Minimum ROI target for informal portfolio (22%)*	(22%)
• Active as a consultant, board member, or employee (80%)	(81%)
+ • Does not seek voting control (95%)	(85%)
• Wants to invest 35% more than opportunity permitted	(35%)

SUCCESSFUL ENTREPRENEURS/FIRMS

+ • $493,000 total Angel financing* (equity and loans)	($176,700)
+ • $150,000 in equity and $343,000 more in loans/guarantees*	($112,500) ($64,200)
• Four private individuals supply funding*	(Three)
• Entrepreneur is a white male, age 25–35 (85%)	(79%)
• Zero to nine employees at time of investment (67%)	(74%)
• Start-up or infant stage of firm growth (68%)	(69%)
+ • FIRE industry firms are most frequently financed (21%)	(17% in service)
• 50 miles or less from investor's home or office (69%)	(72%)
+ • Has a comprehensive business plan (70%)	(61%)
• Has detailed marketing and financing plans	

HIGH-PROBABILITY DEAL STRUCTURE

• $37,500 in equity per investor*	($37,500)
+ • $85,700 in loans/guarantees by Angels*	($21,400)
• 30% voting power transferred to investor	(37%)
• Majority control to Angel in 25% of investments	(27%)
• 30% capital risk seen by Angel*	(30%)
• 25% expected annual ROI (27% average)	(25%) (27%)
• Common stock or partner equity instrument (83%)	(79%)
• Four-year liquidation horizon*	(Four years)
+ • Liquidation buyback by insiders planned (32%)	(50%)
+ • Investor is or becomes an employee in 25% of investments	(39%)

---

*Median value—half higher, half lower.   + = Differs importantly from U.S. Composite.

Daddy Warbucks says he rarely seeks majority control in his investments, but the actual level of his ownership share is consistent with market standards. The percentages of Daddy Warbucks' voting power per investment are:

- Under 25% voting share   49%
- 25–49%   11%
- 50%   15%
- Over 50%   25%

The total risk capital committed by Daddy Warbucks per investment is very large by composite standards; $123,000 versus $59,000, respectively. The large size of loans/guarantees and not equity accounts for the difference. The range of deal sizes suggests that Daddy Warbucks accommodates the needs of good deals of any size and is not solely interested just in "big" deals. The percentages of Daddy Warbucks' total risk capital commitment per investment are:

- Under $30,000   10%
- $30,000–$79,999   20%
- $80,000–$159,999   23%
- $160,000–$324,999   17%
- $325,000–$800,000   20%
- Over $800,000   10%

Daddy Warbucks both prefers and invests in FIRE firms, in contrast to the U.S. Composite Angel, who most often invests in the service industry. The percentages of industries Daddy Warbucks actually invests in are:

- Natural resources/mining   5%
- Construction   10%
- Manufacturing—high-technology   11%
- Manufacturing—industrial   9%
- Manufacturing—consumer   6%
- Transportation, communication, utilities   1%
- Wholesale trade   5%
- Retail trade   12%
- Finance/insurance/real estate   21%
- Services   18%
- Other   2%

When the time for liquidating the investment arrives, Daddy Warbucks has planned more frequently than other Angels to exit by selling to outsiders or by using combinations of methods. The percentages of expected liquidation methods are:

- None   26%
- Sell to company   22%
- Sell to coinvestor   11%
- Merge or sell to another company 7%

- Public offering   8%
- Other and combinations   26%

The "bottom line," as always, is performance, and here Daddy Warbucks excels. Over 8 out of 10 financings meet or exceed initial expectations, in contrast to 7 out of 10 for all Angels. One in 5 Daddy Warbucks deals performed *well above* expected, compared to 1 in 8 for all Angels. The percent of Daddy Warbucks investments in each level of actual performance is:

- Well above expected performance   21%
- Above expectations   22%
- Equal to expected   39%
- Below expected   11%
- Well below expected   7%

Key Points about Daddy Warbucks

- Daddy Warbucks Angels are all millionaires. They are also male business owners more than usual. They make up one-third of the Angels but provide two-thirds of the total risk capital.
- Business associates are the prime information channel, followed by friends and the entrepreneurs themselves.
- Total risk capital funding averages twice the size of that of other Angels, with an emphasis on large loan/guarantee amounts. Majority control is not a high priority but is acquired in the usual number of cases.
- Daddy Warbucks prefers FIRE deals supported by comprehensive business plans.
- Investment success is unusually high.
- Like their namesake, Daddy Warbucks appear benevolent.

HIGH-TECH ANGELS

Media hype has raised high-technology manufacturing firms to almost a cult status in financial markets, seemingly the last hope of American economic leadership. Along with these high-tech firms and their touted entrepreneurs, the Angels who provide the fuel for this reportedly awesome industry have also attained an inflated importance among business Angels. Here we see what kind of Angels the High-Techies really are.

A High-Tech Angel is an individual investor who is interested *only* in investing in firms that manufacture high-technology products. This should not be confused with the high-tech industry investor profiled in Chapter 9. Those Chapter 9 investors (13 percent of total Angel pool) have invested in other firms in addition to high-technology companies. The concept of High-Tech Angels used here is much narrower and more highly specialized, and their number is accordingly smaller; about 45,000 nationwide (6 percent of the Angel pool).

High-Tech Angels are a special subtype of wealthier, more experienced businesspeople who form larger-than-usual coinvestor Angel
groups to finance very small, capital-intensive firms. High-Tech investors
stick close to their deals by being unusually active in the firm's operations. Despite investing typical amounts they rarely obtain voting control and often receive smaller-than-usual equity shares. They are more
patient than other Angels in waiting for equity liquidation, which they
plan to get by cashing in through outsiders. The full set of market characteristics for High-Tech Angels is presented in Profile 4-6.

Real Differences Between High-Techs and the Composite Angel

Profile 4-6 gives us only a broad-brush portrait of the real differences
that exist between High-Tech Angels and the U.S. Composite Angel,
because the High-Tech Angels are themselves composites of diverse
market experience.

High-Techs have an unusually high concentration of business owners/
managers but no more than the expected degree of experienced entrepreneurs. The only other sizeable occupational group within High-Tech Angels besides business owners is sales occupations, which account for only
9 percent of High-Tech Angels. Interestingly enough, science and engineering occupations provide almost no High-Tech Angels (3 percent of total). High-Techs are wealthy businesspeople with a median net worth of
$1 million or more. The percentages of High-Techs by net worth class are:

- $300,000 or less   12%
- $300,000–$499,999   4%
- $500,000–$1,000,000   28%
- Over $1,000,000   56%

Apparently those Angels with a net worth of only half a million or less
are the "true believers," making large financial sacrifices and taking big
risks by scraping together every penny they can find to back their entrepreneurs. High-Tech Angels are almost totally white male—compared
to the Composite Angels' 84 percent.

Where do these Angels find out about High-Technology investment
opportunities? By three-to-two majority, they rely on information from
friends, and they get information directly from entrepreneurs more frequently than they do from business associates.

Capital-intensive High-Technology firms receive about two-thirds
more total risk capital investment than the composite of all industries.
In order to supply that capital, High-Tech Angels combine into larger
coinvestor groups. The percentage of High-Tech Angels in each coinvestor
group size is:

- 1 Angel   8%
- 2   0%

- 3   13%
- 4   25%
- 5–10   38%
- More than 10   16%

These Angels stick close to their money by being an active part of the entrepreneur's firm. Their type of participation can be broken down as:

- None   10%
- Board member   15%
- Consultant (as needed)   39%
- Full-time employee   16%
- Part-time employee   20%

Their investment goals rarely include ownership control (4 percent, compared to the composite goal of 15 percent). Perhaps this simply reflects the larger number of Angels involved.

The successful High-Tech entrepreneur needs and gets 166 percent of the usual total risk capital. This larger amount is due entirely to more coinvestors involved, not to larger investments per Angel. The percentage of High-Tech firms receiving each size class of total risk capital is:

- Under $75,000   19%
- $75,000–$199,999   25%
- $200,000–$399,999   9%
- $400,000–$799,999   28%
- $800,000–$2,000,000   11%
- Over $2,000,000   8%

The capital intensiveness of high-technology firms is clearly seen from their small employment size relative to the total risk capital involved. High-Tech firms have under 10 employees in 84 percent of the financings, compared to 74 percent for all industries. The major difference lies in the 5 to 9 employee size group, in which the composite makes only 17 percent of its investments. The percentages of High-Tech firms' employment size at deal time is:

- 0–4 employees   46%
- 5–9   38%
- 10–19   3%
- 20 or more   13%

High-Tech deals generate less ownership share and absolute control for the Angels than usual. High-Tech Angels envision a longer waiting period prior to cashing in (seven and a half years). When they do liquidate, they clearly favor cashing in by selling to outsiders, and they favor eventual public stock offering disproportionately more than the composite Angel.

MARKET PROFILE 4-6. High-Tech Angels

<u>ANGELS</u>   U.S. **Composite**

+ • Business owner/manager is principal occupation (81%)   (69%)
  • Has personal entrepreneurial experience (85%)   (83%)
  • 49 years old*   (47 years)
+ • White male (96%)   (84%)
  • College degree (77%)   (72%)
  • $90,000 annual family income*   ($90,000)
+ • $1,000,000 net worth*   ($750,000)
+ • Friends and entrepreneurs are the primary   (Friends and associates)
    information channel
  • Accepts 3 of 10 investment opportunities*   (3)
  • Rejects deals mostly due to lack of personal knowledge   (Growth potential)
    about entrepreneur/key personnel and inadequate
    growth potential
  • Invests about every 18 months and has 3.5 firms in
    portfolio*   (18) (3.5)
  • Satisfied with past investments (78%)   (72%)
+ • Four other coinvestors*   (Two)
  • $131,000 equity invested in informal portfolio*   ($131,000)
  • $75,000 more via loans/guarantees to portfolio firms*   ($75,000)
+ • Prefers investing in high-technology firms (63%)   (Service/FIRE)
  • Minimum ROI target for informal portfolio (22%)*   (22%)
+ • Active as a consultant, board member, or employee (90%)   (81%)
+ • Does not seek voting control (96%)   (85%)
  • Wants to invest 37% more than opportunity permitted   (35%)

SUCCESSFUL ENTREPRENEURS/FIRMS

+ • $295,000 total Angel financing* (equity and loans)   ($176,700)
+ • $187,500 in equity and $107,000 more in
    loans/guarantees*   ($112,500) ($64,200)
+ • Five private individuals supply funding*   (Three)
  • Entrepreneur is a white male, age 25–35 (82%)   (79%)
+ • Zero to nine employees at time of investment (84%)   (74%)
  • Start-up or infant stage of firm growth (65%)   (69%)
  • High-technology firms are most frequently
    financed   (100%)   (17% in service)
  • 50 miles or less from investor's home or office (68%)   (72%)
  • Has a comprehensive business plan (66%)   (61%)
  • Has detailed marketing and financing plans

HIGH-PROBABILITY DEAL STRUCTURE

  • $37,500 in equity per investor*   ($37,500)
  • $21,400 in loans/guarantees by Angel*   ($21,400)
+ • 23% voting power transferred to investor   (37%)
+ • Majority control to Angel in 15% of investments   (27%)
  • 30% capital risk seen by Angel*   (30%)
  • 25% expected annual ROI (24% average)   (25%) (27%)
  • Common stock or partner equity instrument (83%)   (79%)
+ • Liquidation horizon of seven and a half years*   (Four years)
+ • Limited liquidation buyback by insiders planned (19%)   (50%)
  • Investor is or becomes an employee in 36% of
    investments   (39%)

---

*Median value—half higher, half lower.   + = Differs importantly from U.S. Composite.

Key Points about High-Tech Angels

- High-Tech Angels, who invest only in firms manufacturing high-technology products, are only 6 percent of all Angels, despite media hype.
- These Angels should not be confused with those in Chapter 9's section "Angels in the high-tech Industry" because the latter include any Angels that have made a high-technology industry investment, and the two sets of Angels are far from the same.
- High-Tech Angels are almost exclusively wealthy, white male business owners/managers.
- Most often High-Tech investment opportunities are discovered through friends and directly via enterpreneurs themselves, while business associates as information channels come in third place.
- The extraordinarily large amount of risk capital High-Tech firms receive is the result of larger Angel coinvestor groups. Each High-Tech Angel has only average amount of money committed.
- High-Tech Angels participate actively more than expected in the very small firms they finance, thus adding experience and expertise to their dollars.
- Techies accept unusually low ownership shares given the size of their investment. They're more patient than other Angels, waiting over seven years to cash in.

THE STOCKHOLDER

Angel participation can be a mixed blessing in a firm's daily operation. Some entrepreneurs welcome help from any quarter, while other entrepreneurs see it as meddling. The least-intrusive Angel involvement comes in the traditional share owner role. These Stockholder Angels occasionally read reports and may vote their shares at stockholders meetings, but they play no other role in firm operations. About 11 percent of all Angels fit this mold. The other participation extreme is the full-time employee Angels, who are sufficiently common (accounting for about 17 percent of all Angels) that their market profile shows no important differences from the U.S. Composite. Our interest here is with the Stockholder.

Angels who do not participate in the firm except in the traditional share owner role are less likely to be business owners/managers themselves. They invest infrequently and usually along with many other Angels. Their investment is typically small in terms of both equity and loans, and Stockholder Angels reject deals primarily due to insufficient personal knowledge of the entrepreneur/key personnel. The firms they choose to invest in are in finance, insurance, and real estate, often more than 50 miles away. Stockholders view their investments as more risky than usual, but their return on investment expectations are not higher.

Because of the small dollar commitment to any one entrepreneur, the Stockholder Angel ownership share is well below the composite. The full market profile of the Stockholder is presented in Profile 4-7.

Real Differences Between the Stockholder and the Composite Angel

The composite Stockholder is more diverse than implied by the profile line items. Stockholders' personal characteristics are similar to the composite, but when we look at market activity important differences begin to appear. Stockholders are very sensitive about personally knowing the entrepreneur they invest in. This issue is so important to them that lack of this information is the leading deal killer. The top four Stockholder rejection reasons, in rank order, are:

1. Insufficient personal knowledge about entrepreneur/key personnel
2. Limited growth chances
3. Insufficient information generally
4. Management's lack of necessary talent

Stockholders do not invest often and consequently have small portfolios. Generally they invest only about once each 36 months. The percentages of the number of their investments are:

- 1 investment   61%
- 2   22%
- 3   8%
- 4   4%
- 5 or more   4%

When the Stockholder does invest, he or she is only one of a large group of typically seven coinvestors, compared to two coinvestors for the composite Angel. The percentages of Stockholder Angels by number of coinvestors are:

- None   15%
- 1   10%
- 2   7%
- 3   7%
- 4   10%
- 5–10   34%
- Over 10   17%

The dollar size of Stockholders' capital contribution is unusually small, with a median equity value of only $17,500 and another $14,700 in loan guarantees. The percentages of Stockholders by equity investment per deal are:

- Under $10,000   30%
- $10,000–$24,999   30%

MARKET PROFILE 4-7. The Stockholder

ANGELS   U.S. Composite

- Business owner/manager is principal occupation (73%)   (70%)
- Has personal entrepreneurial experience (77%)   (83%)
- 49 years old*   (47 years)
- White male (76%)   (84%)
- College degree (67%)   (72%)
- $90,000 annual family income*   ($90,000)
- $750,000 net worth*   ($750,000)
+ Friends are the primary information channel   (Friends and associates)
- Accepts 3 of 10 investment opportunities*   (3)
+ Rejects deals mostly due to inadequate personal   (Growth potential)
  knowledge of entrepreneur/key personnel
+ Invests about every 36 months and has 1.7 firms in   (18) (3.5)
  portfolio*
- Satisfied with past investments (77%)   (72%)
+ Seven other coinvestors*   (Two)
+ $29,800 equity invested in informal portfolio*   ($131,000)
+ $25,000 more via loans/guarantees to portfolio firms*   ($75,000)
- Prefers investing in FIRE firms (43%)   (Service/FIRE)
- Minimum ROI target for informal portfolio (22%)*   (22%)
+ Active as a consultant, board member, or employee (0%)   (81%)
- Does not seek voting control (91%)   (85%)
- Wants to invest 41% more than opportunity permitted   (35%)

SUCCESSFUL ENTREPRENEURS/FIRMS

+ $257,600 total Angel financing* (equity and loans)   ($176,700)
+ $140,000 in equity and $117,600 more in
  loans/guarantees*   ($112,500) ($64,200)
+ Eight private individuals supply funding*   (Three)
- Entrepreneur is a white male, age 24–35 (82%)   (79%)
- Zero to nine employees at time of investment (69%)   (74%)
- Start-up or infant stage of firm growth (70%)   (69%)
+ FIRE firms are most frequently financed (34%)   (17% in service)
+ 50 miles or less from investor's home or office (53%)   (72%)
- Has a comprehensive business plan (64%)   (61%)
- Has detailed marketing and financing plans

HIGH-PROBABILITY DEAL STRUCTURE

+ $17,500 in equity per investor*   ($37,500)
+ $14,700 in loans/guarantees by Angel*   ($21,400)
+ 12% voting power transferred to investor   (37%)
+ Majority control to Angel in 10% of investments   (27%)
+ 40% capital risk seen by Angel*   (30%)
- 25% expected annual ROI (29% average)   (25%) (27%)
- Common stock or partner equity instrument (77%)   (79%)
- Four-year liquidation horizon*   (Four years)
- Liquidation buyback by insiders planned (51%)   (50%)
+ Investor is or becomes an employee in 0% of investments   (39%)

---

*Median value—half higher, half lower.   + = Differs importantly from U.S. Composite.

- $25,000–$49,999   9%
- $50,000–$99,999   11%
- $100,000–$250,000   16%
- Over $250,000   5%

The small investment size may reflect the fact that Stockholders view informal investments as more risky than do most Angels. However, the higher risk does not show up as a higher return when the Stockholder does invest.

Rarely do Stockholders gain major voting control, and generally the ownership share they receive for their investment is very small. The size of the ownership share Stockholders obtain in any one investment is:

- Under 25% voting control   81%
- 25–49%   4%
- 50%   5%
- Over 50%   10%

Stockholder Angels most frequently invest in finance, insurance, and real estate and often more than 50 miles away. The percentages of Stockholder Angels by industry they invest in are:

- Natural resources/mining   11%
- Construction   5%
- Manufacturing—high-technology   6%
- Manufacturing—industrial   4%
- Manufacturing—consumer   4%
- Transportation, communication, and utilities   1%
- Wholesale trade   2%
- Retail trade   8%
- Finance/insurance/real estate   34%
- Services   22%
- Other   4%

The distance from the entrepreneur's firm to the Stockholder's home or office is:

- 10 miles away or less   30%
- 10–50 miles   23%
- 50–150 miles   8%
- Over 150 miles   38%

Key Points about the Stockholder

- Stockholder Angels are the least active in firm operations of all Angel types and represent about 1 out of every 10 Angels. (The most active investors, full-time employee Angels, are more common, representing 17 percent of all Angels. They do not differ in any important characteristic from the profile of all Angels.)

- The Stockholder is an infrequent investor who invests small amounts, usually as part of a large group of coinvestors. The share of voting power is correspondingly small.
- Stockholder Angels target the FIRE industry and firms far from home. They view these circumstances as unusually risky but do not receive any higher ROI for that risk.

VERY HUNGRY ANGELS

There is a subtype of Angel who not only wants to invest more than opportunity has allowed but who desires to *more than double* the level of informal risk capital commitments. These Angels I call "Very Hungry Angels." Among all Angels, a majority of 53 percent would have invested more than they did. Those who would have more than doubled their investment represent a much smaller group of only 15 percent of all investors. In this section I examine what this special group looks like and which market factors make them special.

Very Hungry Angels are most often not business owners/managers. They make smaller-than-usual dollar commitments to their entrepreneurs but expect and hold out for high rates of return. They rely on friends more than on business associates for investment opportunity information and aggressively seek majority control as an investment goal (but succeed no more than usual). Very Hungry Angels invest in larger-size firms than usual, in conflict with both their pattern of seeking majority control and making small capital contributions. Their characteristics are shown in full in Market Profile 4-8.

Real Differences Between
Very Hungry Angels and the Composite Angel

Profile 4-8 shows only composite, summary differences that exist between Very Hungry Angels and the U.S. Composite Angel. The objective now is to look behind the summary to discern the range of real characteristics of Very Hungry Angels.

Perhaps the single most distinguishing mark of a Very Hungry Angel is that he is not generally in the business sector of the economy. Sales, medicine, law, accounting, and miscellaneous nonbusiness occupations are heavily overrepresented among Very Hungry Angels, and science and engineering are largely unrepresented. This occupational difference may account in part for their unusually high minimum ROI goals and the inconsistency of their majority control objective coupled with small dollar commitments and the habit of investment in larger-size firms. The percentages of Very Hungry Angels by principal occupation are:

MARKET PROFILE 4-8. Very Hungry Angels

ANGELS   U.S. Composite

+ • Business owner/manager is principal occupation   (43%)   (69%)
  • Has personal entrepreneurial experience   (81%)   (83%)
  • 49 years old*   (47 years)
  • White male   (81%)   (84%)
  • College degree   (70%)   (72%)
+ • $70,000 annual family income*   ($90,000)
  • $750,000 net worth*   ($750,000)
+ • Friends are the primary information channel   (Friends and associates)
  • Accepts 3 of 10 investment opportunities*   (3)
  • Rejects deals mostly due to inadequate growth
    potential   (Growth potential)
  • Invests about every 18 months and has 3.5 firms in   (18) (3.5)
    portfolio*
  • Satisfied with past investments   (71%)   (72%)
  • Two other coinvestors*   (Two)
+ • $61,000 equity invested in informal portfolio*   ($131,000)
+ • $25,000 more via loans/guarantees to portfolio firms*   ($75,000)
  • Prefers investing in FIRE firms   (41%)   (Service/FIRE)
+ • Minimum ROI target for informal portfolio   (27%)*   (22%)
  • Active as a consultant, board member, or employee   (81%)   (81%)
+ • Does not seeking voting control   (58%)   (85%)
+ • Wants to invest over 100% more than opportunity
    permitted   (35%)

SUCCESSFUL ENTREPRENEURS/FIRMS

+ • $73,800 total Angel financing* (equity and loans)   ($176,700)
+ • $52,500 in equity and $21,300 more in loans/guarantees*   ($112,500) ($64,200)
  • Three private individuals supply funding*   (Three)
+ • Entrepreneur is a white male, age 25–35   (67%)   (79%)
+ • Zero to nine employees at time of investment   (58%)   (74%)
  • Start-up or infant stage of firm growth   (64%)   (69%)
  • Service firms are most frequently financed   (19%)   (17% in service)
  • 50 miles or less from investor's home or office   (70%)   (72%)
+ • Has a comprehensive business plan   (76%)   (61%)
  • Has detailed marketing and financing plans

HIGH-PROBABILITY DEAL STRUCTURE

+ • $17,500 in equity per investor*   ($37,500)
+ • $7,100 in loans/guarantees by Angel*   ($21,400)
  • 33% voting power transferred to investor   (37%)
  • Majority control to Angel in 29% of investments   (27%)
  • 30% capital risk seen by Angel*   (30%)
  • 25% expected annual ROI   (32% average)   (25%) (27%)
  • Common stock or partner equity instrument   (75%)   (79%)
+ • Liquidation horizon of seven and a half years   (Four years)
  • Liquidation buyback by insiders planned   (42%)   (50%)
  • Investor is or becomes an employee in 41% of investments   (39%)

---

*Median value—half higher, half lower.   + = Differs importantly from U.S. Composite.

- Business owner/manager   43%
- Sales   12%
- Science and engineering professionals   2%
- Other professionals   11%
- Others   32%

The 27 percent minimum ROI target for Very Hungry Angels is the highest of all Angel subgroups. The single biggest difference from all Angels is in the 50 to 99 percent ROI class, where all Angels report only 10 percent of their deals. Surely these extremely high ROI demands must be severe limiting factors preventing the "Hungries" from investing more. The percentages of Very Hungry Angels by expected ROI are:

- Under 20% ROI   39%
- 20–29%   32%
- 30–39%   4%
- 40–49%   4%
- 50–99%   18%
- 100% or more   4%

Despite their high ROI expectations, Very Hungry Angels do not put up much capital. They generally invest only $17,500 per investment, with another $7,100 in loans/guarantees. Both these amounts are well below half the size for all Angels. The size of equity dollars committed by Very Hungry Angels is:

- Under $10,000   33%
- $10,000–$24,999   23%
- $25,000–$49,999   12%
- $50,000–$99,999   11%
- $100,000–$250,000   9%
- Over $250,000   13%

Over three-fourths of Very Hungry Angels require comprehensive business plans prior to investing (close to the highest rate found). Very Hungry Angels also claim one of the highest voting control objectives of all—42 percent say they want majority control when they invest. When it comes to actually achieving majority ownership, however, they do no better than the composite. No wonder, since Very Hungry Angels make small capital investments in larger-than-usual firms. These Angels invest in small firms with zero to nine employees only 58 percent of the time, compared to the usual 74 percent for all Angels. The largest gap is for the 20 and over employee firm size where all Angels placed 12 percent of their deals. The percentages of Very Hungry Angel investment by employment size of firms are:

- 0–4 employees   52%
- 5–9   6%
- 10–19   19%
- 20 or more   23%

Very Hungry Angels rely more on friends than on business associates for information. This is the only Angel group that pays much attention to (unpaid) investment banker/broker information. Nevertheless, that channel still lags behind both friends and business associates. The percentages of information channels used by Very Hungry Angels are:

- Business associates   35%
- Friends   29%
- Entrepreneurs   12%
- Investment
  bankers/brokers   24%
- Others   0%

Key Points about Very Hungry Angels

- Very Hungry Angels want to invest 100 percent or more than past opportunity has allowed, and they represent 15 percent of all Angels.
- They want a high return but do not put up much risk capital.
- They want majority control more than others do, but they don't get it because of their small investments in larger-than-usual service industry firms.
- They primarily listen to friends as information sources but pay attention to unpaid investment bankers/brokers more than do other Angel groups.
- Very Hungry Angels come from a variety of occupations, with business owners/managers in the minority. This lack of daily business environment contact probably accounts for the rather odd and conflicting mix of market characteristics and results that are typical of this Angel group.

As the market profiles in this chapter indicate, there is an encouraging variety of Angel subtypes—many of whom share the composite characteristic of wanting to invest more than opportunity has permitted! Details of how to locate and approach this cast of Angels are given in the next chapter, "Where to Look and What to Say."

5

WHERE TO LOOK
AND WHAT TO SAY

Where are Angels found? How do they learn about investment opportunities? What information do they require for an investment decision? How can we pinpoint frequent, "high-probability" Angels? Why are some seriously considered proposals rejected? This chapter provides some answers to these and related questions. Each year the pool of U.S. Angels sees about 2.1 million investment proposals; they seriously consider some 740,000, reject 250,000, and eventually fund 490,000 deals with 87,000 entrepreneurs. A giant exchange of information is required to handle this volume of investment proposals as they work through the investment decision stages. Unfortunately, the giant is lame, blind, and confused. It cannot be said to function beyond the hit-or-miss personal searching typical of both entrepreneurs and Angels. From an outside point of view the whole matchup process resembles an almost random game of "Pin the Deal on the Angel" with everyone blindfolded and constantly moving.

Nevertheless, some investment information is transmitted between entrepreneurs and Angels, no matter how inefficient or costly the process. Until now, this complex, localized information exchange was not much studied, and definitive descriptions of how the system works may be a long time coming. But the facts presented here shed some first light, allowing plans for more economical and rational seed capital strategies. Again, the facts will raise more questions than they answer, but they do suggest some important answers about network geography, Angel information sources, types of information they want, high-probability Angel characteristics, and, finally, why some seriously considered deals fail to jell. We will also look at some new developments that employ computer matching to put Angels and entrepreneurs in touch with each other.

ANGEL GEOGRAPHY

Angels invest where they live, and they live everywhere. The Angels in the survey are not clustered in major financial centers or limited to large urban areas. They live throughout the United States. In fact the single best predictor of the size of the local Angel pool is simply local population. There are about 4 Angels in almost any 1000 adults selected at random. Survey evidence says that this proportion remains fairly constant whether the local population is large or small. This relatively uniform distribution of Angels among the general population should not surprise us since the bulk of Angels as we know are local businesspeople and professionals.

Dorothy's dilemma in *The Wizard of Oz* was where to look for happiness. Entrepreneurs do not face that uncertainty. Angels have solved the question of where to look rather neatly by rarely (only 7 percent of the time) investing more than 150 miles from their own home or office. Angel capital is even more homegrown than implied by the 150-mile limit—40 percent of all deals are inside 10 miles! The geographical perspective says Angel capital doesn't travel far and that Angel markets are highly Balkanized. A radius of 50 miles probably exceeds the size of most urban areas in the United States. Thus your chances are 7 in 10 that your deal will find its Angel in your city. Save your travel time and money for more productive use. The facts present an unequivocal lesson: "Stay in Kansas." The percentages of all Angel deals by the miles between the firm's location and the Angel's home or office are repeated here from Chapter 2 for convenience:

- Under 10 miles   40%
- 10–50   32%
- 51–150   10%
- Over 150   11%
- Unimportant   7%

ANGEL INFORMATION SOURCES

Nothing happens until an Angel becomes aware of a business investment opportunity. How does this awareness come about? The Angels who responded to the survey were asked to rate potential information channels for both frequency and reliability of use, with the following scale index:

1 = Frequent and highly reliable information source
2 = Often a reliable source
3 = Occasionally a source or sometimes reliable
4 = Seldom a source or slightly reliable
5 = Not a source or unreliable

The sum of the 416 responses gives this picture: Angels rely about equally on either friends or business associates as their primary investment information sources. This combined, indirect channel is followed in second place by the direct channel of entrepreneurs themselves as the source of initial contact. Other channels are rated by Angels as too infrequent and/or unreliable to be of much value. The rank order of information sources and an index of use are:

Rank	Information Sources	Frequency and Reliability Index
1	Business associates	2.2
2	Friends	2.4
3	Entrepreneurs	2.9
4	Investment bankers*	3.4
5	Investment/business brokers*	3.6
6	Others*	3.9

* = No fees involved.

Because most Angels report using a mixture of both direct and indirect channels, they cannot tell us about differences between the two approaches since their market profile characteristics are virtually identical to the U.S. Composite. However, some Angels show definite patterns of using either direct or indirect sources. From them we can get some idea how the profile patterns change between these two main sources. Market Profile 5-1 is a side-by-side comparison of Angels, entrepreneurs, and deals that exposes channel differences. The column labeled "Direct" shows the market characteristics associated with actual deals initiated by direct contact between the entrepreneurs and Angel. The second column ("Indirect") shows the market characteristics associated with deals that begin indirectly via either friends or business associates. Criteria in Profile 5-1 for distinguishing "important" differences between information channels is wider than usual because the number of cases is smaller. Nevertheless, a glance at the plus (+) signs in the profile reveals many differences. For comparison purposes I will focus on the direct, entrepreneurial approach channel.

Direct-Approach Angels

Angels who primarily learn about investment opportunities directly from entrepreneurs differ markedly from both indirect channel users and the U.S. Composite. Angels accepting a direct approach are young Angels with a high frequency of being entrepreneurs themselves (sympathy?). However they do not consider business ownership as their prime occupation. They are less often white males and have far lower incomes and

---

MARKET PROFILE 5-1.
Comparison of Investment Opportunity Information Sources

ANGELS

	Direct	Indirect
• Business owner/manager is principal occupation	40%	80%+
• Has entrepreneurial experience	100%	84%+
• Age*	39 years	49 years+
• White male	60%	74%+
• College degree	60%	71%
• Annual family income*	$50,000	$70,000+
• Net worth*	$300,000	$750,000+
• Deal acceptance rate (%)*	30	50+
• Main deal rejection reason	Equity price	Growth potential
• Investment frequency*	12 months	18 months+
• Satisfied with past investments	40%	59%+
• Number of coinvestors*	Three	Two
• Total equity invested in portfolio firms*	$188,000	$131,000
• Total loans/guarantees to portfolio firms*	$25,000	$25,000
• Minimum ROI target for informal portfolio*	17%	22%+
• Active as a consultant, board member, or employee	82%	82%
• Does not seek voting control	67%	93%+
• Wants to invest more than opportunity permitted	45%	38%

SUCCESSFUL ENTREPRENEURS/FIRMS

	Direct	Indirect
• Total Angel financing* (equity and loans)	$170,000	$152,000
• Equity to loan ratio*	7.5	6.2
• Number of private individuals supplying funding*	Four	Three
• Entrepreneur is a white male, age 25–35	70%	83%
• Zero to nine employees at time of investment	100%	78%+
• Start-up or infant stage of firm growth	100%	77%+
• 50 miles or less from investor's home or office	64%	66%
• Has a comprehensive business plan	50%	70%+

HIGH-PROBABILITY DEAL STRUCTURE

	Direct	Indirect
• Equity per investor*	$37,500	$37,500
• Loans/guarantees by Angel*	$5,000	$7,100+
• Voting power transferred to investor	32%	35%
• Majority control to Angel (% of investments)	42%	22%+
• Capital risk seen by Angel*	40%	30%
• Expected annual ROI	25%	27%
• Common stock or partner equity instrument	60%	84%+
• Liquidation horizon*	Four years	Seven and a half years
• Liquidation buyback by insiders planned	60%	43%+
• Investor is or becomes an employee (% of investments)	40%	48%

---

*Median value—half higher, half lower.   + = Differs importantly from Direct Channels.

wealth. Direct-approach Angels set lower minimum ROI targets but more aggressively seek majority control. They invest more frequently, with an emphasis on committing equity dollars relative to loans/guarantees. They are not especially happy with the results; the majority of direct-approach Angels feel that their deals have performed below initial expectations.

Direct-Approach Entrepreneurs

Entrepreneurs who are successful by directly contacting Angels have three unusual characteristics. First, they *all* have very small firms of less than 10 employees; second, their firms are *all* in the earliest stages of start-up or growth; and, third, they prepare fewer comprehensive business plans for Angels prior to closing the deal.

Direct-Approach Deals

Deals that result from entrepreneurs directly approaching Angels provide the entrepreneurs with the usual amount of equity capital but far less in loans/guarantees, as previously mentioned. The deals shift majority control to the Angel more frequently than indirectly initiated deals. Simple common stock equity instruments are often replaced by the use of notes with warrants. This equity instrument is suspected of contributing to the entrepreneur's loss of majority control. (Discussion in Chapter 11 regarding Corporate Achiever Angels notes an association between Angels obtaining absolute majority and the use of notes with stock warrants.) Lastly, the majority of directly initiated deals contain plans for eventual return of equity to the entrepreneur or other insider.

Key Points about Angel Information Sources

The vast majority of Angels use both direct and indirect communication channels to learn of investment opportunities. As a consequence they also have the same profile characteristics as the U.S. Composite. However, some Angels show a marked use of either direct or indirect information channels. A comparison of their profiles reveals that the direct approach by the entrepreneur has the following features:

- Angels are young, professionally employed people with relatively low income and net worth. They are active investors, interested in getting majority control, but so far their deals are not working out as well as expected.

- Direct-approach entrepreneurs are notable because they always have very small, start-up firms and they are somewhat casual about providing complete business plans.

- Direct-approach deals come up short on total risk capital because loans/guarantees are well below the usual size. Notes with warrants are frequently involved, and majority control often ends up with the Angel.

Often voting control loss is potentially offset by plans to eventually resell the equity back to the entrepreneur when liquidation time arrives.

INFORMATION ANGELS RELY ON

"Always prepare a comprehensive business plan" is good advice, but this "must do" is only part of what Angels want for decision facts. The other part is the information that is not part of the written business plan but that results from a well-executed "due diligence" investigation.

Business Plan Requirements

How often do Angels require a comprehensive business plan before they make their investment decision? Angels were asked to indicate the percentages of their deals in which a comprehensive business plan was available prior to investing. Almost two out of every three Angels always require such planning and documentation. The other one-third frequently require such plans. The specifics are as follows:

- Plan required 100% of time   62%
- 61–99%   6%
- 41–60%   11%
- 20–40%   5%
- Under 20%   16%

Decision Information Content

Investment information reaches the Angel in several forms ranging from a formal written plan, to personal endorsements by others, to informal facts that come only from face-to-face contact with the entrepreneur. Regardless of the source, what is it that Angels want to know most, and how important is each piece of information compared to others? Each Angel, of course, has his or her own list of required facts and own ranking of their importance. A fair idea of what is generally expected can be seen in Table 5-1, which shows the composite Angel's information requirements and their relative importance. The descriptions appear in rank order of importance, and the index shows their relative importance to each other. For example, a clear description of the proposed financing is rated by Angels as twice as important as identifying the entrepreneurs' principal customers and suppliers.

The information descriptions in Table 5-1 are not surprising, but their ranking may give food for thought. For example, notice that item number 6 (direct personal knowledge) occupies a relatively low importance rank, but it is a real killer when it comes to reasons why deals drop dead. Its low rank doesn't mean it's unimportant. Later in this chapter we will see

**TABLE 5-1. Investment Information Content
and Its Relative Importance (U.S. Composite)**

Rank	Content Description	Importance Index*
1	Clear description of proposed financing needed from start to maturity	100
2	Marketing plans, including segment of market sought or controlled by company, data on market size and characteristics, present and potential market competition, and future market strategy	100
3	Summary statement of the purpose and goals of the enterprise	92
4	History of the firm, financial statements, and background (résumés) of key personnel	80
5	Clear description of the technical aspects of the proposed project	67
6	Direct personal knowledge about firm's principals and key personnel	67
7	Names of principal suppliers and customers	52

*100 = most important.

that the second-most-common deal killer is "insufficient" personal knowledge of the firm's principals and key personnel. This suggests that direct personal knowledge of entrepreneurs comes from more than résumés and references. In fact, personal knowledge of the entrepreneur may be the most difficult requirement for entrepreneurs to meet because it is not easily established or documented.

The information requirements listed in Table 5-1 do not exhaust the possibilities that may be of key importance to any given deal. Special circumstances require special knowledge, and each investment proposal is a special circumstance to its participants. The list in Table 5-1, then, is not a final statement but only a beginning.

ANGELS WHO SAY "YES" OFTEN

Investment frequency clearly affects the likelihood that a given Angel will fund your proposal. The focus of this section is to distinguish high-probability Angels from their colleagues who invest only seldom. The frequency with which Angels say "yes" to an investment proposal varies over a wide range. Some invest only once in a lifetime, while others finance several deals a year. The comparison profile in this section illuminates what is most characteristic of high-potential Angels, what these Angels look for in an entrepreneur/firm, and how subsequent deals are put together. Angel behavior can be categorized in three classes of investment frequency:

- One investment only ("One Shot")
- Two only
- Three or more ("Fast Track")

The profile in this section compares the One-Shot Angel with Fast-Track Angels. Two-investment Angels are not profiled because they resemble the U.S. Composite. The text highlights Fast-Track Angels and concludes with a summary of key points.

Fast-Track Angels account for one in four surveyed Angels, and collectively they reported the details of 348 investments averaging a little over 3 per Angel. The total value of these investments exceeds $34 million. Market Profile 5-2 shows how Fast-Track Angels differ from One-Shot Angels and the U.S. Composite. They are less often business owners/managers and have higher incomes than One-Shot Angels but not higher than the U.S. Composite. Fast Trackers have an overriding concern for the quality of the entrepreneur's management talent that is shared by One-Shot Angels but not by the U.S. Composite. They invest most frequently in the finance, insurance and real estate (FIRE) industry and routinely require comprehensive business plans. The ownership share they obtain is smaller than usual, but their dollars invested are not. They have more holding period patience and are more likely to look to outsiders for eventual liquidation.

Fast-Track (and One-Shot) Angels

The most outstanding difference between Fast-Track Angels and others is their relatively low proportion of business owners/managers: 57 percent versus the composite's 70 percent. An unusually large number of Fast Trackers belong in the "all other" occupational class. Unfortunately the 24 percent in that class is hidden from view since a finer breakdown of this group is not available. The percentages of Fast-Track Angels by occupation are:

- Business owner   38%
- Business manager   19%
- Sales   6%
- Science/engineering professionals   6%
- Other professionals   7%
- All other   24%

When they reject deals, Fast-Track Angels do so because of lack of day-to-day contact with entrepreneurs. They make negative decisions mostly

MARKET PROFILE 5-2.
Comparison of Frequent and Infrequent Angels

ANGELS	One-Shot	Fast-Track
• Business owner/manager is principal occupation	72%	57% + #
• Has entrepreneurial experience	81%	83%
• Age*	49 years	49 years
• White male	82%	86%
• College degree	69%	80%
• Annual family income*	$70,000	$90,000+
• Net worth*	$750,000	$750,000
• Primary information channel	Friends & associates	Friends & associates
• Deal acceptance rate*	30%	30%
• Main deal rejection reason	Inadequate personal knowledge	Inadequate personal knowledge
• Investment frequency*	36 months	12 months
• Satisfied with past investments	73%	73%
• Number of coinvestors*	Two	Three
• Total equity invested in portfolio firms*	$37,500	$187,500 + #
• Total loans/guarantees to portfolio firms*	$75,000	$300,000 + #
• Prefers investing in	Service	FIRE + #
• Minimum ROI target for informal portfolio*	22%	22%
• Active as a consultant, board member, or employee	83%	77%
• Does not seek voting control	84%	82%
• Wants to invest more than opportunity permitted	37%	29%

SUCCESSFUL ENTREPRENEURS/FIRMS

• Total Angel financing* (equity and loans)	$237,000	$390,000 + #
• Equity to loan ratio*	.89	.63
• Number of private individuals supplying funding*	Three	Four + #
• Entrepreneur is a white male, age 25–35	71%	86% +
• Zero to nine employees at time of investment	74%	73%
• Start-up or infant stage of firm growth	72%	71%
• Industry most frequently financed	Service	FIRE +
• 50 miles or less from investor's home or office	71%	64%
• Has a comprehensive business plan	90%	70% + #

(continued)

MARKET PROFILE 5-2. Continued

HIGH-PROBABILITY DEAL STRUCTURE	One-Shot	Fast-Track
• Equity per investor*	$37,500	$37,500
• Loans/guarantees by Angel*	$75,000	$60,000 + #
• Voting power transferred to investor	34%	23% + #
• Majority control to Angel (% of investments)	24%	30%
• Capital risk seen by Angel*	30%	30%
• Expected annual ROI	29%	31%
• Common stock or partner equity instrument	82%	80%
• Liquidation horizon*	Seven and a half years	Seven and a half years #
• Liquidation buyback by insiders planned	50%	40%
• Investor is or becomes an employee (% of investments)	42%	38%

---

*Median value—half higher, half lower.   + = Differs importantly from One-Shot Profile.
= Differs importantly from U.S. Composite.

because their personal knowledge of the entrepreneur and/or key personnel is insufficient to generate confidence of success. As expected, frequent investment leads to large informal portfolios, which average five investments at any one time, with a $490,000 total commitment.

Two aspects distinguish One-Shot Angels from all others: the larger proportion of female and minority entrepreneurs and the very heavy emphasis on comprehensive business plans. The major demographic difference is that female entrepreneurs succeed 13 percent of the time with One-Shot investors, compared to their 9-percent success rate with all Angels. The percentages of entrepreneurs by demographic class are:

- White male   71%
- Female   13%
- Minority   16%

Ninety percent of successful entrepreneurs provide written comprehensive business plans to the One-Shot Angel prior to the deal. This is the highest rate of planning for any Angel group. It exceeds the U.S. norm by half again as often.

Successful Fast-Track Entrepreneurs/Firms

Frequent investors provide double the usual total capital to successful entrepreneurs because of a combination of larger coinvestor groups and larger loans and guarantees. Fast-Track Angels both prefer and actually fund FIRE industry firms as No. 1; however, service industry firms are a very close second. The percentages of Fast-Track investments made in the various sectors are:

- Natural resources/mining   5%
- Construction   10%
- Manufacturing—high-technology   14%
- Manufacturing—industrial   6%
- Manufacturing—consumer   3%
- Transportation, communication, and utilities   1%
- Wholesale trade   3%
- Retail trade   12%
- Finance/insurance/real estate   21%
- Services   20%
- Other   4%

Entrepreneurs who attract Fast-Track Angels provide written comprehensive business plans in 7 out of 10 cases, compared to 61 percent of the U.S. Composite. In all other respects successful entrepreneurs resemble the U.S. Composite.

Fast-Track Deals

The Fast-Track deal contains an unusually large proportion of Angel loans/guarantees relative to equity capital, as mentioned above. This is not because the equity dollars are low (they are average) or because of more frequent lending but because Fast-Track loans are almost triple normal size: $60,000 and $21,400, respectively. The percentages of Fast-Track deals by size of Angel loans/guarantees are:

- None   11%
- Under $20,000   37%
- $20,000–$100,000   31%
- Over $100,000   21%

Large loans apparently do not help these Angels acquire ownership shares, because they achieve only 23 percent control, compared to the 37 percent of the composite Angel. The percentages of Fast-Track deals by size of ownership share are:

- Under 25% share   47%
- 24–49%   8%
- 50%   15%
- Over 51%   30%

Frequent investors' deals have patient liquidation horizons of seven and a half years compared to the U.S. Composite's four years. The percentages of deals by expected holding period are:

- 3 years or less   23%
- 4–5   26%
- 6–10   32%
- Over 10 or not important   18%

When the holding period is complete, the Fast Trackers frequently (60 percent) plan to cash out by selling to outsiders or combinations of buyers, which is more often than the U.S. Composite (50 percent).

Key Points about Angel Investment Frequency

In this section the key characteristics of high-probability Fast-Track Angels (three or more investments) were contrasted to their One-Shot colleagues and the U.S. Composite Angel. The picture that emerges from the profile comparisons tells an interesting story of the close resemblance between Fast-Track and One-Shot Angels. While these Angels both differ from the U.S. Composite, they still tend to resemble each other. Yet there are also some important differences worth noting. The special characteristics shared by both that set them apart from the U.S. Composite are:

- Both reject deals because of a lack of personal knowledge of the entrepreneur/key personnel.
- Both make unusually large loans/guarantees but only typical equity commitments.
- Both insist on receiving comprehensive business plans beyond the composite's requirements.
- Both have longer holding periods.

Contrary to expectations, Fast-Track Angels are not especially wealthy, but they are different from both the U.S. Composite and their One-Shot counterparts because they are:

- Less often business owners/managers (but not professionals either)
- Heavy investors in the FIRE industry
- Part of larger Angel coinvestor groups
- Smaller voting control shareholders
- Looking frequently to outsiders for eventual cash-out

One-Shot Angels are distinguished from both the composite and their Fast-Track associates by only two characteristics: They have lower incomes, and they invest more often in female and minority entrepreneurs. Overall, One-Shot Angels could be called "First-Shot" Angels because their characteristics suggest that they will invest again.

WHY ANGELS REJECT DEALS

One in three seriously considered deals is rejected because of unfavorable due diligence results or failed negotiations over terms and conditions. I can't say exactly how many fail in each of those two stages, but Angels did report the leading reasons for rejecting seriously considered proposals. These deal killers are shown in Table 5-2, along with an index of their relative lethalness. Angels rated their rejection reasons as Very, Moderately, Slightly, or Not Important. These ratings are shown in the ''Importance Index'' in the table.

The first four reasons are all ranked closely together and clearly rated more important than the next four. Notice that two of the top four deal killers relate directly to the Angels' knowledge (or lack of it) about entrepreneurs. By combining reasons 2 and 3, we can say the top three deal killers are problems with (1) market potential, (2) the entrepreneur/key personnel, and (3) equity pricing. This rank order represents a commonsense decision sequence that first emphasizes whether a sufficient market exists; next, whether the entrepreneur is the person who can do it; and third, whether the Angel can buy in at an attractive price.

The list of rejection reasons is not necessarily the last word on why investment proposals go awry. Rather it is a warning of what may be ahead and a guide through the most frequent and (now) well-known trouble spots. Looking at the top-ranked deal killers, it seems clear that the entrepreneur should not be unduly modest when providing information

TABLE 5-2. Deal Rejection Reasons

Rank	Content Description	Importance Index*
1	Venture's chances for growth seemed limited	100
2	Inadequate personal knowledge of firm's principals and key personnel	96
3	Firm's management lacked experience or talent necessary for success	93
4	Proposed value of firm's equity was unrealistic	90
5	Did not coincide with Angel's long-term investment objectives	74
6	Venture concept needed further development	71
7	Not enough time for adequate appraisal	71
8	Insufficient information provided	71
9	Unable to assess technological aspects	43

*100 = most important.

that a potential Angel will use to base investment decisions on. It is advisable to be "bullish" (without stretching facts) on your firm's chances for growth, the talent and experience of its key people (especially you), and why its equity is a good value at the proposed price. Making yourself personally available so that the would-be Angel can make an assessment of your character and motivation may mean the difference between life and death for your deal.

COMPUTERIZED MATCHING SERVICES

The hit-or-miss information networks operating among Angels' friends/associates and entrepreneurs are not very effective, as evidenced by the fact that most Angels want to invest more than their deal flow permits. The need for a better and less costly system has led to the development of Angel-entrepreneur computerized matching services. These services are sometimes called "venture capital hot lines," "computerized dating services for money," and "venture capital networks." They all operate in basically the same manner and are designed to supplement or add to the "invisible network" of friends and associates and not to replace them. There are over a dozen such matching services scattered around North America. A list of their addresses concludes this chapter.

What Matching Services Are

The operational methods of the matching services are remarkably similar because they all stress the vital importance of absolute confidentiality, their nonprofit status, and reliance on subscription fees for support. Confidentiality is a key service attraction for Angels. An Angel hanging out a "shingle" advertising "I'm an investor" will likely attract every nut in the area. Matching services avoid this problem by use of elaborate screening procedures that ensure strict confidentiality, often even from the officers of the matching service itself.

Matching services recruit both Angels and entrepreneurs by inexpensive fee subscription. Fees are usually around $150 for an entrepreneur application and $200 to $250 a year for an Angel. Those subscribing fill out a relatively simple three- or four-page questionnaire outlining their investment interests or business plan. The questionnaire serves to create the data base and to filter out inappropriate applicants (salesmen hunting leads). Properly completed questionnaires are computerized, and then a two-stage, anonymous matching process begins. First, the computer searches among its Angel subscribers for preferences that match certain entrepreneur categories. Second, when matches are found, a brief description of the (anonymous) entrepreneur's plan is sent to the matched-up Angel. At this point an interested Angel can request more information. This double-blind confidentiality is continued until the Angel says that he or she wants to meet the entrepreneur to discuss possible funding. At this stage both sides are provided with names and telephone numbers. The role of the matching service ends here when direct Angel–entrepreneur contact begins. What happens after direct contact is strictly between the individual Angel and entrepreneur.

The success of the matching services depends upon their subscriber pools of Angels and entrepreneurs. They generally number 50 to 300 Angels and 100 to 500 entrepreneurs, which amounts to a small fraction of the total market. Some services report that several thousand matchups are made yearly, but the actual number of deals is unknown because matching service involvement ends at the introduction stage. Some successes have been announced featuring deals cut in only 40 days and valued at over $85,000 in new equity capital.

Matching services are often sponsored during their own start-up stage by grants from chambers of commerce, private economic development committees, banks, public utility companies, CPA firms, and others having an interest in local economic growth. A drawback of this type of sponsorship is that most matching services limit their geographical coverage to a small area or at most a single state. Two services listed later are exceptions and operate nationwide.

What Matching Services Are Not

Knowing what computer matching services do not do is as important as knowing how they operate. They have no money themselves, do not go beyond the introduction stage, and do not evaluate or recommend investments. Consequently they do not compete with venture capital professionals, banks, investment brokers, the SBA, or any other organization except perhaps the invisible "good-old-boy" system. No advising, counseling, planning, research, or other such service is offered by the companies. Not only is this consistent with their main objective of an efficient computerized matching system, but it is also required by Securities and Exchange Commission (SEC) regulations that permit the services to operate under virtually no other restrictions. The services recognize that many aspiring entrepreneurs need planning help, and they will usually recommend help sources elsewhere. The element of confidentiality and applicant screening means that matching services cannot be used as a client source by financial advisors, CPAs, lawyers, brokerage houses, or others. Entry into the computer system is limited to bona fide Angels and entrepreneurs only. Finally, matching services have no financial interest in the outcome of any investment negotiation. They receive no fees other than by subscription. In other words, the services have no ax to grind beyond introducing Angels to entrepreneurs.

Who and Where

At the time of this writing, the organizations that link Angels with entrepreneurs via computer matchups are as follows.

Matching Service	Geographical Limits
Seed Capital Network, Inc. Operations Center 8905 Kingston Pike, Suite 12493 Knoxville, TN 37923 (615) 693-2091	
Indiana Seed Capital Network Institute of New Business Ventures, Inc. One North Capital, Suite 420 Indianapolis, IN 46204 (317) 634-8418	Indiana
Upper Peninsula Venture Capital Network, Inc. 206 Cohodas Administration Center Northern Michigan University Marquette, MI 49855 (906) 227-2406	Michigan
Heartland Venture Capital Network Evanston Business Investment Corporation 1710 Orrington Avenue Evanston, IL 60201 (312) 864-7970	Illinois
Venture Capital Network of Texas P. O. Box 690870 San Antonio, TX 78269-0870 (512) 691-4318	Texas
The Computerized Ontario Investment Network (COIN) Ontario Chamber of Commerce 2323 Yonge Street Toronto, Ontario Canada M4P 2C9 (416) 482-5222	Ontario
Midwest Venture Capital Network P. O. Box 4659 St. Louis, MO 63108 (314) 534-7204	Missouri

Matching Service	Geographical Limits
Venture Capital Network of New York, Inc. TAC State University College of Arts and Science Plattsburgh, NY 12901 (518) 564-2214	New York
Investment Contact Network Institute for the Study of Private Enterprise University of North Carolina The Kenan Center 498A Chapel Hill, NC 27514 (919) 962-8201	North Carolina
Venture Capital Network, Inc. P. O. Box 882 Durham, NH 03824 (603) 862-3556	None
Casper College Small Business Development Center 125 College Drive Casper, WY 82601 (307) 235-4825	Wyoming
University of South Carolina at Aiken 171 University Parkway Aiken, SC 29801 (803) 648-6851	South Carolina
Mississippi Venture Capital Clearinghouse Mississippi Research and Development Center 3825 Ridgewood Road Jackson, MS 39211 (601) 982-6425	Mississippi
Venture Capital Network of Atlanta, Inc. 230 Peachtree Street, N.E., Suite 1810 Atlanta, GA 30303 (404) 658-7000	Georgia

BEYOND INITIAL CONTACT

You can't make a deal with an Angel unless you can make contact. But whatever the initial information channel—direct, indirect, or computerized—the heart of the deal making occurs after contact is made. The entrepreneur will take precautions to keep unwanted killers from sitting in on the deal making. And, as negotiations continue, attention should be given to other areas as well. Consideration of the issues of investment size, risk, control, and return, discussed in the next chapter, will help you pitch your deal successfully after contact has been made.

6

PRICING THE DEAL: ISSUES OF INVESTMENT SIZE, RISK, CONTROL, AND RETURN

Each deal is unique, and so too is its equity pricing. There is no magic formula for pricing equity. The wide range of circumstances surrounding each Angel deal can easily lead to disagreement, even among intelligent people of good will. This is why "overpriced equity" is one of the leading reasons for deal failure. Despite the uniqueness of any particular equity price, there is a common core of influences that are present in almost all pricing situations, including investment size, risk and profit expectations, alternative opportunities, and equity share (voting power) at stake. Survey results shed light on these important pricing issues but emotional and psychological factors, unique to individual bargainers, defy neat categorization.

Universal pricing rules do not exist because there is no "cookbook" method to take into account all of the possible combinations and degrees of circumstances that can exist for every possible deal. Here, I can only isolate and examine a few of the most important pricing factors as they appear in actual deals between Angels and entrepreneurs. By looking at some broad measures of key pricing issues and assessing how they are systematically associated with market performance, we can find some initial answers to the following questions:

- Does the dollar amount of equity invested change market events?
- How do increasing risk expectations alter the actual market performance of Angels, entrepreneurs, and deals?
- What impact does increasing Angel equity share (voting power percentage) have on the composite market profile?
- What market changes occur in actual deals between low and high levels of return on investment (ROI)?

This chapter presents, with interpretation, four comparative market profiles that highlight the differences between high and low investment size, risk perception, level of Angel voting power, and ROI expectation. Analysis of the differences cannot answer all our questions, but the profiles do suggest the actual impact on real investment deals stemming from each of those major pricing factors.

Some important data limitations should be kept in mind. The market profiles and their underlying facts are one-sided—they represent only deals that have been successfully negotiated. Thus, they cannot tell what deals did not occur. Another limit is that the facts do not necessarily show cause-and-effect relationships—they only suggest that there is or is not an apparent association. For example, the second profile (6-2) shows that Angels who see informal deals as highly risky are also less satisfied with their past investments' performance. What it does not tell us is whether these disappointments cause high risk perceptions or vice versa. Another example: Do lower-income Angels see higher risk, or do high risks lead to lower income? We don't know. What we can say is that less-satisfied Angels and lower-income Angels do see higher risks when investing.

INVESTMENT SIZE

Angel market profiles change dramatically as the amount of equity investment increases. The purpose of this section is to reveal these market differences. Equity investments ranging from $250 to $800,000 are among the 891 deals that form the basis of this discussion. These Angel investments represent only the equity portion of risk capital—the most important capital element. Recall that total funding is rarely provided by a single Angel: there are usually three to five coinvestors involved. Moreover, equity dollars themselves usually represent only about two-thirds (64 percent) of the total financing package. The balance, of course, is in Angel loans/guarantees. In other words, the typical entrepreneur receives $177,000 in total risk capital from a group of three Angels, each of whom typically invests a median of $37,500 equity and another $21,400 in loans. The percentages of all U.S. Angel deals by size of equity dollars invested (detailed in Chapter 3) can be more generally grouped into three size classes for ease of comparison of market behavior. The classes are:

- $100,000 or more in any deal ("Deep Pockets")   22%
- $25,000 to $99,999 ("Mid-Scale")   35%
- Under $25,000 in all deals ("Small Scale")   43%

(A special group of Angels who always invest under $10,000 per deal is examined in Chapter 11 under the heading "Nickel and Dime Angels.")

The main objective here is to highlight the important market differences between Small-Scale Angels and Deep-Pocket Angels. A scan of the comparison data given in Market Profile 6-1 will reveal many such market differences. These differences, however, mainly reflect the special characteristics of the Small-Scale Angel; Deep Pockets bear a close resemblance to the U.S. Composite (apart from wealth, income, and related items). The comparison discussion will focus on Small-Scale investors because they have the clearest distinction among all size groups. Little direct attention is given to the Mid-Scale Angel class, which is indistinguishable from the U.S. Composite.

Angels in the Small-Scale class of equity investors account for over one out of five Angels and collectively they reported 169 investments with a total portfolio value of a little over $9 million. Deep Pockets represent almost one in three Angels and their profile reflects the composite experience of 352 actual deals, whose total portfolio commitments exceed $321 million. The comparison of Deep-Pocket and Small-Scale Angels is made in terms relative to Deep Pockets. That is, the fact that Small-Scale Angels are younger means younger compared to Deep-Pocket Angels and not necessarily to the U.S. Composite.

Small-Scale Angels

Small-Scale Angels are younger than Deep-Pocket Angels, have lower incomes and wealth, and invest less frequently. They kill deals most often because of either insufficient personal knowledge about the entrepreneur/ key personnel or insufficient growth potential. They have a clear preference for service industry investments and invest disproportionately more in very small size and early development stage firms. In other respects their entrepreneurs resemble those financed by Deep-Pocket Angels and the U.S. Composite. They pay less attention to their firms' daily operations than do Deep-Pocket Angels. As might be expected, they are further away from achieving their investment volume goals than are their larger-scale colleagues.

Quite naturally, Small-Scale Angels obtain absolute voting control at only half the rate of Deep-Pocket Angels, and they see a higher level of risk. Small-Scale Angels more commonly plan the investment's eventual liquidation via insider buy-out.

Deep-Pocket Angels

Deep-Pocket Angels have personally invested at least $100,000 equity in any single deal and, not surprisingly, are most often millionaires with high incomes. The primary source of their information about deal

MARKET PROFILE 6-1. Comparative Investment Equity Size

ANGELS	Small Scale	Deep Pockets
• Business owner/manager is principal occupation	64%	72%
• Has entrepreneurial experience	82%	87%
• Age*	39 years	49 years +
• White male	78%	85%
• College degree	69%	66%
• Annual family income*	$70,000	$150,000 +
• Net worth*	$400,000	$1,000,000 +
• Primary information channel	Friends and associates	Friends +
• Deal acceptance rate*	30%	30%
• Main deal rejection reason:	Personal knowledge, growth potential	Growth potential, + pricing, personal knowledge
• Investment frequency*	36 months	18 months +
• Satisfied with past investments	66%	76% +
• Number of coinvestors*	Two	Two
• Total equity invested in portfolio firms*	$22,400	$613,000 +
• Total loans/guarantees to portfolio firms*	$25,000	$300,000 +
• Preferred industry	Service	FIRE +
• Minimum ROI target for informal portfolio	22%	22%
• Active as a consultant, board member, or employee	73%	86% +
• Does not seek voting control	85%	85%
• Wants to invest more than opportunity permitted	43%	26% +

SUCCESSFUL ENTREPRENEURS/FIRMS

	Small Scale	Deep Pockets
• Total Angel financing* (equity and loans)	$84,000	$782,000 +
• Equity to loan ratio*	0.9	2.0 +
• Number of private individuals supplying funding*	Three	Three
• Entrepreneur is a white male, age 25–35	72%	82% +
• Zero to nine employees at time of investment	78%	66% +
• Start-up or infant stage of firm growth	80%	63% +
• Industry most frequently financed	Service	FIRE +
• 50 miles or less from investor's home or office	74%	67%
• Has a comprehensive business plan	65%	62%

HIGH-PROBABILITY DEAL STRUCTURE

	Small Scale	Deep Pockets
• Equity per investor*	$13,200	$175,000 +
• Loans/guarantees by Angel*	$14,700	$85,700 +
• Voting power transferred to investor*	30%	33%
• Majority control to Angel (% of investments)	16%	31% +
• Capital risk seen by Angel*	40%	30% +
• Expected annual ROI	28%	29%
• Common stock or partner equity instrument	79%	80%
• Liquidation horizon*	Four years	Four years
• Liquidation buyback by insiders planned	53%	36% +
• Investor is or becomes an employee (% of investments)	40%	33%

* Median, value—half higher, half lower.   + = Differs importantly from Small-Scale profile.

opportunities is personal friends. The opportunities they reject after serious consideration fail for any one of three main reasons: unattractive growth projections, overpriced equity, and perceived lack of sufficient talent among the proposed management. Deep Pockets' informal portfolios are average in terms of number of investments but very large in dollar size, totaling over $900,000 in equity and loans. Their preference runs strongly to deals in the finance, insurance, and real estate industry. Entrepreneurs who are successful with large-equity Angels generally have FIRE firms that are larger and older than usual. Deep-Pocket deal structure, apart from the size of the capital involved, is remarkably normal. The only important difference is the higher frequency of planning to liquidate to outsiders rather than insiders.

Summary of Key Points about Investment Size

Small-Scale Angels (no deals above $25,000) are not like the U.S. Composite but can be summarized as fledgling Angels testing new wings. To be sure, their typically small investments do reflect a limited wealth and income capacity, but it seems to reflect more than that. When the sum of their market characteristic differences is considered, these angels appear to be younger businesspeople who are making their first, hesitant, perhaps very conservative steps toward building their informal portfolios. Their high risk perception bears out this portrait of inexperienced young investors moving a step at a time.

Mid-Scale Angels are similar to the U.S. Composite, which is why there was no separate discussion of their characteristics.

Deep-Pocket Angels (any deals over $100,000) show market differences, such as higher income and wealth, that are directly or indirectly linked to their ability to make large investments. This suggests that they are otherwise ordinary Angels who simply have a larger capacity and are able to accommodate entrepreneurs with unusually large capital needs. Market performance does not suggest that Deep Pockets are really much different than other Angels.

Entrepreneurs should bear in mind that the facts suggest a direct ability to substitute the number of Angels for Angel dollar size. That is, large capital needs can be met by a few Deep Pockets or a few more Mid- or Small-Scale Angels. Given the similarity in their overall market characteristics, it seems to be entrepreneurial luck or choice of strategy that determines the type or mixture of Angel financing.

RISK PERCEPTIONS

The element of perceived risk is important in making deals. Chapter 3 detailed how Angels' views of informal investment risk are measured, and the discussion need not be repeated here. It is important, however, to restate that the 30-percent risk anticipated by the U.S. Composite Angel means that for any given deal the median Angel believes there is a 3 in 10 chance that the deal will eventually result in the loss of over half the original investment. Half of all Angels see 3 or fewer losers out of 10, and the most frequent expectation is that 2 deals (20 percent) will be losers. The average (mean) is 3.3, or 33 percent. The full range of Angel risk perception was shown in Chapter 3. For convenience, the risk responses can be grouped in three classes:

- Expectation of 20% or less risk ("Low-Risk")   36%
- 21–49% risk ("Mid-Risk")   26%
- 50% or more risk ("High-Risk")   37%

A comparison of Low- and High-Risk Angels is given in Market Profile 6-2. The Mid-Risk Angel profile is not shown since it repeats the U.S. Composite.

Angels in the Low-Risk group account for 36 percent of all Angels. They represent a similar proportion of all deals and total risk capital invested. High-Risk Angels similarly add up to 37 percent of the Angel pool, but since they invest fewer dollars and less frequently, they account for only 19 percent of all deals and dollars invested. The remaining 26 percent are Mid-Risk Angels. It can easily be seen from Profile 6-2 that rising risk is associated with many differences in market results. Indeed, almost half the line items change with the perceived level of risk. From the viewpoint of the entrepreneur it may be preferable to avoid negotiating price with an Angel who generally sees high risk and wants a higher return than usual. The focus of this section, then, will be the market behavior of High-Risk Angels, for two reasons. First, by becoming familiar with their market profile one can more easily avoid them or at least anticipate them and be prepared. Second, High-Risk Angels are a more distinctive group than either Low- or Mid-Risk Angels and thus are easier to identify beforehand. The comparison characteristics are stated in terms relative to the Low-Risk Angel. For example, when I say that High-Risk Angels have lower incomes, it means that their income is lower compared to Low-Risk Angels. For those readers who wish to emphasize Low-Risk Angels, simply reversing the relative conclusion will usually (but not always) pinpoint the Low-Risk side.

High-Risk Angels

As the level of perceived capital risk shifts from low to high, as shown in Profile 6-2 the typical Angel has lower income, relies on friends for information, individually invests fewer dollars and invests less frequently, prefers service industry firms, and in general is less happy with investment performance.

MARKET PROFILE 6-2. Investment Risk Comparison

	Angels' Expected Capital Risk	
ANGELS	**Low**	**High**
• Business owner/manager is principal occupation	70%	73%
• Has entrepreneurial experience	82%	85%
• Age*	49 years	49 years
• White male	86%	84%
• College degree	69%	73%
• Annual family income*	$90,000	$70,000 +
• Net worth*	$750,000	$750,000
• Primary information channel	Associates	Friends +
• Deal acceptance rate	30%	30%
• Main deal rejection reason	Growth potential	Growth potential
• Investment frequency	18 months	36 months +
• Satisfied with past investments	81%	53% +
• Number of coinvestors*	Three	Two
• Total equity invested in portfolio firms*	$131,000	$64,000 +
• Total loans/guarantees to portfolio firms*	$75,000	$75,000
• Preferred industry	FIRE	Service +
• Minimum ROI target for informal portfolio*	22%	22%
• Active as a consultant, board member, or employee	81%	84%
• Does not seek voting control	90%	92%
• Wants to invest more than opportunity permitted	32%	34%

SUCCESSFUL ENTREPRENEURS/FIRMS

• Total Angel financing* (equity and loans)	$236,000	$326,000 +
• Equity to loan ratio*	1.7	0.9 +
• Number of private individuals supplying funding*	Four	Three
• Entrepreneur is a white male, age 25–35	80%	75%
• Zero to nine employees at time of investment	74%	68%
• Start-up or infant stage of firm growth	69%	78% +
• Industry most frequently financed	FIRE	Service +
• 50 miles or less from investor's home or office	73%	73%
• Has a comprehensive business plan	70%	57% +

HIGH-PROBABILITY DEAL STRUCTURE

• Equity per investor*	$37,500	$37,500
• Loans/guarantees by Angel*	$21,400	$44,100 +
• Voting power transferred to investor	33%	34%
• Majority control to Angel (% of investments)	27%	26%
• Capital risk seen by Angel*	10%	50% +
• Expected annual ROI	26%	41% +
• Common stock or partner equity instrument	83%	80%
• Liquidation horizon*	7½ years	4 years +
• Liquidation buyback by insiders planned	41%	59% +
• Investor is or becomes an employee (% of investments)	12%	40% +

---

*Median value—half higher, half lower.   + = Differs importantly from Low-Risk profile.

As a group, High-Risk Angels supply their chosen entrepreneurs with one-third more risk capital, but the increase is all in the form of loans/guarantees. The entrepreneur's firm is younger, less well developed, and usually in the service industry group. Lastly, fewer comprehensive business plans are received by High-Risk Angels. When the level of Angel risk perception reaches the 50 percent or higher mark, the deal structure changes radically. The number of equity dollars invested does not change, but the level of loans doubles and exceeds the amount of equity dollars. Not surprisingly, the mean ROI rises from 26 to 41 percent. Expected holding periods decline, and insiders are increasingly designated as the source for the deal's eventual liquidation. Finally, the High-Risk Angel is or becomes a firm employee three times more often than Low-Risk Angels.

What kind of portrait do the preceding facts paint? The picture of a High-Risk Angel is necessarily speculative since definitive evidence of causation is not available. Few identifying personal characteristics stand out except for low income, but the pattern of investment suggests some reasons for the perception of high risk. The primary fact is that past deals have not worked out as well as for other investors. Perhaps this is because the High-Risk Angel only invests infrequently when led by friends to young, underdeveloped service industry firms or where business planning is not common. Rationally, the High-Risk investor seems to be trying to minimize or compensate for perceived risk by more lending instead of equity investment, demanding higher ROI over shorter holding periods, and sticking closer to his or her money by participating in the firm. Whatever the rationale really is, the facts remain unchanged.

Key Points about Risk Perceptions

Low-Risk Angels are those who anticipate no more than 2 chances in 10 of substantial capital loss for any given informal investment. High-Risk Angels see the odds of loss at 5 in 10 chances or higher!

The market profile of High-Risk Angels reveals major differences in almost half the profile line items. High-Risk Angels compared to Low-Risk are associated with relatively low income, more friends as information sources, more unsatisfactory deals, small informal portfolios, more preference for service industry firms, younger/less-developed firms, fewer comprehensive business plans, more loans compared to equity dollars per deal, higher ROI, shorter holding period, more frequent insider liquidation sources, and more frequent Angel employment by entrepreneur.

The profile characteristics of High-Risk Angels point to relatively inexperienced investors whose investment techniques are undeveloped or rather casual. They learn of investment opportunities from friends and seem to invest in young, undeveloped firms. These Angels are less satisfied than most.

ACTUAL VOTING POWER SHARE
(OWNERSHIP PERCENT)

Ownership share and control of the firm are sensitive issues during deal negotiations. The voting share results reflect the interplay of numerous factors. It is not the purpose here to determine how shares are divided but rather to survey the whole range of investment characteristics associated with low and high levels of attained voting power.

The voting power that changes hands among actual deals ranges widely. I define "low voting power" as any under 25 percent (41 percent of U.S. Composite Deals) and "high" as 51 percent or more—or majority control (27 percent of U.S. Composite)—for purposes of comparison. Those Angels who achieve majority control are the subject of a section of Chapter 11 titled "Business Devils," which presents their complete profile. The purpose now is to see how market profiles change as ownership share rises. The comparative profile of low- and high-voting-power deals is presented in Profile 6-3. Caution in interpreting the facts is again advisable because the direction of causation is not known.

From the entrepreneur's viewpoint, avoiding the loss of absolute majority control is often paramount. Consequently, the comparative view will focus on the changing market characteristics as voting control rises from low to high.

High-Voting-Power Angels

As actual voting power increases, the Angels are more frequently experienced entrepreneurs themselves and contain a larger proportion of females and minorities. Family income is low for Angels in high-control deals and equity price becomes the top deal killer in place of limited growth potential. Both investment frequency and size of the informal portfolio increase with voting share levels. Oddly enough, the total capital input falls as Angel voting power rises, which suggests that it is small firms with small capital needs that give up larger percentage shares to recruit Angels. More control by Angels is also related to fewer Angels involved in the financing. The firms that give up more control to Angels are smaller in terms of employment size and are most often in the service industry. Geographical proximity to the Angel's home or office and the frequency of comprehensive business plans both rise as Angel control increases. Not surprisingly, Angel loans/guarantees and perceived risk increase as ownership share rises. Lastly, Angel-employee combinations are more common as Angel control increases.

Key Points about Voting Power

Low Angel voting power includes all deals in which the Angel gets less than a 25 percent share. They are 41 percent of all deals, with an average of 12 percent ownership share to the Angel.

MARKET PROFILE 6-3. Comparative Angel Voting Power Share

ANGELS	Voting Share Obtained by Angel	
	Low	High
• Business owner/manager is principal occupation	70%	71%
• Has entrepreneurial experience	77%	89% +
• Age*	49 years	49 years
• White male	88%	77% +
• College degree	72%	63% +
• Annual family income*	$90,000	$70,000 +
• Net worth*	$750,000	$750,000
• Primary information channel	Associates	Friends
• Deal acceptance rate*	30%	30%
• Main deal rejection reason	Growth potential	Price +
• Investment frequency*	36 months	18 months +
• Satisfied with past investments	69%	73%
• Number of coinvestors*	Seven	Two +
• Total equity invested in portfolio firms*	$64,000	$131,000 +
• Total loans/guarantees to portfolio firms*	$25,000	$75,000 +
• Preferred industry	High-technology	Service +
• Minimum ROI target for informal portfolio*	22%	22%
• Active as a consultant, board member, or employee	65%	94% +
• Does not seek voting control	93%	55% +
• Wants to invest more than opportunity permitted	34%	31%

SUCCESSFUL ENTREPRENEURS/FIRMS

• Total Angel financing* (equity and loans)	$418,000	$176,000 +
• Equity to loan ratio*	2.5	1.8
• Number of private individuals supplying funding*	Eight	Three +
• Entrepreneur is a white male, age 25–35	86%	72% +
• Zero to nine employees at time of investment	70%	82% +
• Start-up or infant stage of firm growth	69%	64%
• Industry most frequently financed	FIRE	Service +
• 50 miles or less from investor's home or office	64%	80% +
• Has a comprehensive business plan	61%	71% +

HIGH-PROBABILITY DEAL STRUCTURE

• Equity per investor*	$37,500	$37,500
• Loans/guarantees by Angel*	$14,700	$21,400 +
• Voting power transferred to investor	12%	51% +
• Majority control to Angel (% of investments)	0%	100% +
• Capital risk seen by Angel*	30%	40% +
• Expected annual ROI	30%	28%
• Common stock or partner equity instrument	76%	71%
• Liquidation horizon*	Four years	Four years
• Liquidation buyback by insiders planned	43%	45%
• Investor is or becomes an employee (% of investments)	18%	57% +

*Median value—half higher, half lower.   + = Differs importantly from Low profile.

High voting power includes all deals where one Angel gets more than 50 percent of the voting power (majority control). This group represents 27 percent of all deals.

Rising Angel ownership share is clearly linked to relatively more Angel entrepreneurial experience, more female and minority Angels and entrepreneurs, lower Angel income, higher equity price sensitivity by Angels, more frequent Angel investments and portfolio size, fewer co-investors, less total risk capital received by the firm, small firms (employment size), more service industry firms, nearby firms (close to Angel), more frequent use of comprehensive business plans, larger loans per deal, greater risk seen by Angels, and more Angels as firm employees.

EXPECTED RETURN ON INVESTMENT

Equity price per share and total ownership shares combine with anticipated profit growth to determine the Angel's expected return on investment, a very important element in many deals. The Angels surveyed reported expectations of ROI at deal time varying from less than 12 percent to well over 100 percent per year. For purposes of seeing how market profiles change with the expected level of ROI, we can compare low ROI to high. Low is defined to include any Angel who has invested where the ROI is below 12 percent, and High means above 40 percent. The average ROI expectations of these two groups is 16 and 79 percent, respectively, and they account for 28 and 11 percent of all Angels.

In Chapter 11, the detailed market profile for very High-ROI Angels is presented under the heading "High Fliers." Our interest here is to compare low with high ROI expectations and reveal associated changes in market performance. The comparative market profile of Low- and High-ROI is contained in Profile 6-4. As pointed out earlier, the reader should exercise caution in interpreting these facts since the direction of cause and effect is not always clear.

High-ROI Angels

As the expected level of payoff increases, we find Angels with relatively higher income and net worth who increasingly rely on information channels composed of friends more than business associates. Overpriced equity becomes the leading deal killer, replacing insufficient growth potential. High-ROI Angels make fewer informal investments, have smaller informal portfolios, and are less happy with the performance of their investments than Low-ROI Angels. The desire for voting control increases for High-ROI Angels, along with the desire to have invested more dollars in that past than deal flow allowed.

MARKET PROFILE 6-4. Comparative Expected Return on Investment

---

	Expected ROI at Deal Time	
ANGELS	**Low**	**High**
• Business owner/manager is principal occupation	85%	90%
• Has entrepreneurial experience	77%	80%
• Age*	49 years	49 years
• White male	87%	85%
• College degree	66%	75% +
• Annual family income*	$90,000	$150,000 +
• Net worth*	$1,000,000	$1,000,000
• Primary information channel	Associates	Friends +
• Deal acceptance rate*	30%	30%
• Main deal rejection reason	Growth potential	Price +
• Investment frequency*	18 months	36 months +
• Satisfied with past investments	78%	50% +
• Number of coinvestors*	Two	Two
• Total equity invested in portfolio firms*	$131,000	$64,000 +
• Total loans/guarantees to portfolio firms*	$75,000	$25,000 +
• Preferred industry	FIRE	FIRE
• Minimum ROI target for informal portfolio*	17%	22% +
• Active as a consultant, board member, or employee	83%	70% +
• Does not seek voting control	96%	85% +
• Wants to invest more than opportunity permitted	24%	47% +

SUCCESSFUL ENTREPRENEURS/FIRMS

	Low	High
• Total Angel financing* (equity and loans)	$177,000	$157,000
• Equity to loan ratio*	1.8	2.5
• Number of private individuals supplying funding*	Three	Three
• Entrepreneur is a white male, age 25–35	84%	83%
• Zero to nine employees at time of investment	76%	65% +
• Start-up or infant stage of firm growth	76%	72%
• Industry most frequently financed	Service	Manufacturing—industrial +
• 50 miles or less from investor's home or office	78%	60% +
• Has a comprehensive business plan	54%	59%

HIGH-PROBABILITY DEAL STRUCTURE

	Low	High
• Equity per investor*	$37,500	$37,500
• Loans/guarantees by Angel*	$21,400	$14,700 +
• Voting power transferred to investor	35%	31%
• Majority control to Angel (% of investments)	20%	16%
• Capital risk seen by Angel*	30%	50% +
• Expected annual ROI	16%	79% +
• Common stock or partner equity instrument	86%	82%
• Liquidation horizon*	Four years	Seven and a half years +
• Liquidation buyback by insiders planned	42%	47%
• Investor is or becomes an employee (% of investments)	35%	30%

---

*Median value—half higher, half lower.   + ⁵ Differs importantly from Low profile.

Relatively few changes in the characteristics of successful entrepreneurs occur as ROI expectation increases. The changes that do occur
reflect a more-frequent association between High-ROI Angels and larger
firms that are farther from the Angels' home or office. In addition, higher
ROI is associated with increasing size of equity relative to loans. High-
ROI deals increase the risk expected by Angels and also increase the
length of time anticipated before deal liquidation.

Key Points about ROI

The Low-and High-ROI groups include Angels with less than 12 percent
ROI expectations and more than 40 percent, respectively. On average the
Low-ROI Angel expects 16 percent, and the High-ROI Angel expect 79
percent.

Low-ROI Angels represent 28 percent of Angels and total risk capital,
while High-ROI Angels account for 11 percent of all Angels but only 6
percent of all informal risk capital.

High expected ROI is associated with relatively high Angel income
and wealth, reliance on friends for investment information, more Angel
sensitivity to equity price as a deal killer, small informal portfolios and
less-frequent deals, more Angel emphasis on absolute voting control, less
happiness with past investment performance, large size of financed firms,
more deals for firms manufacturing industrial products, more miles between Angels and entrepreneurs, more dollars of equity compared to
loans/guarantees, higher expected risk, and a longer waiting time before
deal liquidation.

"Pricing a deal" involves more than dollar amounts alone. The differences highlighted in this chapter between low-level and high-level
Angels in the areas of investment size, perceived risk, voting control, and
ROI may help guide the entrepreneur to Angels who will be more
favorably disposed to meeting your capital needs. The next chapter delves
into the question of increasing the prospects for success by looking at
"super matchups" between entrepreneur and Angel.

7

SUPER ANGEL-
ENTREPRENEUR MATCHUPS
(AND OTHERS)

Some combinations of Angels and entrepreneurs are much more successful than others. Achieving the right combination does not ensure a firm's success, but the wrong matchup can spell disaster. This chapter exposes the distinctive characteristics of both winning and losing matchups. A "winning matchup" as used here is one in which actual investment performance has *greatly* exceeded the Angel's initial expectations. Losing is the reverse. In Chapter 1, I reported the level of satisfaction surveyed Angels experienced with the performance of their informal investments. Performance "well above" expectations was reported by 14 percent of Angels, whom I call here "Super Combos." Losing Angel-entrepreneur matchups are the 11 percent with investment performance "well below" expectations, who are called "Odd Couples."

In addition to looking at winners and losers, we will also see what happens when Angels and professional venture capital firms invest in the same entrepreneur in a section titled "Mixed Couples." In a summary of key points at chapter's end each market profile line item is assessed for its relationship to winning and losing. This assessment results in a three-fold identification of performance characteristics seemingly related to: investment success, investment disappointment (not to say failure), and neutrality or coincidental characteristics.

SUPER COMBOS

In my sample the 14 percent of all Angels in very successful Angel-entrepreneur matchups collectively reported 142 deals valued at $14 million. Their portfolios represent a total commitment of $127 million. The full array of their market behavior and experience is shown in Profile 7-1. In a direct comparison of the 40 item profile with the U.S. Composite,

---

MARKET PROFILE 7-1. Super Combos

ANGELS	U.S. Composite
+ • Business owner/manager is principal occupation (64%)	(71%)
+ • Has personal entrepreneurial experience (91%)	(83%)
+ • 39 years old*	(47 years)
• White male (86%)	(84%)
• College degree (77%)	(72%)
+ • $150,000 annual family income*	($90,000)
+ • $1,000,000 net worth*	($750,000)
• Friends are the primary information channel	(Friends and associates)
• Accepts 3 of 10 investment opportunities*	(3)
• Rejects deals mostly due to inadequate growth potential	(Growth potential)
+ • Invests about every 18 months and has 5 firms in portfolio*	(18) (3.5)
• Satisfied with past investments (100%)	(72%)
• Three other coinvestors*	(Two)
+ • $187,500 equity invested in informal portfolio*	($131,000)
+ • $300,000 more via loans/guarantees to portfolio firms*	($75,000)
• Prefers investing in service/FIRE firms (46%)	(Service/FIRE)
• Minimum ROI target for informal portfolio (22)%*	(22%)
+ • Active as a consultant, board member, or employee (88%)	(81%)
• Does not seek voting control (81%)	(85%)
+ • Wants to invest 43% more than opportunity permitted	(35%)

SUCCESSFUL ENTREPRENEURS/FIRMS	
+ • $390,000 total Angel financing* (equity and loans)	($176,700)
+ • $150,000 in equity and $240,000 more in loans/guarantees*	($112,500) ($64,200)
• Four private individuals supply funding*	(Three)
• Entrepreneur is a white male, age 25–35 (82%)	(79%)
• Zero to nine employees at time of investment (75%)	(74%)
+ • Start-up or infant stage of firm growth (78%)	(69%)
• Service firms are most frequently financed (21%)	(17% in service)
• 50 miles or less from investor's home or office (71%)	(72%)
• Has a comprehensive business plan (69%)	(61%)
• Has detailed marketing and financing plans	

HIGH-PROBABILITY DEAL STRUCTURE	
• $37,500 in equity per investor*	($37,500)
+ • $60,000 in loans/guarantees by Angel*	($21,400)
• 36% voting power transferred to investor	(37%)
• Majority control to Angel in 31% of investments	(27%)
+ • 20% capital risk seen by Angel*	(30%)
• 25% expected annual ROI (24% average)	(25%) (27%)
• Common stock or partner equity instrument (83%)	(79%)
+ • Liquidation horizon of seven and a half years*	(Four years)
+ • Liquidation buyback by insiders planned (37%)	(50%)
• Investor is or becomes an employee in 40% of investments	(39%)

---

*Median value—half higher, half lower.   + = Differs importantly from U.S. Composite.

Super Combos stand out on 16 characteristics. In a comparison with unsuccessful Angels, there is a set of 22 characteristic differences, which are reviewed at the end of the chapter. This section addresses questions like:

- What Angel characteristics and behavior result in very successful investments?
- What do Angels look for in firms/entrepreneurs that subsequently become extraordinary performers?
- What are the central features of the investment deals that confirm super combinations?

The Angel half of Super Combos consist of young, experienced Angels with high income and wealth. They rely on friends for information about investing opportunities and most often reject deals because growth potential is uninteresting. They generally have five investments going at any one time, making a new deal about once every 18 months. Their total commitment to informal investment is in the half-million dollar range. They are noticeably more active in the firm's operations than the U.S. Composite and much more active than Angels belonging to Odd Couples. Probably as a result of their success, they would like to have invested 43 percent more in the past than they were able to.

The entrepreneurial half of Super Combos obtain over twice the level of risk capital funding as the U.S. Composite—especially loans, which are four times normal amounts. The most successful firms are very young when Angel investments arrive, and comprehensive written business plans are more common than usual. Contrary to what might be anticipated, Angels do not expect the deal to be especially risky; on the contrary, they expect less risk. Deal liquidation horizons of over seven years mean that deals are cut for the long haul. Eventual liquidation to outsiders was more commonly planned than usual.

Super Combo Angels

Very successful Angels are 10 years younger than usual (median) and have more hands-on personal entrepreneurial experience (91 percent) than the U.S. norm (83 percent). The percentages of Super Combo Angels by age class are:

- 34 years or less   16%
- 35–44   35%
- 45–54   20%
- 55–64   18%
- Over 65   12%

Family income and net worth are substantially above the U.S. Composite, but this may be the result of success rather than a cause of it, since income and wealth are measured after the investment success. The breakdown of Super Combo Angels by income and net worth is:

Income		Net Worth	
• Under $40,000	6%	• $300,000 or less	14%
• $40,000–$59,999	19%	• $300,001–$499,999	14%
• $60,000–$79,999	13%	• $500,000–$1,000,000	16%
• $80,000–$99,999	8%	• Over $1,000,000	55%
• $100,000–$200,000	29%		
• Over $200,000	25%		

Despite a typical rate of investing once each 18 months, Super Combo Angels have informal portfolios of five investments because of their longer-than-usual holding periods. These larger portfolios are also reflected in total risk funds committed of almost half a million dollars per Angel, compared to the U.S. Composite of about $200,000. Another important characteristic of Super Combo Angels is that they are more active than usual in their firms' day-to-day operations. Eighty-eight percent are active, compared to 81 percent for the U.S. Composite. While this percentage level falls just inside the sampling error range, it is an important difference because it is 14 points higher than the participation percentage of unsuccessful Angels. It is not surprising, given the degree of their success, that Super Combo Angels wanted to invest 43 percent more if they had sufficient opportunity. This contrasts with 35 percent for the U.S. Composite and 25 percent for Odd Couple Angels.

Super Combo Entrepreneurs/Firms

Outstanding success is associated with over twice the usual amount of total risk capital. Highly successful firms obtained a median of $390,000 from four Angels, in contrast to the U.S. Composite's $177,000 from three Angels. Apart from the number of Angels, the major source of this additional risk capital is four times the usual amount of Angel loans/guarantees: $240,000 versus $64,000 for the composite. Super Combo entrepreneurs include a disproportionately high level of very young firms; 78 percent were in their start-up or infant stage, whereas only 69 percent are usually so young. The percentages of super-successful entrepreneurs by growth stage (age) of their firm at deal time are:

- Start-up   66%
- Infant   12%
- Young   8%
- Established   14%

In all other characteristics the Super Combo firm is similar to the U.S. Composite.

Super Combo Deals

The principal differences between the U.S. Composite Deal and highly successful deals lie in the amount of risk capital loaned to the firm, the perceived level of risk, and liquidation expectations. Super Combo deals include four times the usual level of Angel loans over and above a normal-size equity commitment. Thus the high loan proportion is not a substitute for equity but a complement. The percentages of deals by loan/guarantee size per Angel are:

- None   9%
- Under $20,000   38%
- $20,000–$99,999   34%
- $100,000 or more   19%

Angels in Super Combo deals are optimistic about the success probability of informal markets in general, or at least they are confident in their ability to pick winners. Angels see only 20 percent risk, in contrast to the U.S. Composite's 30 percent and the Odd Couple's 50 percent risk! The risk capital loss expectations of Super Combo Angels at deal time are:

- 20% or less risk   55%
- 21–39%   9%
- 40–49%   5%
- 50% or more   31%

Patience is the norm in liquidating Super Combo deals. The median holding period is anticipated at seven and a half years, compared to four years for the U.S. Composite. The percentages of expected holding period are:

- 3 years or less   12%
- 4–5   37%
- 6–10   25%
- Over 10 years or not important   26%

When cash-out plans are included in the deal, Super Combo deals plan liquidation via outsiders more often than usual. The percentages of planned methods of investor cash-out are:

- None   23%
- Resell to firm   29%
- Sell to existing coinvestor 8%
- Sell or merge with another firm   4%
- Public stock offering   14%
- Other and combinations   22%

THE ODD COUPLE

Angels admit getting stung in about 1 in 10 cases. Those "losers" in my sample made a total of 75 recent deals valued at $3 million and had invested $31 million in their collective portfolios. Their market characteristics are presented in Profile 7-2. These Angels differ from the U.S. Composite on 14 out of 40 characteristics. Some of these differences are important because they seem to be associated with later investment disappointment, while others appear to be no more than coincidence or just risky circumstances. Risk has both up and down sides. These points will be examined later in the summary of key points.

Odd couples, those with very unsuccessful performance, stand in stark contrast to both the U.S. Composite and Super Combos. Odd Couple Angels have lower incomes and less wealth and comprise larger proportions of female and minority Angels. Their reasons for rejecting deals are topped by "not enough time for sufficient appraisal." Judging by the performance of the deals they did accept, one might think that insufficient time may have been spent on them too. Unsuccessful Angels invest normally as far as size and frequency of investment, but they are less actively involved in their firms' day-to-day activities than usual and much less active than Super Combo Angels. Predictably, Odd Couple Angels have a low desire to have invested more—but it is still larger than zero!

The entrepreneurial half of this losing team displays telltale signs of undercapitalization and especially a heavy burden of Angel loans. Loan-heavy capital is not because Odd Couple Angels provided big loans but because they put up too little equity. Like Super Combos, the Odd Couple firms are mostly young start-ups, but in this down-side case an unusually large number of them are more than 50 miles distant from the Angel (which may account for the Angels' low participation level in firm operations).

Odd Couple deals are marked from the beginning by smaller equity per investor (half the usual amount). They are viewed as highly risky even at the time the deal is cut. Complex investment instruments appear frequently and simple common stock or partnership equity interests less often.

Odd Couple Angels

Low income, low net worth, and a standard-size portfolio suggest that Odd Couple Angels are personally overextended and can invest only minimal amounts in any given deal. Moreover, these Angels' ranks include a larger-than-usual number of female and minority investors (who nonetheless claim to be experienced business owners and entrepreneurs themselves). The demographic mix of Odd Couple Angels is:

- White male   71%
- White female   6%
- Minority male   23%
- Minority female   0%

As a group, Odd Couple Angels are less well educated than the U.S. Composite and Super Combos, with 60 percent university degree holders versus a 72 percent U.S. norm. The percentages of unsuccessful Angels by education level are:

- High school or less   18%
- Some college   24%

MARKET PROFILE 7-2. Odd Couple

ANGELS   U.S. Composite

• Business owner/manager is principal occupation (73%)	(71%)
• Has personal entrepreneurial experience (81%)	(83%)
• 49 years old*	(47 years)
+ • White male (71%)	(84%)
+ • College degree (59%)	(72%)
+ • $70,000 annual family income*	($90,000)
+ • $400,000 net worth*	($750,000)
• Friends are the primary information channel	(Friends and associates)
• Accepts 3 of 10 investment opportunities*	(3)
+ • Rejects deals mostly due to insufficient evaluation time	(Growth potential)
• Invests about every 18 months and has 3.5 firms in portfolio*	(18) (3.5)
• Satisfied with past investments (0%)	(72%)
• Two other coinvestors*	(Two)
• $131,000 equity invested in informal portfolio*	($131,000)
• $75,000 more via loans/guarantees to portfolio firms*	($75,000)
• Prefers investing in service firms (33%)	(Service/FIRE)
• Minimum ROI target for informal portfolio (22%)*	(22%)
+ • Active as a consultant, board member, or employee (74%)	(81%)
+ • Does not seek voting control (96%)	(85%)
+ • Wants to invest 25% more than opportunity permitted	(35%)

SUCCESSFUL ENTREPRENEURS/FIRMS

+ • $116,700 total Angel financing* (equity and loans)	($176,700)
+ • $52,500 in equity and $64,200 more in loans/guarantees*	($112,500) ($64,200)
• Three private individuals supply funding*	(Three)
• Entrepreneur is a white male, age 25–35 (81%)	(79%)
• Zero to nine employees at time of investment (74%)	(74%)
+ • Start-up or infant stage of firm growth (78%)	(69%)
• Service firms are most frequently financed (19%)	(17% in service)
+ • 50 miles or less from investor's home or office (63%)	(72%)
• Has a comprehensive business plan (56%)	(61%)
• Has detailed marketing and financing plans	

HIGH-PROBABILITY DEAL STRUCTURE

+ • $17,500 in equity per investor*	($37,500)
• $21,400 in loans/guarantees by Angel*	($21,400)
• 29% voting power transferred to investor	(37%)
• Majority control to Angel in 23% of investments	(27%)
+ • 50% capital risk seen by Angel*	(30%)
• 25% expected annual ROI (29% average)	(25%) (27%)
+ • Common stock or partner equity instrument (66%)	(79%)
• Liquidation horizon of four years*	(Four years)
• Liquidation buyback by insiders planned (54%)	(50%)
• Investor is or becomes an employee in 38% of investments	(39%)

---

*Median value—half higher, half lower.   + = Differs importantly from U.S. Composite.

- College degree   33%
- Graduate degree   26%

Odd Couple Angels have $20,000 less income than the U.S. Composite and half the median net worth. The breakdown of Odd Couple Angels by income and net worth is:

Income		Net Worth	
Under $40,000	19%	Under $300,000	37%
$40,000–$59,999	22%	$300,000–$499,999	13%
$60,000–$79,999	30%	$500,000–$1,000,000	26%
$80,000–$99,999	10%	Over $1,000,000	24%
$100,000–$200,000	19%		
Over $200,000	0%		

The main reason given by Odd Couple Angels for rejecting deals stands out from all other groups. The leading reason is "insufficient time to adequately assess the proposal," followed in a tie for second place by "overpriced equity" and "lack of talent in the entrepreneurs." Perhaps these Angels did not reject *enough* deals for insufficient time, or so it would seem from subsequent performance. Odd Couples are the only Angels to cite hurried decisions as an important rejection reason. Another noteworthy difference from both the U.S. Composite and Super Combo Angels is the relative inattention that Odd Couple Angels give to their firms' day-to-day operations. Only 74 percent are active with the firm, compared to 88 percent for Super Combo Angels. It should surprise no one that Odd Couple Angels have a very low desire to have invested more than they did.

Odd Couple Entrepreneurs/Firms

The firms in losing combinations are undercapitalized by their Angels. The risk capital shortfall is due entirely to insufficient equity investment, which averages less than half the U.S. norm and only one-third the level of Super Combo's. In part this shortfall is due to one less Angel coinvestor (three versus four), but mainly it reflects less equity per Angel, as shown in the subsection on Odd Couple deals.

Odd Couple firms include a high proportion of very young start-up and infant stage firms—but so do Super Combos. The percentages of Odd Couple firms by growth stage (age) at deal time are:

- Start-up   62%
- Infant   18%
- Young   8%
- Established   12%

A factor that may contribute to subsequent investment performance is the greater geographical distances (miles) between the Odd Couple Angel and the firm. The U.S. Composite reports 72 percent of investments are within 50 miles of the Angel, yet for the Odd Couple only 63 percent are so close. Perhaps the benefits of Angels' experience and the probability of active participation rapidly dissipate over extra miles. The percentages of Odd Couple firms by miles from their Angel are:

- 10 miles or less   31%
- 11–50   32%
- 51–150   19%
- Over 150   18%

Odd Couple Deals

Three elements stand out in Odd Couple deals: small equity dollars, high risk expectations, and complex investment instruments. The equity contribution per Angel to unsuccessful deals is half as large as that of the U.S. Composite and Super Combos. This suggests that it is small equity that hurts and not large equity that necessarily helps. The percentages of Odd Couple Angels by size of their equity input per deal are:

- Under $10,000   25%
- $10,000–$24,999   24%
- $25,000–$49,999   16%
- $50,000–$99,999   11%
- $100,000–$250,000   15%
- Over $250,000   9%

The pattern of smaller equity per deal may partly reflect the extraordinarily high risk expected by Odd Couple Angels for informal investments. It could also be a reflection of their unsuccessful experience. Since risk is measured after the fact, the high risk expectation may be caused by poor investment performance, or it may be related to the Angel's lack of self-confidence in picking winners. Whatever the cause, the Odd Couple Angel sees informal deals as a 50–50 proposition at best! (With this level of expected risk, betting red/black on a roulette wheel would be quicker and more fun!) The percentages of Odd Couple Angels by expected levels of capital risk are:

- Under 30% risk of loss   27%
- 30–39%   19%
- 40–49%   3%
- 50% or more   51%

Unsuccessful deals are encumbered by complex investment instruments; only 66 percent are simple common stock or partnership equity transactions, compared to the U.S. Composite of 79 percent. The major differences occur with a one-fourth less use of partnership equity documentation and with almost twice as frequent use of notes with warrants. The increased frequency of notes with warrants probably reflects the loan-heavy risk capital committed by Odd Couple Angels. The percentages of unsuccessful deals by type of equity instrument are:

- Common stock   35%
- Partnership equity interest   31%
- Notes with warrants   17%
- Convertible preferred stock   3%
- Convertible debentures   0%
- Other and combinations   14%

In all other aspects the deals resemble the composite.

MIXED COUPLES

Mixing Angels and professional venture capital firms is not common but not unknown either. Angels in 2 out of 3 cases coinvest only with private individuals, but 1 in 25 (4 percent) has a venture capital firm as a coinvestor. I call these Angel–venture capital coinvestors "Mixed Couples."

What happens when Angels and professional venture capitalists invest in the same entrepreneur? From the viewpoint of the Angel, the simplest, most basic answer is that it works out just fine, thank you! Eight out of 10 Angels who have professional venture capital firms as coinvestors say that the performance of their investment has equalled or exceeded initial expectations. The profile of the Mixed Couple presented in Profile 7-3 shows one of the most diverse sets of market characteristics. Out of 40 possible comparisons, Mixed Couples differ from the U.S. Composite on 22 points. These numerous differences, however, can be summed up neatly: Almost everything about Mixed Couple Angels makes them and their market behavior look like junior versions of professional venture capitalists.

Angels in Mixed Couples

Compared to all Angels, those who are part of a Mixed Couple are well-educated, wealthy, high-income businesspeople who rely on business associates for information on investment opportunity. They invest frequently and have large portfolios in terms of the number of firms and the amount of equity and loan dollars committed. They prefer to invest in firms manufacturing high-technology products, usually together with many other Angels. If professional venture capital is the "big league," then Angels who team up with venture capital firms are the big leaguers among Angels—or at least rising stars on the farm teams.

Successful Entrepreneurs/Firms

Those firms that have Mixed Couple investors are unusual. Their typical risk capital base exceeds $1 million and is supplied by eight investors, including the venture capital firm. The company most frequently manufactures high-technology products and is larger and more fully developed

MARKET PROFILE 7-3. Mixed Couples

ANGELS	U.S. Composite
• Business owner/manager is principal occupation (67%)	(69%)
• Has personal entrepreneurial experience (86%)	(83%)
• 49 years old*	(47 years)
• White male (82%)	(84%)
+ • College degree (86%)	(72%)
+ • $150,000 annual family income*	($90,000)
• $750,000 net worth*	($750,000)
+ • Associates are the primary infomation channel	(Friends and associates)
• Accepts 3 of 10 investment opportunities*	(3)
• Rejects deals mostly due to inadequate growth potential	(Growth potential)
+ • Invests about every 12 months and has 5 firms in portfolio*	(18) (3.5)
• Satisfied with past investments (80%)	(72%)
+ • Seven other coinvestors*	(Two)
+ • $375,000 equity invested in informal portfolio*	($131,000)
+ • $300,000 more via loans/guarantees to portfolio firms*	($75,000)
+ • Prefers investing in high-technology and FIRE firms (38%)	(Service/FIRE)
• Minimum ROI target for informal portfolio (22%)*	(22%)
• Active as a consultant, board member, or employee (79%)	(81%)
+ • Does not seek voting control (98%)	(85%)
• Wants to invest 36% more than opportunity permitted	(35%)

SUCCESSFUL ENTREPRENEURS/FIRMS

+ • $1,080,000 total Angel financing* (equity and loans)	($176,700)
+ • $600,000 in equity and $480,000 more in loans/guarantees*	($112,500)($64,200)
+ • Eight private individuals supply funding*	(Three)
• Entrepreneur is a white male, age 25–35 (80%)	(79%)
+ • Zero to nine employees at time of investment (56%)	(74%)
+ • Start-up or infant stage of firm growth (58%)	(69%)
+ • High-technology firms are most frequently financed (32%)	(17% in service)
• 50 miles or less from investor's home or office (71%)	(72%)
+ • Has a comprehensive business plan (74%)	(61%)
• Has detailed marketing and financing plans	

HIGH-PROBABILITY DEAL STRUCTURE

+ • $75,000 in equity per investor*	($37,500)
+ • $60,000 in loans/guarantees by Angel*	($21,400)
+ • 19% voting power transferred to investor	(37%)
+ • Majority control to Angel in 8% of investments	(27%)
• 30% capital risk seen by Angel*	(30%)
• 25% expected annual ROI (23% average)	(25%) (27%)
• Common stock or partner equity instrument (73%)	(79%)
+ • Liquidation horizon of seven and a half years	(Four years)
+ • Liquidation buyback by insiders planned (24%)	(50%)
+ • Investor is or becomes an employee in 29% of investments	(39%)

*Median value—half higher, half lower.   + = Differs importantly from U.S. Composite.

than most Angel-financed firms. Moreover, the sophistication of these investors requires that entrepreneurs provide comprehensive business plans far more than usual.

Deals with Mixed Couples

Angels with venture capital firm coinvestors put up more risk capital than any other Angel group. The single Angel deal commits $75,000 equity, with another $60,000 in loans/guarantees. Because of the large number of coinvestors the deal for one Angel nets only a 19-percent equity share, and gaining majority control is rare (8 percent). The expected holding period in the Mixed Couple deal is long (seven and a half years), and exit plans call for outsiders to provide the liquidation cash. While Mixed Couple Angels participate in the firm's operations with typical frequency, they are less often employees.

Key Points about Mixed Couples

Mixed Couple Angels are those who have a professional venture capital firm as a coinvestor; they account for 1 in 25 Angels. The profile of a Mixed Couple Angel adds up to a portrait of a junior version of a professional venture capitalist—educated, mature, experienced, high income, and a frequent investor of large sums. Preference is for high-technology manufacturing firms.

Successful entrepreneurs represent high-technology manufacturing firms that are relatively large and in more advanced growth stages. The entrepreneurs provide a comprehensive business plan almost always and in return attract over $1 million of risk capital from an average of eight Angels.

Deals between Mixed Couple Angels and successful entrepreneurs involve equity and loan dollars that exceed the composite amounts by a factor of over twice as much. The deals transfer relatively little voting share to any one Angel, perhaps due to the large number of Angels involved. Majority control is rarely transferred in the deal. Long holding periods are typically expected when investing, and eventual liquidation is planned via outside sources. Both before and after the deal, the Angel is less likely to be a company employee.

SUMMARY OF KEY POINTS

This chapter highlights the main market characteristics of very successful as well as very unsuccessful Angel-entrepreneur combinations. Almost one in four Angels fall into one or the other of these groups. The contrast between success and failure is stark, though not always easy to explain. One in 4 of the market profile's 40 line items seems prominently associated in some way with either success or failure, as explored in the next subsection.

Characteristics Seemingly Related to Investment Performance

Direct comparison of the market profiles of Super Combos with Odd Couples (leaving out the leveling effect of the U.S. Composite) suggests the following as factors that are directly associated with either the success or failure of investments. This list is not scientifically valid; it is only a rough product of a simple comparison of groups representing very complex members. Nevertheless, it may be useful as a baseline for due diligence and as a pointer toward important questions that should be asked and answered in the investment process. The success/failure characteristics are:

- Angel occupation and entrepreneurial experience
- Angel age and demographics
- Education level
- Rejection reason
- Equity and loan size
- Angel participation in operations
- Geographical distance between firm and Angel
- Written comprehensive business plan
- Angel risk expectations
- Equity instrument
- Liquidation horizon and cash-out method

It could take years of analysis and model building to disentangle the interrelationships among items in this list, let alone trying to assign some degree of relative importance to each one. Indeed, careful analysis and further research may show that some of the list items have nothing to do with success or failure. I leave that task to others in the interest of "spreading the work." What can be said now is that all the above items showed such a large difference between the success and failure groupings of Angels that they must at the very least be subject to suspicion and concern until further evidence is available. In any case the market experience items provide a crude but convenient checklist for the cautious investor/entrepreneur. In sum, the success/failure associations appear to be as follows.

Very Successful Profile Characteristics. The Super Combo profile elements that distinguish them from both the U.S. Composite and Odd Couples are:

- Angels' more frequent entrepreneurial experience and relative youth (energy?)
- High family income and net worth
- Large dollar commitments to informal portfolios
- Higher level of activity in firm operations

- Double the average funding (especially loans) for firms
- More frequent existence of comprehensive business plans
- Relatively low risk expectations
- Long investment holding periods (5 to 10 years)
- Planned liquidation via outsiders

Very Unsuccessful Profile Characteristics.   Odd Couple profile elements
that set them apart from both the U.S. Composite and Super Combos are:

- Less-educated Angels
- More frequent minority and female Angels
- Lower family income and net worth
- Insufficient time for due diligence
- Lower level of activity in firm operations
- Underfunded firms
- Over 50 miles between Angel and firm
- Small Angel equity contribution (equity starvation)
- High risk perceptions
- More frequent use of complex equity instruments

Be forewarned!

Seemingly Coincidental or Neutral Characteristics

Some of the market profile differences from the U.S. Composite for both
Super Combos and Odd Couples suggest an element of coincidence or
that the investment experience is simply risky and can end up either very
successful or very unsuccessful. These "neutral" items are common to
both Super Combos and Odd Couples and thus seem independent of the
results (at least superficially). Comparison of profiles 7-1 and 7-2 shows
that the following elements are common to both successful and unsuccessful deal results:

- Communication channels
- Investment frequency and acceptance rate
- Number of coinvestors
- Industry preference
- Minimum ROI target
- Entrepreneur demographics
- Firm employment size
- Growth stage of firm
- Industry of firm
- Desired and actual voting control
- Expected ROI
- Investor-employee status

Becoming part of a "super" Angel-entrepreneur combination may de-
pend partly on luck and partly on advance work. A discussion of the
firm's "age factor" in matchups, presented in the next chapter, may aid
in the timing of deal approaches.

8

WHEN TO LOOK
FOR ANGELS

When entrepreneurs need external growth capital, their firm will likely occupy one of four growth or life-cycle stages. Angels have definite preferences among these growth stages that influence market behavior, what they look for in investments, and how subsequent deals are structured. This chapter focuses on the specific Angel market for each of the four business growth stages defined below:

- *Start-Up Firms:* Business ventures in the idea stage or in the process of being organized. No formal financing may exist at this point. Equity funds may be provided to individuals or to inventors/innovators developing a new product, process, or other marketable concept.
- *Infant Firms:* Firms that may be losing money but that have the potential for attractive profits in one to three years. Often they are about a year old.
- *Young Firms:* Firms still establishing a track record, expecting to enter a period of rapid and profitable growth, and generally less than five years old.
- *Established Firms:* Small, profitable firms that are growing too fast to finance their growth from retained earnings.

Surveyed Angels reported their 908 investments were made in each growth stage as follows:

- Start-up   56%
- Infant   13%
- Young   11%
- Established   20%

Few important differences exist between start-up and infant firms, which for convenience are combined into a single market profile. The allocation of Angel investment dollars forms a different pattern because each growth stage does not average the same number of dollars per deal. The percentages of total risk capital invested by growth stage are:

- Start-up and infant stage   32%
- Young   16%
- Established   51%

Start-up and infant firms attract Angels with lower incomes who hear about investment opportunities more through friends than through business associates. These Angels are very concerned about how well they know the entrepreneur, and more deals die for lack of this personal knowledge than for any other reason. Early stage Angels invest on a small scale and infrequently. Entrepreneurs of start-up and infant stage firms who are successful in attracting Angel financing quite naturally receive smaller total risk capital, consistent with their early stage needs. The firms have fewer employees than the composite company. Otherwise, the characteristics of start-up and infant stage firms are normal by composite standards. The only thing unusual about their deal structure is, again, the small number of investment dollars committed per Angel. In other aspects the market profile for start-up and infant stage firms does not differ from the expected.

Angels who have made deals with the entrepreneurs of *young* firms account for about 1 in 10 deals. These Angels rely more on business associates as information sources and are less likely to discover investment opportunities through friends or other information sources. Perhaps because of the larger capital needs of young firms relative to start-up/ infant firms, the Angels for young firms assemble larger investment groups. The result is that each successful entrepreneur receives three times more total risk capital than earlier stage counterparts. In other respects successful entrepreneurs resemble the U.S. Composite. Deals cut between Angels and entrepreneurs of young firms are unremarkable except for the greater flexibility afforded by the extraordinarily large amount of Angel loans/guarantees made available through the deal.

Angels investing in *established* firms are the real mavericks of the market. Despite their small numbers, they differ from the composite and from less-developed-firm profiles on 15 out of 40 characteristics. These Angels have below usual incomes, invest infrequently, and put up large loans instead of equity dollars. They are perhaps the most frustrated investors, judging by the fact that they wanted to invest almost twice as much as opportunity allowed. As expected, these firms have more employees than does the U.S. Composite. They commonly prepare comprehensive business plans and are most often found in the FIRE industry. The established firms and their successful entrepreneurs receive the largest amounts of total risk capital of any growth stage firm, but the investment is top-heavy with loans. The structure of the large deals made between individual Angels and established firms is dominated by heavy doses of loans and about average equity dollars. It almost looks as if the firm is gaining a banker instead of an investor. But bankers are not as aggressive about taking majority control as these Angels are, especially when compared to Angels for start-up and infant stage firms. The deal's ROI is lower for established firms than for either the composite or Angels in more risky growth stages. The market profiles for each of the three development stages will detail more specifically the deals made on behalf of these firms.

START-UP AND INFANT STAGE FIRMS

Each year some 600,000 new business establishments begin life, and 6 percent (33,000) of them have Angel backing. While this may seem like a small porportion, when you deduct those who don't qualify for Angel financing (proprietorships and most partnerships), the percent with Angel financing rises to 22 percent, or almost one in every four new eligible companies. A market profile for these Angel-assisted new firms is presented in Profile 8-1. The Angels in this profile include only those who have invested in start-up and infant firms. Compared to the composite, this market differs on nine items mostly related to the Angels themselves, whom I call "Early Birds."

Early Bird Angels

Investors who ante up early in a firm's development hear about the opportunity mostly from friends, have lower-than-expected levels of income, do not invest very often, and are most sensitive about getting to know the entrepreneur and key people well enough to entrust their money to them.

Friends as the main information source is a switch from the typical reliance on both friends and business associates equally. The percentages of Early Bird Angels' information sources are:

- Friends   35%
- Business associates   25%
- Entrepreneurs   14%
- Brokers   10%
- Others   16%

The median Angel investing in a start-up or infant firm has a lower income than Angels who invest at later stages of the firm's growth: $70,000 versus $90,000, respectively. The percentages of Early Bird Angels by income size are:

MARKET PROFILE 8-1. Start-up and Infant Stage Firms

ANGELS

		U.S. Composite
	• Business owner/manager is principal occupation (69%)	(69%)
	• Has personal entrepreneurial experience (86%)	(83%)
	• 49 years old*	(47 years)
	• White male (84%)	(84%)
	• College degree (73%)	(72%)
+	• $70,000 annual family income*	($90,000)
	• $750,000 net worth*	($750,000)
+	• Friends are the primary information channel	(Friends and associates)
	• Accepts 3 of 10 investment opportunities*	(3)
+	• Rejects deals mostly due to inadequate personal knowledge	(Growth potential)
+	• Invests about every 36 months and has 1.7 firms in portfolio*	(18) (3.5)
	• Satisfied with past investments (68%)	(72%)
	• Two other coinvestors*	(Two)
+	• $63,800 equity invested in informal portfolio*	($131,000)
+	• $25,000 more via loans/guarantees to portfolio firms*	($75,000)
	• Prefers investing in service/FIRE firms (38%)	(Service/FIRE)
	• Minimum ROI target for informal portfolio (22%)*	(22%)
	• Active as a consultant, board member, or employee (85%)	(81%)
	• Does not seek voting control (81%)	(85%)
	• Wants to invest 34% more than opportunity permitted	(35%)

SUCCESSFUL ENTREPRENEURS/FIRMS

+	• $156,600 total Angel financing* (equity and loans)	($176,700)
+	• $112,500 in equity and $44,100 more in loans/guarantees*	($112,500) ($64,200)
	• Three private individuals supply funding*	(Three)
	• Entrepreneur is a white male, age 25–35 (81%)	(79%)
+	• Zero to nine employees at time of investment (83%)	(74%)
	• Start-up or infant stage of firm growth (100%)	(69%)
	• Service firms are most frequently financed (19%)	(17% in service)
	• 50 miles or less from investor's home or office (71%)	(72%)
	• Has a comprehensive business plan (68%)	(61%)
	• Has detailed marketing and financing plans	

HIGH-PROBABILITY DEAL STRUCTURE

	• $37,500 in equity per investor*	($37,500)
+	• $14,700 in loans/guarantees by Angel*	($21,400)
	• 33% voting power transferred to investor	(37%)
	• Majority control to Angel in 24% of investments	(27%)
	• 30% capital risk seen by Angel*	(30%)
	• 25% expected annual ROI (26% average)	(25%) (27%)
	• Common stock or partner equity instrument (85%)	(79%)
	• Liquidation horizon of four years*	(Four years)
	• Liquidation buyback by insiders planned (47%)	(50%)
	• Investor is or becomes an employee in 38% of investments	(39%)

---

*Median value—half higher, half lower.   + = Differs importantly from U.S. Composite.

- Under $40,000   10%
- $40,000–$59,999   21%
- $60,000–$79,999   19%
- $80,000–$99,999   17%
- $100,000–$200,000   22%
- Over $200,000   11%

Seriously considered deals are most frequently killed by the Early Bird Angels' inability to acquire sufficient knowledge about the entrepreneur/ key people or by their belief that the entrepreneur lacks necessary talent. The leading rejection reasons for early stage funding proposals are:

1. Inadequate personal knowledge of entrepreneurs
2. Growth potential too limited
3. Management lacks talent necessary for success
4. Overpriced equity value

Early stage Angels do not invest frequently. Exactly half have never invested before, which means that the entrepreneurs have successfully recruited brand-new Angels in half the cases. It clearly pays entrepreneurs of start-up and infant firms to approach people who have never before invested. The percentages of Angels by the number of investments they made (including this one) are:

- 1 investment   50%
- 2   34%
- 3   9%
- 4   3%
- 5 or more   4%

The size of Angel loans and guarantees to start-up and infant firms is small by composite standards: $25,000 versus $75,000, respectively. Perhaps the strain of making the normal size of equity investment coupled with lower incomes straps these Angels when it comes to further loans/ guarantees. The major difference in loans is not that they are fewer in number but that they tend to be smaller in amount. This of course may not be a major disadvantage so long as the firm is small. In any event, the percentages of Early Bird Angels by size of total loans to their informal portfolio firm are:

- None   16%
- Under $50,000   37%
- $50,000–$99,999   14%
- $100,000–$500,000   22%
- Over $500,000   10%

Early Stage Entrepreneurs/Firms

About the only notable characteristics of successful early stage entrepreneurs are those we might expect: smaller total risk capital invested and smaller size (employment) of firm. The total Angel financing for start-up and infant stage firms ($157,000) is smaller than the composite ($177,000) by 11 percent. The percentages of entrepreneurs by size of total risk capital obtained are:

- Under $40,000   22%
- $40,000–$99,999   25%
- $100,000–$199,999   23%
- $200,000–$399,999   14%
- $400,000–$1,000,000   11%
- Over $1,000,000   5%

The employment sizes of successful Early Bird firms are:

- 0–4 employees   67%
- 5–9   16%
- 10–19   12%
- 20 or more   5%

Early Stage Deals

The structure of deals between Angels and early stage firms is typical, with the exception previously mentioned of the size of Angel loans/guarantees, which are only about two-thirds normal size.

Key Points about Start-up and Infant Firms

- Firms in their start-up and infant growth stage receive two out of three Angel financings but only about one-third of all Angel risk capital.
- Half of all Early Bird Angels have never invested before and hear about the opportunity through friends more than through business associates.
- Angel income, equity, and loans are all smaller than usual, but so are the firms financed.
- Lack of knowledge by the Angel about the entrepreneur or key people kills more deals than any other factor.
- The characteristics of the successful early stage entrepreneur and the deal itself are similar to the U.S. Composite in almost all respects.

YOUNG FIRMS

Firms in their "youth" stage of growth are involved in about 1 in every 10 Angel deals. They are the least popular target for Angels. Despite the fact that they are such a small minority of the Angel financial market, their market characteristics differ little from the composite of all firms. Exceptions include Angel information channel, size of investor group, leading deal killer, and Angel loans sizes, which can be seen in Market Profile 8-2.

MARKET PROFILE 8-2. Young Firms

ANGELS

U.S. Composite

- Business owner/manager is principal occupation (69%) — (69%)
- Has personal entrepreneurial experience (78%) — (83%)
- 49 years old* — (47 years)
- White male (82%) — (84%)
- College degree (71%) — (72%)
- $90,000 annual family income* — ($90,000)
- $750,000 net worth* — ($750,000)
+ • Associates are the primary information channel — (Friends and associates)
- Accepts 3 of 10 investment opportunities* — (3)
+ • Rejects deals mostly due to price, inadequate growth potential — (Growth potential)
- Invests about every 18 months and has 3.5 firms in portfolio* — (18) (3.5)
- Satisfied with past investments (75%) — (72%)
+ • Three other coinvestors* — (Two)
- $131,000 equity invested in informal portfolio* — ($131,000)
+ • $300,000 more via loans/guarantees to portfolio firms* — ($75,000)
- Prefers investing in FIRE firms (34%) — (Service/FIRE)
- Minimum ROI target for informal portfolio (22%)* — (22%)
- Active as a consultant, board member, or employee (81%) — (81%)
- Does not seek voting control (92%) — (85%)
- Wants to invest 31% more than opportunity permitted — (35%)

SUCCESSFUL ENTREPRENEURS/FIRMS

+ • $493,000 total Angel financing* (equity and loans) — ($176,700)
+ • $150,000 in equity and $343,000 more in loans/guarantees* — ($112,500) ($64,200)
+ • Four private individuals supply funding* — (Three)
- Entrepreneur is a white male, age 25–35 (79%) — (79%)
- Zero to nine employees at time of investment (66%) — (74%)
- Start-up or infant stage of firm growth (0%) — (69%)
- Service firms are most frequently financed (20%) — (17% in service)
- 50 miles or less from investor's home or office (71%) — (72%)
- Has a comprehensive business plan (65%) — (61%)
- Has detailed marketing and financing plans

HIGH-PROBABILITY DEAL STRUCTURE

- $37,500 in equity per investor* — ($37,500)
+ • $85,700 in loans/guarantees by Angel* — ($21,400)
- 32% voting power transferred to investor — (37%)
- Majority control to Angel in 30% of investments — (27%)
- 30% capital risk seen by Angel* — (30%)
- 25% expected annual ROI (28% average) — (25%) (27%)
- Common stock or partner equity instrument (73%) — (79%)
- Liquidation horizon of four years* — (Four years)
- Liquidation buyback by insiders planned (50%) — (50%)
- Investor is or becomes an employee in 40% of investments — (39%)

---

*Median value—half higher, half lower.   + = Differs importantly from U.S. Composite.

Market Profile

The Angel information channels that young firms find most productive
is Angels' business associates more so than friends or other sources. The
frequency of information channel productivity for Angels is:

- Business associates   35%
- Friends   29%
- Entrepreneurs   14%
- Brokers   10%
- Others   12%

When deals fall through, it is most likely that no equity price agreement
could be reached and growth potential seemed inadequate. However,
many reasons crowd together near the top killer position. The leading
four reasons why Angels reject a young firm investment proposal are:

1. Overpriced equity and too-limited growth potential (tied)
2. Lack of knowledge of entrepreneurs and management's lack of talent for
   success (tied)
3. Venture's need of further development
4. Failure to meet Angels' long-term objectives

When Angels do invest in young firms, the amount of loans provided
is unusually large. The difference in total loans reflects both more frequent lending (14 percent of U.S. Composite make no loans) and a
disproportionate concentration of loans (35 percent) to young firms in
the $100,000 to $500,000 bracket (U.S. Composite equals only 27 percent).
The percentages of Angels by size of portfolio loans/guarantees are:

- None   9%
- Under $50,000   25%
- $50,000–$99,999   14%
- $100,000–$500,000   35%
- Over $500,000   17%

Angels who support young firms form larger coinvestor groups to boost
total finances to match the firms' needs. The percentages of Angels and
the number of coinvestors per firm are:

- None   8%
- 1   19%
- 2   23%
- 3   11%
- 4   11%
- 5 or more   28%

Deals and successful entrepreneurs closely match the composite firm,
with the exceptions just illustrated above.

Key Points about Young Firms

- Young firms are least popular with Angels and account for only 1 in 10 financings.
- With few exceptions young-firm Angel markets closely resemble the U.S. Composite.
- When a deal occurs, it was initially discovered by the Angel through a business associate more often than through any other source, and it survived the Angel's special sensitivity to both equity pricing and growth goals.
- Total risk capital funding is usually top-heavy with loans relative to equity dollars.

ESTABLISHED FIRMS

The role of maverick belongs to the supporters of established firms. More than any other stage of development, established firms and their Angels stand out from the rest. Established firms account for only one in five Angel deals but receive 51 percent of their total capital dollars. This disproportionate market share reflects the larger capital needs of firms that are on the steep upswing portion of their growth curves. The odd part is that established-firm Angels, as shown in Market Profile 8-3, have relatively low incomes, invest infrequently, and accept a low ROI at standard risk levels. To top this off, they want to double their commitment, and they say they're happy with their investment performance. But oddity is what makes mavericks.

Angels for Established Firms

The $70,000 median income of established-firm Angels is similar to that of start-up and infant firms. However, the frequency of Angel investments shows that few repeat the process once they make one established-firm investment. The percentages of established-firm Angels and the number of their investments are:

- 1 investment   70%
- 2   17%
- 3   9%
- 4   2%
- 5 or more   2%

Perhaps this infrequency reflects the large amount of informal capital committed per firm, which is almost five times larger than usual—a median of $855,000, compared to the composite's $177,000. The percentages of established firms by size of total risk capital invested are:

MARKET PROFILE 8-3. Established Firms

ANGELS   U.S. Composite

- Business owner/manager is principal occupation   (68%)   (69%)
- Has personal entrepreneurial experience   (78%)   (83%)
- 49 years old*   (47 years)
- White male   (83%)   (84%)
- College degree   (67%)   (72%)
+ • $70,000 annual family income*   ($90,000)
- $750,000 net worth*   ($750,000)
- Friends and associates are the primary information channel   (Friends and associates)
- Accepts 3 of 10 investment opportunities*   (3)
- Rejects deals mostly due to inadequate growth potential   (Growth potential)
+ • Invests about every 36 months and has 1.7 firms in portfolio*   (18) (3.5)
- Satisfied with past investments   (77%)   72%
+ • Three other coinvestors*   (Two)
+ • $63,800 equity invested in informal portfolio*   ($131,000)
+ • $300,000 more via loans/guarantees to portfolio firms*   ($75,000)
- Prefers investing in service/FIRE firms   (33%)   (Service/FIRE)
- Minimum ROI target for informal portfolio (22%)*   (22%)
- Active as a consultant, board member, or employee   (79%)   (81%)
- Does not seek voting control   (80%)   (85%)
+ • Wants to invest 47% more than opportunity permitted   (35%)

SUCCESSFUL ENTREPRENEURS/FIRMS

+ • $855,000 total Angel financing* (equity and loans)   ($176,700)
+ • $150,000 in equity and $705,000 more in loans/guarantees*   ($112,500) ($64,200)
+ • Four private individuals supply funding*   (Three)
- Entrepreneur is a white male, age 25–35   (79%)   (79%)
+ • Zero to nine employees at time of investment   (46%)   (74%)
- Start-up or infant stage of firm growth   (0%)   (69%)
+ • FIRE firms are most frequently financed   (31%)   (17% in service)
- 50 miles or less from investor's home or office   (77%)   (72%)
+ • Has a comprehensive business plan   (77%)   (61%)
- Has detailed marketing and financing plans

HIGH-PROBABILITY DEAL STRUCTURE

- $37,500 in equity per investor*   ($37,500)
+ • $176,000 in loans/guarantees by Angel*   ($21,400)
- 34% voting power transferred to investor   (37%)
+ • Majority control to Angel in 36% of investments   (27%)
- 30% capital risk seen by Angel*   (30%)
+ • 10% expected annual ROI (17% average)   (25%) (27%)
- Common stock or partner equity instrument   (75%)   (79%)
- Liquidation horizon of four years*   (Four years)
- Liquidation buyback by insiders planned   (45%)   (50%)
- Investor is or becomes an employee in 34% of investments   (39%)

---

*Median value—half higher, half lower.   + = Differs importantly from U.S. Composite.

- Under $225,000   23%
- $225,000–$574,999   17%
- $575,000–$1,099,999   21%
- $1,100,000–$2,299,999   10%
- $2,300,000–$5,500,000   14%
- Over $5,500,000   16%

When asked, two out of three Angels wanted to invest more than opportunity allowed by an amount that averaged 47 percent more when spread
out over all Angels. The percentages of established-firm Angels and their
professed desires to invest more than they were able are:

- None   32%
- Up to 100% more   43%
- Over 100% more   25%

Successful Entrepreneurs with Established Firms

As expected, established firms need and receive more total risk capital.
They have more employees at the time of investment, they are often in
the FIRE industry, and they usually prepare a comprehensive business
plan. When Angel money is received, over half the established firms
have more than 10 employees. The big differences are in the 20 or more
employee class, where the U.S. Composite finds only 12 percent of its
firms, and in the 0 to 4 employee class, where 57 percent of the composite's firms are found. The percentages of successful established firms
and their employment size at deal time are:

- 0–4 employees   25%
- 5–9   21%
- 10–19   25%
- 20 or more   29%

Successful firms are located in the FIRE industry more than any other.
The actual percentages of successful established-firm industries are:

- Natural resources/mining   3%
- Construction   3%
- Manufacturing—high technology   7%
- Manufacturing—industrial   14%
- Manufacturing—consumer   5%
- Transportation, communication, utilities   1%
- Wholesale trade   1%
- Retail trade   12%
- Finance/insurance/real estate   31%
- Services   20%
- Other   3%

Even if you add up all manufacturing (26 percent), it does not surpass
FIRE in popularity.

Comprehensive business plans for successful firms are the norm. The percent of successful firms with such plans is 77 percent; the U.S. Composite is 61 percent.

Established-Firm Deals

The typical investment agreement between the established-firm entrepreneur and any one Angel involves a total of $214,000, compared to the composite's $58,900. This total risk capital is made up of $37,500 equity and $176,000 in loans/guarantees. The equity size is equal to the U.S. Composite, but loans exceed the composite by a factor of eight times ($176,000 versus $21,400, respectively). The percentages of loan sizes in established-firm deals are:

- None   17%
- Under $50,000   22%
- $50,000–$99,999   9%
- $100,000–$500,000   26%
- Over $500,000   26%

The high proportion of loans to equity is as unusual as the ability of the Angel's small equity commitment to gain majority control in one out of every three deals (36 percent). The percentages of deals by the proportion of voting power transferred to the Angel are:

- Under 25% voting power   40%
- 25–49%   8%
- 50%   16%
- Over 50%   36%

A final element of this unusual deal is the ROI expected by established-firm Angels. Their 17 percent average ROI is the lowest reported, yet the Angels' view of risk is no lower than for composite deals. The percentages of deals by size of expected ROI are:

- Under 20% ROI   57%
- 20–29%   38%
- 30–39%   5%
- 40% or more   0%

Key Points about Established Firms

- Established firms account for one in five Angel deals and half of all Angel capital invested.
- Two out of three Angels have never invested before when they invest here, and two-thirds of them want to invest even more than they were able.
- Total risk capital is large, exceeding the composite standard by almost a factor of five ($855,000 and $177,000, respectively). This capital is disproportionately made up of loans and not equity dollars.

- Large firms in the FIRE industry with over 10 employees are most popular with these Angels, who almost always require a comprehensive business plan before investing.
- Angels gain majority control from the entrepreneur in almost 4 in 10 deals.
- Return is low for Angel dollars, with a median ROI of only 10 percent and an average of 17 percent.

The age of your firm, as this chapter shows, is a special factor in attracting Angel dollars. The wise entrepreneur will use the information given here to help achieve an optimum matchup. Finer points about Angels who are predisposed to investing in your firm's particular industry will be found in the next chapter, "Angels Who Like Your Business Already."

9

ANGELS WHO ALREADY LIKE YOUR BUSINESS

Each specific industry, such as manufacturing, retail, services, and so forth, has its own unique market profile. What succeeds in attracting Angels to retail trade firms is not necessarily useful if your industry happens to be manufacturing. This chapter highlights market profile elements for each of seven major industry groups: manufacturing—high-technology products, manufacturing—all, retail trade, wholesale trade, services, finance/insurance/real estate (FIRE), and construction.

"Custom-tailored" profiles for the seven industries (along with the U.S. Composite) are presented side by side for ease of comparison in Market Profile 9-1. As usual, all three components of the deal—Angel, entrepreneur, and deal structure—are profiled. Breakdowns of individual elements appear in the sections discussing each industry and the Angels who seek to invest in it.

Custom tailoring of the U.S. Composite into individual industry profiles allows much more accurate pinpointing of market facts needed for actual business planning. In fact, the seven industry profiles that are presented in Profile 9-1 form the foundation for assembling more highly customized profiles described in Chapter 12. In that chapter, a series of step-by-step examples shows how to assemble a custom market profile incorporating six important business parameters specifically tailored to your particular needs. Each industry portrait shown in Profile 9-1 is unique in some way, yet some industries resemble the U.S. Composite and others are quite different. The discussions of the specific industries show these differences and highlight the special features that allow the industries to compete with others for Angel capital. The industry-specific sections first look at the industry's success in attracting Angel dollars, followed by a preview sketch of the market elements that set it apart from other industries. Each distinguishing market characteristic is disaggregated into its probability ranges. Finally, each industry section concludes with a summary of key points.

OVERVIEW OF MARKET DIFFERENCES

A brief overview of market differences will help add perspective before we begin our close examination of the characteristics of each industry. (Readers may want to study only the section or sections that apply to their situations and interests.) Almost every U.S. Composite market characteristic is applicable in one industry or another. Yet the overall similarities across widely different industries are often striking. Two industries, retail trade and services, almost match the U.S. Composite. But each departs from the composite on several key profile elements (but not the same ones). The most deviant industry in terms of U.S. Composite standards is manufacturing and its special subgroup, manufacturing—high-technology products. Together their financial market profiles show nine major exceptions to U.S. patterns. The risk capital market for both categories of manufacturing firms commonly involves five interrelated market features: Total capital invested is much larger compared to nonmanufacturing industries, larger groups of Angel coinvestors join to finance the entrepreneur, ownership share per Angel is less, investment holding periods are longer, and cash-out methods look to outsiders for eventual liquidation. In high-technology manufacturing, funding comes at a later development stage, and their Angels are almost completely dominated by white males who do not usually seek voting control.

Nonmanufacturing industries have their own wide-ranging patterns of market distinction that separate them from manufacturing firms and from each other. They typically have Angels with lower incomes than usual who invest early in the firm's growth curve. Angels in nonmanufacturing kill serious deals for a wider variety of reasons, unlike the U.S. Composite or manufacturing where insufficient growth potential is the main deal rejection reason.

MANUFACTURING FIRMS—HIGH-TECHNOLOGY PRODUCTS

Media hype touting the high-technology industry is solidly backed by Angel dollars. There is no reliable data on the actual number of high-technology firms, but their number is relatively small compared to all other types of firms. Despite these small numbers, they attracted about 10 percent of all Angel financing between 1982–1987—some 8700 high-technology entrepreneurs succeeded each year in recruiting about 43,500 Angels who in turn invested $2.6 billion, or about 15 percent of all Angel risk capital. The $2.6 billion is fully one-half of all Angel capital committed to all manufacturing firms and is exceeded only by Angel capital commitment to the service sector.

The term "high-technology" in this chapter is used differently than in the Chapter 1 subsection "High-Tech Angels." There, I focused on

MARKET PROFILE 9-1. Industry-Specific Profiles

	U.S. Composite	Manufacturing— High-Technology Products	Manufacturing— All	Retail Trade	Wholesale Trade	Service	FIRE	Construction
ANGELS								
• Business owner/manager	69%	73%	76%	69%	66%	74%	60%+	61%
• Personal entrepreneurial experience	83%	81%	81%	83%	81%	81%	91%	91%
• Age*	47 years	49 years	49 years	49 years	49 years	49 years	49 years	39 years+
• White male	84%	92%+	88%	87%	89%	75%+	89%	84%
• College degree	72%	78%	79%	59%+	63%+	76%	73%	72%
• Annual family income*	$90,000	$90,000	$90,000	$70,000+	$70,000+	$90,000	$90,000	$70,000+
• Net worth*	$750,000	$750,000	$750,000	$750,000	$750,000	$750,000	$750,000	$750,000
• Primary information channel	Friends and associates	Friends and associates	Friends and associates	Friends and associates	Friends+	Friends and associates	Friends and associates	Friends+
• Deal acceptance rate*	30%	30%	30%	30%	30%	30%	30%	30%
• Main deal rejection reason(s)	Growth	Talent, growth+	Growth	Growth	Price+	Talent, personal knowledge+	Personal knowledge+	Time, talent, personal knowledge+
• Investment frequency/ firms in portfolio	18 mos./3.5	18 mos./3.5	18 mos./3.5	18 mos./3.5	18 mos./3.5	18 mos./3.5	18 mos./3.5	18 mos./3.5
• Satisfied with past investments	72%	72%	68%	71%	73%	74%	78%	76%
• Number of coinvestors*	Two	Four+	Three+	Two	Two	Two	Two	Two
• Equity invested in informal portfolio*	$131,000	$131,000	$131,000	$131,000	$131,000	$131,000	$131,000	$131,000
• Loans/guarantees to portfolio firms*	$75,000	$75,000	$75,000	$75,000	$75,000	$75,000	$300,000+	$75,000
• Preferred industry	Service/FIRE 35%	High-Tech. mfg. 56%+	High-Tech. mfg. 37%+	Retail trade 58%+	Whsle. trade /FIRE 43%+	Service 50%+	FIRE 67%+	Construction 57%+
• Minimum ROI target*	22%	22%	22%	22%	22%	22%	22%	22%
• Active as consultant, board member, or employee	81%	84%	85%	88%	89%+	82%	80%	87%
• Does not seek voting control	85%	97%+	88%	81%	85%	86%	80%	78%
• Dollars available for more investment than opportunity permitted	35%	34%	38%	33%	34%	38%	31%	30%

MARKET PROFILE 9-1. Continued

	U.S. Composite	Manufacturing—High-Technology Products	Manufacturing—All	Retail Trade	Wholesale Trade	Service	FIRE	Construction
ENTREPRENEURS/FIRMS								
• Total Angel financing* (equity and loans)	$176,700	$294,500 +	$235,600 +	$176,700	$176,700	$176,700	$370,000 +	$176,700
• Equity	$112,500	$187,500 +	$150,000 +	$112,500	$112,500	$112,500	$112,500	$112,500
• Loans/guarantees*	$64,200	$107,000 +	$85,600 +	$64,200	$64,200	$64,200	$257,000 +	$64,200
• No. of individuals supplying funding*	Three	Five +	Four +	Three	Three	Three	Three	Three
• Entrepreneur while male, age 25–35	79%	87%	85%	78%	80%	74%	83%	77%
• Zero to nine employees	74%	75%	70%	81%	78%	78%	71%	88% +
• Start-up or infant stage firm	69%	60% +	62%	74%	79% +	68%	73%	80% +
• 50 miles or less from investor's home or office	72%	69%	67%	76%	67%	73%	75%	70%
• Comprehensive business plan	61%	66%	63%	62%	64%	56%	71% +	53%
HIGH-PROBABILITY DEAL STRUCTURE								
• Equity per investor*	$37,500	$37,500	$37,500	$37,500	$37,500	$37,500	$37,500	$37,500
• Angel loans/guarantees*	$21,400	$21,400	$21,400	$21,400	$21,400	$21,400	$86,000 +	$21,400
• Voting power transferred to investor	37%	27% +	27% +	37%	35%	32%	34%	39%
• Majority control to Angel	27%	15% +	21%	35%	31%	31%	27%	35%
• Capital risk seen by Angel*	30%	30%	30%	30%	30%	30%	30%	30%
• Expected annual ROI* (average ROI)	25% (27%)	25% (24%)	25% (25%)	25% (23%)	25% (35%) +	25% (27%)	25% (27%)	25% (34%) +
• Common stock or partner equity instrument	79%	80%	80%	82%	81%	76%	86%	87%
• Liquidation horizon*	Four years	Seven and a half years +	Seven and a half years +	Four years	Four years	Four years	Four years	Four years
• Buyback by insiders planned	50%	52%	35% +	46%	45%	52%	42%	57%
• Investor is or becomes employee	39%	33%	35%	43%	45%	40%	36%	38%

*Median value—half higher, half lower.   + = Important difference from U.S. Composite.

the special type of Angel who invests only in high-technology firms. The focus here is on all Angels who have made any high-technology investments, whether they invest in other industries or not. The different meanings are important, and the number of sample Angels here is over twice the number profiled in Chapter 1. The high-technology industry differs from the U.S. Composite on 10 profile elements, as can be seen in Profile 9-1 and as will be detailed in the following subsections.

Angels in the High-Tech Industry

Investors with any investments in high-technology firms are disproportionately males who form large coinvestor groups, they often kill deals due to perceived lack of management talent, and they place less emphasis on obtaining voting control. High-tech industry Angels include fewer women or minorities than usual, and a complete absence of minority females was reported. The percentages of Angels by demographics are:

- White male   92%
- White female   4%
- Minority male   4%
- Minority female   0%

The size of coinvestor groups is double the usual number (four versus two). The percentages of industry Angels by number of coinvestors are:

- None   7%
- 1–2   17%
- 3–5   30%
- 6–10   35%
- 10 or more   11%

The large number of coinvestors combines with lower voting share objectives to produce the lowest actual voting share per Angel of any industry, as shown later. The U.S. Composite Angel claims not to seek voting control in over 8 out of 10 cases, but for high-tech manufacturing it's almost universal.

Successful Entrepreneurs

High-technology entrepreneurs obtain two-thirds more risk capital from their Angels because more Angels coinvest, not because each commits more dollars. The larger risk capital total probably reflects the fact that high-tech firms are more capital-intensive and have reached a more advanced growth stage than typical. The percentages of successful firms by growth stage (age) at time of investment are:

- Start-up   44%
- Infant   16%

- Young   18%
- Established   22%

Deal Structure

The specific agreements that make up a high-tech industry deal are similar to the U.S. Composite, with the exception of voting control and investment holding period. The high-tech industry investor averages only a 27-percent ownership share, compared to the composite's 37 percent. Moreover, Angels gain voting control far less often than any other industry group (15 percent versus the composite's 27 percent). The percentages of deals by voting power obtained by the Angel are:

- Under 25% share   60%
- 25–49%   13%
- 50%   11%
- Over 50%   15%

The deal also anticipates a long holding period of seven and a half years, compared to the usual four years. The percentages of high-tech industry deals by anticipated holding period are:

- Under 3 years   13%
- 3–5   23%
- 6–10   40%
- Over 10 years or
  unimportant   24%

Key Points about High-Tech Industry Group

Of all industry groups, high-tech is the least common. Its market profile differs from the U.S. Composite more than any other, including:

- High-tech industry Angels are dominated by white males who form large coinvestor teams to provide 67 percent more total risk capital than the U.S. industry standards.
- Angels generally claim less interest in corporate control than is typically the case, and actual deals provide Angels with less ownership share and fewer cases of absolute control than in other industries.
- Despite the fact that successful high-tech entrepreneurs are at a more advanced growth stage than other industries at deal time, a long (seven-and-a-half years) holding period is expected before the firm is mature enough for investment liquidation.

MANUFACTURING FIRMS (ALL)

Manufacturing firms represent 9.5 percent of all U.S. business enterprises and are a favorite target for Angel dollars. In the five years ending in

1987, each year 54,000 Angels (21 percent) provided financing for 23,600 manufacturing industry entrepreneurs. The total Angel capital invested and loaned to manufacturing firms amounted to $5.6 billion annually (27 percent of all Angel dollars). Because manufacturing firms are such a large sector of the Angel market we might expect that their market profile would closely resemble the U.S. Composite. Indeed, there are many profile similarities, but important differences exist also. As usual, the differences are highlighted here.

Manufacturing Industry Angels

The manufacturing industry Angel differs from composite colleagues by coinvesting with larger groups of three versus two for the composite. This reflects the industry's large needs for risk capital per firm, as discussed below. More striking is the Angel's preference for manufacturing in general, highly focused on high-technology manufacturing in particular. This stands in contrast to the composite Angel's preference for investments in the service and/or FIRE industry. The percentages of manufacturing Angels' preferences by industry group are:

- Natural resources/mining   9%
- Construction   12%
- Manufacturing—high-technology   37%
- Manufacturing—industrial   29%
- Manufacturing—consumer   27%
- Transportation, communication, and utilities   10%
- Wholesale trade   15%
- Retail trade   12%
- Finance/insurance/real estate   26%
- Services   21%
- Others   4%

(The percentages do not add to 100 percent since multiple industries can receive "strong" investor preference.)

Successful Entrepreneurs/Firms

The main feature that sets manufacturing apart from the composite profile is that a group of four Angels provides a total of over $250,000 in risk capital, compared to the composite's three Angels committing $177,000. This larger total commitment is due entirely to more Angel coinvestors, and not to more dollars per Angel. The percentages of the total risk capital received by firms are:

- Under $65,000   19%
- $65,000–$159,999   20%
- $160,000–$324,999   17%

- $325,000–$624,999   18%
- $625,000–$1,500,000   17%
- Over $1,500,000   8%

Deal Structure

Manufacturing deals bear a close resemblance to the composite except for voting shares, holding period, and liquidation method. The proportion of voting control achieved by any given Angel is 27 percent versus the composite's 37 percent. This is partly a reflection of the larger number of Angels per firm. The percentages of deals by the amount of voting share per Angel are:

- Under 25% share   53%
- 25–49%   17%
- 50%   10%
- Over 50%   21%

The patience level of manufacturing Angels exceeds the norm by over three years. The median expected holding period for a manufacturing deal is seven and a half years, compared to the U.S. Composite's four years. The actual percentages of deals by expected holding period are:

- Under 3 years   17%
- 3–5   30%
- 6–10   34%
- Over 10 or not important   19%

When Angels do cash out, the provisions written into the deal structure favor liquidation of equity by outsiders more strongly than usual. The percentage of deals for each type of liquidation method is:

- None (no plan)   25%
- Resell to company   26%
- Resell to coinvestor   8%
- Sell/merge with another company   7%
- Public offering   8%
- Other (or combinations)   25%

Key Points about Manufacturing Firms

Manufacturing firms and their Angel capital markets share much the same characteristics as their special subgroup, high-tech manufacturing:

- All manufacturing and high-tech manufacturing obtain between 33 and 66 percent more capital than other industries. This is accomplished by larger groups of coinvestors and not by larger commitments per Angel.
- The Angels in both manufacturing groups receive less equity share than usual, reflecting the dilution of larger coinvestor groups.

• The expected holding period prior to investment liquidation is longer in both industry groups (seven and a half years) than other industries. Sale to outsiders is the most preferred liquidation plan.

RETAIL TRADE

Retailing accounts for 28 percent (1,056,000) of all U.S. business establishments, according to estimates by the U.S. Small Business Administration. In each year between 1982 and 1987 almost 37,000 Angels (14 percent) joined to finance over 12,000 retailing entrepreneurs. The total risk dollars invested added up to almost $2.2 billion per year—about 12 percent of all informal capital invested. These facts paint a picture of a very large industry sector (in terms of firms) that accounts for a much smaller proportion of all Angel investments: 28 percent of all business establishments receiving only 10 percent of Angel capital.

Many small differences in the retail trade industry can be noted in Profile 9-1, but only two stand out significantly, both related to Angel characteristics. Retail trade Angels have lower education achievement and lower family incomes. Only 6 out of 10 retail Angels have completed college, compared to 72 percent of the composite. The percentages of Angels by education level completed are:

• High school   15%
• Some college   26%
• College degree   44%
• Graduate degree   15%

Consistent with their lower education level, retail Angels also earn a lower family income than the U.S. Composite: $70,000 and $90,000, respectively. The percentages of retail Angels by family income class are:

• Under $40,000   17%
• $40,000–$59,999   23%
• $60,000–$79,999   16%
• $80,000–$99,999   15%
• $100,000–$199,999   17%
• Over $200,000   12%

In all other respects the profile characteristics of Angels' finance in the retail trade industry are similar to those of the U.S. Composite.

WHOLESALE TRADE

There are about 416,000 business establishments in the wholesale trade industry, accounting for 11 percent of all U.S. industry. Each year some

5200 wholesale firms receive risk capital from approximately 15,600 Angels. The annual value of this capital funding between 1982 and 1987 is estimated at $920 million, just 5 percent of all Angel dollars invested. Wholesale industry entrepreneurs as a group receive the smallest amount of Angel financing of all industries considered in this chapter. This small capital flow is not because the investment per deal or firm is small but because there are relatively few deals actually made. Perusal of the market elements for wholesale trade presented in Profile 9-1 reveals that major differences between wholesale and other industries occur most often in the Angel characteristics and less so among entrepreneurs or deals.

Angels in Wholesale Trade

Angels who invest in wholesale industry entrepreneurs are more active with their firms, more sensitive to equity pricing, have a lower rate of college completion, and have smaller-than-usual incomes.

Wholesale industry Angels finish their college education less frequently than Angels generally: 63 percent and 72 percent, respectively. The probabilities of Angel financing by education level completed are:

- High school or less   11%
- Some college   26%
- College degree   40%
- Graduate degree   23%

The lower educational attainment is undoubtedly linked to their lower Angel incomes. Median income is $70,000, compared to $90,000 for the U.S. Composite. The percentages of wholesale Angels by income grouping are:

- Under $40,000   13%
- $40,000–$59,999   17%
- $60,000–$79,999   26%
- $80,000–$99,999   17%
- $100,000–$200,000   17%
- Over $200,000   9%

Related to lower income is the extraordinary sensitivity to equity pricing demonstrated by wholesale trade Angels. Their main reason for killing serious deals is because of overpriced equity. Unfortunately we don't know if this difference over equity price is due to Angel or entrepreneurial resistance. Once a deal is cut, the Angel in wholesale trade is more active with the firm than the composite Angel. Almost 9 out of 10 become a consultant, employee, or board member, compared to 8 out of 10 composite Angels. This increase in Angel activity is not primarily due to higher levels of Angel employment but rather to their stepped-up activity as either consultants or board members.

Wholesale Trade Entrepreneurs

The profile of the successful entrepreneur in wholesale trade is very much in line with entrepreneurs everywhere, except when it comes to the firm's growth stage. Wholesale entrepreneurs succeed in attracting Angels when the firm is much younger and less fully developed, compared to the U.S. Composite. Eight out of 10 wholesale trade firms receive Angel risk capital at the start-up or infant stage, but only 7 out of 10 firms do so in other industries. Start-up stage funding by wholesale Angels (71 percent) is particularly "out of sync" with the U.S. Composite (57 percent). The percentages of successful wholesale firms by growth stage are:

- Start-up   71%
- Infant   9%
- Young   9%
- Established   12%

Deals in Wholesaling

Once Angels and entrepreneurs jump the equity pricing barrier, their deals look much like everyone else's, except for the unusually high ROI that Angels expect. Their average expected return on investment is 35 percent, in contrast to the standard 27 percent. The higher ROI is due primarily to twice the number of deals promising returns of 50 to 99 percent per year. (High-ROI deals in general are examined in Chapter 11's subsection titled "High Fliers.") It would appear that overpriced equity situations are resolved in favor of Angels more frequently than in other industries. These seemingly optimistic ROI plans may be realistic, since Angels report being as satisfied with investment performance as the U.S. Composite. The percentages of deals by Angels' expected ROI are:

- Under 20% per year   35%
- 20–29%   30%
- 30–39%   7%
- 40–49%   2%
- 50–99%   22%
- 100% or more   4%

Key Points about Wholesale Trade Deals

Wholesale trade differs more than any other nonmanufacturing industry when market profile elements are compared to the U.S. Composite. The major points of contrast setting it apart include:

- Wholesale trade Angels are less well educated and have lower incomes than usual.

- Angels reject deals for many reasons, but the leading deal killer is over-priced equity.

- Investors are more active than usual as board members or consultants.

- Successful wholesale trade firms receive financing at younger, less-well-developed stages of growth than the composite of all industries.

- Average ROI expected per Angel deal is extraordinarily high—35 percent per year, compared to the composite's 27 percent. This ROI is the highest recorded in any industry group. (Angels say that they're getting it, too!)

SERVICE INDUSTRY

The service industry's 864,000 business establishments represent one in four (23 percent) of all U.S. business enterprises, according to the U.S. Small Business Administration. Each year about 15,700 entrepreneurs receive Angel risk capital from some 47,000 Angels. The collective size of each year's investment between 1982 and 1987 was $2.6 billion, or 15 percent of all informal risk capital (equity and loans).

The outstanding feature of the profile of service industry character-istics is its close correspondence to the U.S. Composite. This is not unex-pected because service industry Angels represent a large portion of all Angels in the U.S. Composite. Nevertheless, two important differences exist. Service industry Angels are females and minorities more often than expected, and the Angels kill deals mainly because of information they do have and don't have about the potential entrepreneur.

More females and minorities participate as Angels in the service in-dustry than anywhere else. The percent of white male Angels across all industries is 84 percent, but in the service sector it is only 75 percent. The difference exists mostly because of the higher rate of participation by minority males, but all demographic groups other than white males are more frequent. Interestingly enough, the demographics of successful entrepreneurs show a usual percent of white males. The percentages of Angels by demographics are:

- White males   75%
- White females   6%
- Minority males   18%
- Minority females   1%

The fact that personal capabilities and characteristics play a bigger part in the service industry than elsewhere may help explain the two main deal killers. Angels reject service industry deals because they see a lack of management talent in their potential entrepreneurs or because they do not have sufficient personal knowledge about the entrepreneur or the key people to make a sound investment decision. The top five deal rejection reasons in rank order are:

1. Inadequate personal knowledge of the firm's entrepreneurs and key personnel
2. Management's lack of experience or talent necessary for success
3. Limited chance for growth
4. Proposal value of equity unrealistic
5. Not enough time for adequate due diligence

In all other characteristics, service industry Angels, entrepreneurs, and deal structure resemble the U.S. Composite.

Summing up, the service industry shares with retail trade the distinction of being most like the U.S. Composite when market profiles are compared. However, two important exceptions exist:

• The percent of service industry Angels who are white males is smaller than in any other industry, meaning that more females and minorities invest here than elsewhere.

• Deal rejection occurs because of two reasons: Angels do not have sufficient personal knowledge of the entrepreneurs/key personnel to reach a "yes" decision, and what information they do obtain often says that the potential entrepreneurs lack the management talent necessary to achieve success.

FINANCE, INSURANCE, AND REAL ESTATE FIRMS

The U.S. Small Business Administration estimates that there are 261,000 business establishments in the FIRE industry, representing 7 percent of the U.S. total. Each year between 1982 and 1987, some 15,000 entrepreneurs received risk capital financing from approximately 47,000 Angels. The total annual value of Angel risk capital (equity and loans) exceeded $4.3 billion. Only the manufacturing industry receives more Angel capital. The inflow of capital from Angels to the FIRE industry represents one out of every four dollars of all Angel funding. There are six major differences between FIRE and other industry profiles, as shown in Profile 9-1 and detailed in the following subsections.

Angels

Angels who invest in the FIRE industry are less often business owners themselves, are most sensitive to personal knowledge about entrepreneurs as a rejection cause, and lend more dollars than usual. Six out of 10 Angels are business owners, compared to 7 in 10 for the composite industry. The occupational pattern of FIRE Angels reflects twice the usual number of sales and other occupations. The percentages of FIRE Angel occupational groups are:

- Business owner/manager   60%
- Sales   7%
- Science/engineering professional 4%
- Other professional   8%
- All other occupations   20%

Angels reject proposed FIRE industry deals mainly because they have insufficient personal knowledge of the entrepreneur or key personnel. The four leading deal rejection reasons are:

1. Angel has inadequate personal knowledge of the firm's entrepreneurs and key personnel.
2. Firm's chances for growth seem too limited.
3. Firm's management lacks experience or talent necessary for success.
4. Proposal value of equity is unrealistic.

The most striking industry difference is the size of Angel loans/guarantees to firms in their informal portfolio; it is four times larger than the U.S. Composite. Total loans/guarantees were $300,000, versus $75,000 for the composite. The composite's frequency of loans of $100,000 or more is only 40 percent, compared to 51 percent among FIRE Angels. The percentages of Angels by the size of their total loans to all their informal invested firms are:

- None   14%
- Under $50,000   26%
- $50,000-$99,999   9%
- $100,000-$500,000   33%
- Over $500,000   18%

Entrepreneurs and Their Firms

Successful FIRE entrepreneurs obtain two-thirds more total risk capital than usual, but only ordinary amounts of equity dollars. Loans/guarantees provide this large margin of risk capital. The percentages of successful industry entrepreneurs by total risk capital received are:

- Under $100,000   16%
- $100,000-$249,999   19%
- $250,000-$499,999   29%
- $500,000-$999,999   13%
- $1,000,000-$2,500,000   16%
- Over $2,500,000   8%

Risk capital of the above size is not invested haphazardly, and FIRE Angels received a comprehensive written business plan in 7 out of 10 actual financings. As in other deals, detailed marketing and financing plans are also provided, but the exact frequency is unknown. The percentages of successful entrepreneurs with comprehensive business plans are:

- Under 20% of deals   7%
- 20–39%   6%
- 40–59%   8%
- 60–79%   8%
- 80–100%   71%

Key Points about the FIRE Industry

- Non–business owner/manager Angels are more prevalent in FIRE firms than in any other industry group.
- Angels reject deals primarily for lack of sufficient personal knowledge about the entrepreneurs and/or key personnel.
- Angels provide more risk capital as loans/guarantees in FIRE than in any other industry. It averages almost three times more than their equity dollar investments.
- Successful entrepreneurs obtain more total capital than the U.S. Composite firm—by a factor of four times, or about $193,000.
- Comprehensive written business plans are required in an unusually high number of deals (7 out of 10).
- Industry deal structure is similar to the U.S. Composite, with the exception of the large size of loans/guarantees.

CONSTRUCTION INDUSTRY

The construction industry numbers 511,000 business establishments (14 percent of total as estimated by the U.S. Small Business Administration). Each year slightly less than 9000 of these firms succeed in attracting risk capital from about 26,100 Angels. The total value of that capital inflow (both equity and loans) is estimated at $1.2 billion per year, or about 8 percent of all Angel financing.

The construction industry market elements shown in Profile 9-1 differ on eight major points from the U.S. Composite. Angels in construction are younger, have lower incomes, reject deals for a wide variety of reasons, and a majority do not want to invest more than they did. The successful firms are smaller and younger than usual, but the deal structure is similar to the U.S. Composite.

Angels

Angels in construction have a median age of 39 years, versus the composite's 47 years. The under-45 age group here is 53 percent of all Angels, but for the U.S. Composite it is only 42 percent of the total. The percentages of Angels by age group are:

- Under 35 years old   13%
- 35–44   40%
- 45–54   29%
- 55–64   12%
- Over 65   6%

Hand in hand with younger age comes lower income (but not less education). The construction Angel has a median annual family income of $70,000, versus $90,000 for all industries. The difference is accounted for by 40 percent of construction Angels with incomes below $60,000, compared to 32 percent for all industry Angels. The percentages of Angels by income class are:

- Under $40,000   15%
- $40,000–$59,999   25%
- $60,000–$79,999   19%
- $80,000–$99,999   6%
- $100,000–$200,000   25%
- Over $200,000   10%

Construction Angels *equally* rank three reasons to explain why they most often reject serious deals. These reasons are (in no special order):

- Insufficient time to do proper due diligence research
- Lack of management talent
- No sufficient personal knowledge of the entrepreneur and/or key personnel

Except for differences of age, income, and deal rejection reasons, construction Angels look like any others.

Successful Firms

The median construction firm is very small at the time of investment, with almost 9 out of 10 having fewer than 10 employees, compared to 74 percent for all industries. The proportion of very small firms with less than 5 employees tells the story—they account for 73 percent in construction, but only 57 percent in all other industries. The percentages of firms by employment size at deal time are:

- 0–4 employees   73%
- 5–9   15%
- 10–19   10%
- Over 20   2%

Consistent with small average employment size is the high percentage of successful construction entrepreneurs who are in the start-up or infant stage of growth. The proportion of start-up firms is the difference. Start-up construction firms account for 70 percent of all deals, but only 57 percent for the U.S. Composite. The percentages of successful firms by growth stage are:

- Start-up   70%
- Infant   10%
- Young   9%
- Established   11%

Deals

The deal structure documenting the terms and conditions of the investment agreement for construction Angels does not vary from the typical structure for all industries.

Key Points about Construction Deals

- Construction Angels are younger than usual and have lower incomes.
- Angels making deals with construction entrepreneurs invest normal amounts of both equity and loans/guarantees.
- Deals are rejected for a variety of reasons that do not seem to be unique to the construction industry.
- Successful entrepreneurs are typical by composite standards, but their firms obtain Angel financing at an earlier development stage (mostly during start-up), and consequently the firms are smaller than usual in terms of the number of employees.
- Deals cut for Angel investments in construction look like deals in any industry.

10

Angels Where You Live

Angels invest their money close to home. Seven out of 10 deals are made within 50 miles of the Angel's home or office. Moreover, Angels are scattered throughout the country in the same pattern as the general population. All this means that there are no national or regional markets, only local ones. It is potentially misleading for a Houston entrepreneur to plan strategy according to a mythical U.S. Composite market profile, because local conditions are different. Houston Angels and entrepreneurs want and need the specifics of their own market to increase the odds for success, and the profile elements that outline success in Boston are not the same as those in Los Angeles or Miami.

In this chapter the U.S. Composite is partitioned into its major local markets. The characteristics of 26 major metropolitan areas in 10 economic regions are summarized. The cities are:

• Boston and New England	Region I
• New York and New Jersey	Region II
• Washington D.C., Philadelphia, Baltimore, and Mid-Atlantic areas	Region III
• Miami, Atlanta, Memphis, and the Southeast	Region IV
• Chicago, Detroit, Cleveland, Minneapolis, and the industrial Heartland	Region V
• Houston, Dallas, New Orleans, San Antonio, and the Mid-South areas	Region VI
• St. Louis, Kansas City, Omaha, and the Plains states	Region VII
• Denver, Salt Lake City, and the Mountains	Region VIII
• Los Angeles, Phoenix, San Francisco, and the Southwest	Region IX
• Seattle, Portland, and the Pacific Northwest	Region X

The exact areas included in each region are shown in Figure 10-1 and defined in Table 10-1. The regions have been arbitrarily grouped into two market profiles that allow comparison of the components of each region to each other and to the U.S. Composite. Although interregion comparisons are interesting, what will be most useful to you is the specifics of your own region. So, like the preceding chapter, this one is intended for "spot reading" of the section that pertains to you rather than for a complete readthrough.

TABLE 10-1. Definition of Regions

Region I	Region VI
Connecticut	Arkansas
Maine	Louisiana
Massachusetts	New Mexico
New Hampshire	Oklahoma
Rhode Island	Texas
Vermont	
	Region VII
Region II	Iowa
New Jersey	Kansas
New York	Missouri
	Nebraska
Region III	
Delaware	Region VIII
District of Columbia	Colorado
Maryland	Montana
Pennsylvania	North Dakota
Virginia	South Dakota
West Virginia	Utah
	Wyoming
Region IV	
Alabama	Region IX
Florida	Arizona
Georgia	California
Kentucky	Hawaii
Mississippi	Nevada
North Carolina	
South Carolina	Region X
Tennessee	Alaska
	Idaho
Region V	Oregon
Illinois	Washington
Indiana	
Michigan	
Minnesota	
Ohio	
Wisconsin	

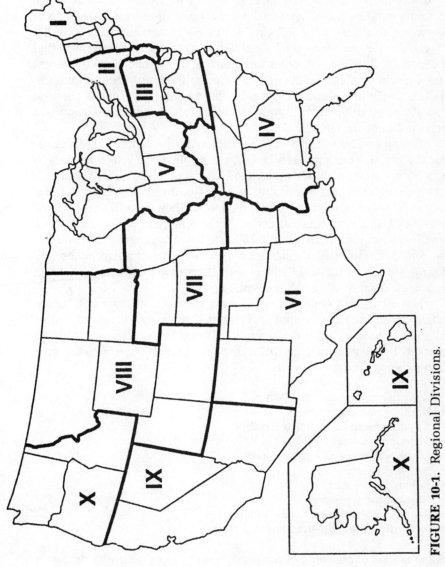

FIGURE 10-1. Regional Divisions.

PREVIEW OF KEY LOCAL DIFFERENCES

The actual market behavior reported for each region results from the interplay of preferences and opportunities for both Angels and entrepreneurs. We cannot decipher from the results which set of factors is the cause of market events, any more than we can say which blade of the scissors cuts the paper. Again, the importance of market differences is determined by the "Rule of Eight," which says that when differences between profiles are larger than eight percentage points there is an actual (important) difference. Another way of saying this is that when differences are eight percentage points or less there is likely no actual difference. When used with judgment, this guideline can help us separate out from the abundant differences in local markets those that are most important to investment decisions.

Boston and New England, along with Miami, Atlanta, and Memphis, are the real maverick markets by U.S. standards. Local Angel markets in the Boston area are at odds with the U.S. pattern on over half of the 40 comparison elements. For Miami and the Southeast the differences are not as frequent (one-fourth of the items) but they are still "off on their own" by U.S. Composite standards. At the other end of the scale, some local markets closely match the U.S. pattern. Washington D.C. and the surrounding Mid-Atlantic markets are almost an exact mirror of the U.S. Composite. St. Louis and its local market area are a close second when it comes to replicating U.S. patterns.

Not all market elements vary across regions; in fact some hardly change from one locale to another. It is safe to say, however, that all typical U.S. characteristics are at odds with local conditions in at least one local market. The market characteristics that change most often from one area to another include:

- Total risk capital invested per firm
- Equity invested per firm
- Angel loans and guarantees per firm
- Angel income and wealth
- Angel experience as entrepreneurs
- Top deal killers
- Risk of capital loss
- Most-popular industry
- Use of comprehensive business plans
- Investment holding period and exit method

Some market characteristics are persistent in their uniformity despite a wide range of local conditions and circumstances. Below are the Angel characteristics that do not change much, if at all, among local markets. It is not that the items listed never change—just not often.

- Occupation
- Communication channels
- Expected return on investment
- Voting power obtained
- Desire to invest more
- Satisfaction with investment performance
- Involvement in firm's operations

BOSTON AND NEW ENGLAND—REGION I

The area included in the local Boston–New England Angel market is shown in Figure 10-1 and covers the traditional New England areas defined in Table 10–1. The capital markets of this compact region embrace about 6 percent (285,000) of all U.S. business enterprises, as estimated by the U.S. Small Business Administration. The area has about 5 percent of the adult U.S. population and personal income. Businesses with Angel investors (9.4 percent) are close to the national average of 9 percent and total about 27,000 area enterprises. Local markets add up to a total pool of some 40,000 Angels who annually conclude 29,000 investment deals with 5200 entrepreneurs. The value of these deals annually is estimated at $2.0 billion in equity dollars and another $1.4 billion in Angel loans and guarantees. Total risk capital invested thus adds up to $3.4 billion per year. Two-thirds of the reporting Angels (67 percent) say they would have invested another $1.1 billion each year if their deal flow permitted. Combining both the actual and potential risk capital for the Boston–New England local markets gives a total of $4.5 billion each year available for local economic growth and development.

Markets in Region I

The composite profile of local markets in Region I differs greatly from the U.S. Composite, more so than any other local market. Its composite characteristics are compared with the U.S. Composite in Market Profile 10-1. They differ on 22 out of 40 points, especially regarding the structure of deals and the pattern of successful entrepreneurs. When it comes to structuring deals, New England departs from the national pattern 90 percent of the time (9 out of 10 comparisons) and 60 percent for the success characteristics of entrepreneurs (6 out of 10 comparisons). The Angels involved are more like the U.S. Composite, differing on only 7 out of 20 comparisons.

Boston-area Angels

Personal Characteristics. Boston-area Angels differ from U.S. patterns because of lower incomes, higher wealth, and use of direct communication

MARKET PROFILE 10-1. Regions I–V

	U.S. Composite	Boston and New England—Region I	New York and New Jersey—Region II	Washington, D.C., Philadelphia, Baltimore, and Mid-Atlantic—Region III	Miami, Atlanta, Memphis and Southeast—Region IV	Chicago, Detroit, Cleveland, Minneapolis and Industrial Heartland—Region V
ANGELS						
• Business owner/manager	69%	76%	75%	63%	66% +	66%
• Personal entrepreneurial experience	83%	81%	83%	82%	92% +	78%
• Age*	47 years	49 years	39 years +	47 years	47 years	47 years
• White male	84%	85%	88%	85%	78%	90%
• College degree	72%	76%	77%	81%	74%	72%
• Annual family income*	$90,000	$70,000+	$90,000	$90,000	$70,000+	$90,000
• Net worth*	$750,000	$1,000,000+	$750,000	$750,000	$400,000+	$750,000
• Primary information channel	Friends and associates	Entrepreneurs+	Friends and associates	Friends and associates	Friends +	Friends and associates
• Deal acceptance rate*	30%	30%	30%	30%	30%	30%
• Main deal rejection reason(s)	Growth	Personal knowledge+	Growth	Growth	Time, personal knowledge+	Talent+
• Investment frequency/firms in portfolio	18 mos./3.5	36 mos./1.7 +	18 mos./3.5	18 mos./3.5	18 mos./5.0 +	18 mos./5.0 +
• Satisfied with past investments	72%	86%+	75%	75%	61%+	72%
• Number of coinvestors*	Two	Two	Two	Three+	Two	Three+
• Equity invested in informal portfolio*	$131,000	$127,500	$131,000	$131,000	$87,500+	$187,500+
• Loans/guarantees to portfolio firms*	$75,000	$25,000+	$25,000+	$75,000	$35,500+	$75,000
• Preferred industry	Service/FIRE	Service/FIRE	Service	Service	Service	Service
• Minimum ROI target*	35%	45%	46%	39%	46%+	28%
• Active as consultant, board member, or employee	22%	24%	22%	22%	N/A	25%
• Does not seek voting control	81%	87%	85%	84%	84%	82%
• Dollars available for more investment	85%	85%	82%	84%	72%+	90%
	35%	36%	26%+	33%	34%	28%

ENTREPRENEURS/FIRMS

Total Angel financing* (equity & loans)	$176,700	$269,000+	$133,800+	$235,600+	$73,800+	$210,000+
Equity	$112,500	$225,000+	$112,500	$150,000+	$52,500+	$150,000+
Loans/guarantees*	$64,200	$44,100+	$21,300+	$85,600+	$21,300+	$60,000
Number of individuals providing funding	Three	Three	Three	Four+	Three	Four+
Entrepreneur is white male, age 25–35	79%	85%	87%	80%	77%	83%
Zero to nine employees	74%	72%	85%+	75%	90%+	65%+
Start-up or infant stage firm	69%	80%+	78%+	70%	67%	72%
Firms most frequently financed	Service 17%	High-tech 28%+	Service, wholesale trade, mfg.—consumer goods, mfg.—high-tech 15% each+	Retail 20%+	Service 21%	Service 20%
50 miles or less from investor's home or office	72%	89%+	77%	61%+	75%	77%
Comprehensive business plan	61%	50%+	49%+	72%+	72%+	58%

HIGH-PROBABILITY DEAL STRUCTURE

Equity per investor*	$37,500	$75,000+	$37,500	$37,500	$17,500+	$37,500
Angel loans/guarantees*	$21,400	$14,700+	$7,100+	$21,400	$7,100+	$15,000+
Voting power transferred to investor	37%	12%+	31%	32%	40%	32%
Majority control to Angel	27%	13%+	23%	21%	43%+	29%
Capital risk seen by Angel*	30%	40%+	30%	40%+	30%	30%
Expected annual ROI* (average ROI)	25% (27%)	25% (28%)	10% (26%)+	N/A	N/A	25% (29%)
Common stock or partner equity instrument	79%	91%+	96%+	85%	75%	72%
Liquidation horizon*	Four years	Seven and a half years+	Four years	Four years	Seven and a half years+	Seven and a half years+
Buyback by insiders planned	50%	25%+	46%	61%+	59%+	44%+
Investor is or becomes employee	39%	28%+	43%	35%	44%	44%

* Median value—half higher, half lower.   + = Differs importantly from U.S. Composite.   N/A = Not available.

channels. Angels report a median income of $70,000, compared to $90,000 nationwide. The percentages of Region I Angels in each income class are:

- Under $40,000   6%
- $40,000–$59,999   33%
- $60,000–$79,999   11%
- $80,000–$99,999   11%
- $100,000–$199,999   22%
- $200,000 or more   17%

Despite the relatively low median income of local Angels, their median wealth is higher than average. Angels in New England, unlike most other areas, fit the stereotype of "millionaire" investors. Local median net worth is $1,000,000 or more, in contrast to the U.S. median of $750,000. The percentages of Region I Angels in each wealth class are:

- Under $300,000   6%
- $300,000–$499,999   6%
- $500,000–$999,999   35%
- $1,000,000 or more   53%

Region I Angels use more direct communication channels than Angels do anywhere else. They say their primary information source for investment opportunities is directly from the entrepreneur. Friends and business associates share second place. The percentages of local and U.S. Angels who primarily rely on each of the main information sources are:

	Boston/NE (%)	U.S. (%)
• Entrepreneurs	33	14
• Friends	29	30
• Business associates	27	27
• Investment bankers	6	11
• Brokers	0	10
• Others	5	8

Market Activity. Boston-area Angels differ from the U.S. pattern where deal rejection reasons are concerned. The rank order of the local top five deal killers is:

	Boston-Area Rank	U.S. Composite Rank
1.	Angel had inadequate personal knowledge about entrepreneur/key personnel.	2
2.	Growth potential was too limited.	1
3.	Angel had insufficient time for appraisal.	7
4.	Project did not fit Angel's long-term objective.	5
5.	Entrepreneur/key personnel lacked sufficient talent for success.	3

Region I Angels invest less frequently and have smaller informal port-folios than the U.S. median, but they are also much more satisfied with their investment performance. Over half of all New England Angels (52 percent) made only one investment in the three-year survey period, which works out to one investment each 36 months compared to the U.S. pat-tern of one every 18 months. The percentages of New England Angels by the number of months between investments are:

- Every 36 months   52%
- Every 18 months   29%
- Every 12 months or less   19%

The five-year length of the average investment holding period results in typical local Angels having a total of less than 2 investments in their port-folios, compared to the U.S. pattern of 3.5. Apparently these differences do not hurt investment performance—in fact, they may help it. Local Angels report the highest rate of satisfaction with their investments in the United States. Almost 9 out of 10 (86 percent) New England Angels rate the performance of their investments as equal to or better than origin-ally expected, compared with 72 percent nationwide. The percentages of actual investment performance levels are:

- Well above expected   24%
- Above   19%
- About equal   43%
- Below expected   0%
- Well below   14%

Investment Portfolio.   Region I Angels invest equity dollars but tread lightly where loans or loan guarantees are concerned. The size of their equity dollars more than makes up the difference; the per-firm equity investment is $75,000, compared to $37,500 nationwide. Locally the median amount of loans/guarantees to all informal portfolio firms is $25,000, compared to $75,000 nationwide. They not only make smaller loans, but fewer of them as well. The percentages of local Angels in loan/guarantee classes are:

- None   30%
- Under $50,000   45%
- $50,000–$99,999   10%
- $100,000–$500,000   15%
- Over $500,000   0%

Investment Objectives.   The investment objectives of New England An-gels are similar to those of the U.S. Composite.

Region I Entrepreneurs/Firms

New England–area companies backed by Angel dollars are most often high-technology manufacturing firms. These firms receive more capital earlier in their development from very nearby Angels based on fewer comprehensive business plans compared to the U.S. Composite.

Total Risk Capital.   Total funding has a median value of almost $270,000 per firm, of which 83 percent ($225,000) is in equity form. The balance is in loans. The percentages of firms by total risk capital received are:

- Under $45,000   17%
- $45,000–$84,999   17%
- $85,000–$174,999   9%
- $175,000–$349,999   13%
- $350,000–$900,000   39%
- Over $900,000   4%

Firm's Growth Stage.   Eight out of 10 local firms receiving Angel funding are less than one year old. That is, 80 percent are either in their start-up or infant stage, compared to the U.S. Composite's 69 percent. The growth stages of Region I firms at time of Angel funding are:

- Start-up and infant   80%
- Young   7%
- Established   13%

Industry.   New England Angels invest in high-technology manufacturing firms more than any other industry and more than Angels in any other region. Local Angels put 28 percent of their investments into high-tech manufacturing, compared to 10 percent nationwide. Firms in finance, insurance, and real estate are a close second. The percentages of successful entrepreneurs/firms by industry are:

- Natural resources/mining   2%
- Construction   5%
- Manufacturing—high-technology   28%
- Manufacturing—industrial goods   7%
- Manufacturing—consumer goods   5%
- Transportation, communication, and utilities   0%
- Wholesale trade   0%
- Retail trade   7%
- FIRE   26%
- Services   19%
- Other   1%

Miles Between Firm and Angel.   Given the compact size of the Boston–New England area we would expect fewer long-distance deals. Indeed, 9 out of 10 firms are within 50 miles of the Angel's home or office, compared to only 72 percent nationwide. The percentages of firms' distances from the Angel are:

- 10 miles or less   39%
- 10–50 miles   50%
- 51–150 miles   7%
- Other   4%

Comprehensive Business Planning.   Despite the area's level of education and touted financial sophistication, the requirement for comprehensive business plans prior to investing ranks among the nation's lowest.
Only half (50 percent) of local Angels require comprehensive business
plans, compared to 61 percent nationwide. Only Angels in the Pacific
Northwest require them less often. Detailed marketing and financing
plans are provided, but the frequency is not known.

Deal Structure

Almost everything about New England deals is at odds with the U.S. Composite. In this unique market, 9 out of 10 deal elements are different.
Relatively speaking, local Angels: invest more equity dollars, invest fewer
loan dollars, get smaller ownership shares, get control less often, expect
greater risks, use simple equity instruments more frequently, expect longer
holding periods, expect to sell to outsiders more often, and are employed
by the firm less often than the U.S. pattern.

Equity Dollars per Angel.   Region I Angels invest two dollars for every
one invested by the U.S. Composite Angel. The percentages of local equity
investments per deal are:

- Under $25,000   35%
- $25,000–$49,999   9%
- $50,000–$99,999   13%
- $100,000–$249,999   39%
- Over $250,000   4%

Ownership Share and Corporate Control.   The large equity investments
made by New England Angels are not rewarded with large ownership
shares. The median deal conveys only 12 percent of the voting power to
the Angel, who obtains 51 percent or more (absolute) control in only 13
percent of investments. This contrasts with the U.S. Composite shares
of 37 percent and 27 percent absolute control, respectively. The percentages of Angels by ownership share per deal are:

- Under 25% share   64%
- 25–49%   6%
- 50%   17%
- Over 50%   13%

Risk.   Local Angels see greater risk of capital loss than does the U.S. Composite. In New England the median risk is anticipated at 40 percent, compared to 30 percent nationwide. The percentages of Angels by level of anticipated risk are:

- 10% risk or loss   5%
- 11–29%   11%
- 30–39%   32%
- 40–49%   16%
- 50% or more   36%

Investment Instrument.   Boston-region deals are documented with more simplicity than are composite deals. Nine out of 10 are either common stock or partnership equity interest transactions. Other instruments are almost nonexistent. The percentages of local deals by type of equity instrument are:

- Common stock   44%
- Partnership equity interest   47%
- Convertible preferred stock   2%
- Notes with warrants   2%
- Convertible debentures   0%
- Other   5%

Liquidation Horizon and Method.   Deals are made with patient anticipation of a long holding period and eventual sale to outsider buyers. The median expected holding period at deal time is seven and a half years, with a public offering of stock as the most common cash-out method. The percentages of deals by liquidation horizons are:

- Under 3 years   19%
- 3–5 years   24%
- 6–10 years   38%
- Over 10 years or not important 19%

The percentages of local deals favoring various liquidation methods are:

- None   25%
- Sell back to company   15%
- Sell to coinvestor   10%
- Sell or merge with another firm 10%
- Sell to institutional investor 0%
- Public stock offering   25%
- Other   15%

Angel-Employee.   New England deals involve Angel employment considerably less often than the U.S. pattern. Slightly more than one in four deals (28 percent) ends up with an Angel-employee, compared to

39 percent for the U.S. Composite. The percentages of deals involving Angels by type of firm participation are:

- Traditional stockholders   13%
- Board of directors   11%
- Consultant   47%
- Employment   28%
- Other   1%

Summary of New England Markets

The informal risk capital markets in Boston and the rest of the New England region are more at odds with the overall U.S. pattern than any other area. More than half the points of comparison in New England are "outliers," reflecting the individualistic character of the region. The differences are concentrated in the Angel deal structure (where the divergences reach 90 percent), but substantial differences are also exhibited by successful firms (60 percent) and the Angels themselves (36 percent).

Yankee Angels have greater net worth but lower incomes, invest less often, talk directly to entrepreneurs more often, and lend less money less often than is usual nationwide. Successful local entrepreneurs/firms obtain 50 percent more risk capital at an earlier development stage from Angels who live nearer to the firm. Firms also provide comprehensive business plans less often and are high-technology manufacturing firms more often than U.S. patterns. Although Boston–New England informal deals involve much larger equity dollar investments per Angel, the firms give up much less ownership share. Deal holding periods are viewed with more patience and targeted toward selling to outsiders more than deals elsewhere. Yankee deals more often use the simplest equity instruments to document the deal and less often involve the Angel as an employee. In sum, this compact geographical area has an investment mind of its own, one that is highly divergent from the national composite deal pattern.

NEW YORK AND NEW JERSEY—REGION II

The area covered by the New York–New Jersey local markets is shown on Figure 10-1 and defined in Table 10-1. Even though only two states are involved, their informal capital markets contain almost 12 percent of all U.S. business enterprises (572,000), as estimated by the U.S. Small Business Administration. The area has 11 percent of the adult U.S. population and 12 percent of U.S. personal family income. Angels are investors in 9 percent (51,000) of all local enterprises. The size of the regional pool of Angels is estimated at 78,000, and they make about 55,000 investment deals per year with some 18,300 entrepreneurs/firms. This annual deal flow totals $3.7 billion in equity dollars, and Angels lend or guarantee another $2.6 billion each year to their entrepreneurs. Almost half of all Angels (48 percent) wanted to invest more than their opportunities permitted. These uninvested dollars averaged 26 percent of actual financings (another $1.6 billion). In total, the area's available pool of invested and uninvested informal capital is $7.9 billion per year.

Region II Markets

The composite profile of local Angels, entrepreneurs, and deals, shown in Market Profile 10-1 on pages 158 and 159, does not closely resemble the U.S. pattern. Only major differences are noted and discussed in the following subsections.

New York–New Jersey Angels

Personal characteristics of local Angels differ from the U.S. pattern on only 3 out of 20 points. Angels in New York–New Jersey closely resemble their colleagues nationwide, except that they are younger, lend less money, and are more content with their current levels of investment activity.

Age. Angels locally have a median age of only 39 years, versus 47 years for the U.S. Composite. There are twice as many local Angels under 34 years old than in the U.S. Composite, and the region has the highest proportion of young investors in the United States. The percentages of Region II Angels by age group are:

- Under 34 years   23%
- 35–44   32%
- 45–54   31%
- 55–64   5%
- 65 or over   9%

Loans/Guarantees. New York–New Jersey Angels lend to entrepreneurs as frequently as usual, but the amounts loaned are smaller. Locally, the median loans by an Angel to all informal investments is $25,000, compared to $75,000 nationwide. These smaller loan amounts do not simply reflect small Angel investments, income, wealth, or the number of investments, since these are all quite average by U.S. standards. The percentages of investors by sizes of total informal loans are:

- None   13%
- Under $50,000   39%
- $50,000–$99,999   13%
- $100,000–$500,000   22%
- Over $500,000   13%

Region II Entrepreneurs/Firms

Entrepreneurs who achieve success with local Angels are substantially different than their colleagues elsewhere, differing on half of the 10 points of comparison.

Total Financing.   Entrepreneurs in New York–New Jersey receive about $43,000 less from their Angels than the national standard. The gap is entirely due to smaller Angel loans, as previously discussed.

Firm Size and Growth Stage.   Firms receiving Angel funding in Region II are smaller and younger than the U.S. Composite Firm. Firms with less than 10 employees received 85 percent of Angel deals here, compared to 74 percent nationwide. The percentages of successful firms by employment size are:

- 0–4 employees   62%
- 5–9   23%
- 10–19   11%
- 20 or more   4%

The small firm size correlates with Angels investing at the earliest possible moment. Start-up (60 percent) and infant stage (18 percent) firms (all usually one year old or less) combined to receive 78 percent of local Angel funding, compared to 69 percent in the U.S. Composite. Established firms received the other 22 percent of funding—which leaves the in-between "young" firms in search of Angel money completely out of Knickerbocker markets.

Industry.   Nationally, service firms receive the most investments, but local markets here show no clear pattern of industry success. In New York–New Jersey there is a four-way tie for first place among service, wholesale trade, consumer goods manufacturing and high-technology manufacturing firms, each with a 15-percent local market share. The percentages of locally successful entrepreneurs by industry are:

- Natural resources/mining   0%
- Construction   9%
- Manufacturing—high-technology   15%
- Manufacturing—industrial products   8%
- Manufacturing—consumer products   15%
- Transportation, communication, and utilities   2%
- Wholesale trade   15%
- Retail trade   11%
- Finance/insurance/real estate   10%
- Services   15%
- Other   0%

Business Plans.   Six out of 10 successful firms nationally provide Angels with written comprehensive business plans, but only 49 percent of locally successful entrepreneurs do so. This is one of the lowest percentages in the United States.

Region II Deal Structure

New York–New Jersey deals are ordinary by national standards. They differ on only three points: Smaller loans are likely (as discussed in the section on Region II Angels), Angels expect lower returns, and there is more frequent use of the simplest equity instruments. The median ROI is well below composite standards; Angels in New York–New Jersey expect only 10 percent ROI, compared to 25 percent nationwide. The local average (mean) ROI is close to the composite level because of a few unusually high ROI deals. The percentages of actual deals by anticipated ROI are:

- 1–19% ROI   52%
- 20–29%   26%
- 30–39%   3%
- 40–49%   7%
- 50–99%   10%
- 100% or more   3%

Investment instruments other than common stock or partnership equity interest are virtually nonexistent in this region. These two simplest forms account for 96 percent of all local deals, but only 79 percent nationwide. The percentages of actual deals for various types of investment instruments are:

- Common stock   71%
- Partnership equity interest   25%
- Convertible preferred stock   0%
- Notes with warrants   5%
- Convertible debentures   0%
- Other   0%

Summary of New York–New Jersey

Informal risk capital markets here show major differences from U.S. patterns. Comparisons reveal that Angels are younger than usual, lend small amounts to their chosen entrepreneurs, and have a deal flow that more closely matches their desires than in other markets. Area entrepreneurs receive less total risk capital due to smaller Angel loans, their firms are smaller and younger, funding success is spread over a wider range of industries, and fewer comprehensive business plans are written than nationwide patterns predict. Angel-Entrepreneur deals, besides involving smaller (but not less frequent) Angel loans, promise unusually low returns on investment. Deals rely heavily on common stock and partnership equity interests in comparison to deals elsewhere. All other market profile characteristics are similar.

WASHINGTON D.C., PHILADELPHIA, BALTIMORE, AND THE MID-ATLANTIC AREA—REGION III

Region III, shown in Figure 10-1, encompasses local markets in the District of Columbia and the states of Delaware, Maryland, Pennsylvania, Virginia, and West Virginia. Almost 10 percent of all U.S. business firms are in these local markets, along with 11 percent of the U.S. adult population and personal income. The U.S. Small Business Administration estimates that the business community here numbers over 470,000 business enterprises. Out of these enterprises about 12 percent, or 56,000, have an Angel investor at any given time. The total pool of Angels numbers about 78,000, and Angels finance 12,000 successful entrepreneurs each year in 47,000 individual deals. The annual Angel investment totals $5.3 billion, of which $3.1 billion is equity dollars and another $2.2 billion is provided in the form of loans and/or loan guarantees. The majority of Angels want to invest more than they have been able to by about $1.7 billion. In total, the area has an annual Angel risk capital pool of $7.0 billion.

Region III Angels

The local market profile for Angels is more like the U.S. Composite than any other area in the United States. The individual elements can be seen and compared to those of other regions and the U.S. Composite in market profiles 10-1 and 10-2.

Personal Characteristics.   Area Angels differ little in their personal characteristics, except that they are better educated than most. As far as their degree fields are concerned they also mirror the U.S. Composite (41 percent in business and 19 percent in engineering). The percentages of Angels in each education class are:

- High school or less   18%
- Some college   2%
- Bachelor's degree   49%
- Graduate degree   31%

Market Activity.   Mid-Atlantic Angels and the U.S. Composite are noted for rejecting investment opportunities primarily due to inadequate growth potential. However, the top five rejection reasons have a different local pattern. The rank order of top Region III deal killers is:

1. Limited growth potential
2. Inadequate personal knowledge of the entrepreneur or key personnel
3. Lack of necessary talent on part of entrepreneur
4. Insufficient information provided
5. Insufficient time allowed for adequate appraisal

Investment Capacity and Objectives.   In the area of investment objectives and the ability to financially back them up, Region III Angels show no difference from the U.S. Composite.

Region III Entrepreneurs

The highest proportion of local market differences (4 out of 10 comparison elements) appears in the characteristics of successful entrepreneurs. Area entrepreneurs obtain larger amounts of Angel dollars from larger coinvestor groups. Retail trade is the leading local industry, and entrepreneurs are located farther from the Angel's home or office.

Total Angel Dollars.   Median financing in Mid-Atlantic metropolitan areas is $235,600, about one-third larger than the U.S. Composite amount of $176,700. The total risk capital components are 64 percent equity ($150,000) and 36 percent loans/guarantees ($85,600).

Equity Dollars.   The diversity of equity dollar financing is:

* Under $40,000   19%
* $40,000–$99,999   14%
* $100,000–$199,999   32%
* $200,000–$400,000   14%
* Over $400,000   21%

Industry Patterns.   Mid-Atlantic entrepreneurs in retailing receive more Angel financing than any other local industry, in contrast to the U.S. Composite's preference for service industry firms. Locally, service firms rate a distant fourth place. The percentages of locally successful entrepreneurs by major industry group are:

* Natural resources/mining   7%
* Construction   18%
* Manufacturing—high-technology   12%
* Manufacturing—industrial   6%
* Manufacturing—consumer   4%
* Transportation, communication, and utilities   2%
* Wholesale trade   4%
* Retail trade   20%
* Finance/insurance/real estate   15%
* Services   9%
* Other   3%

Loans/Guarantees.   The percentage spread of Angel debt capital provided to successful entrepreneurs is:

* None   18%
* Under $60,000   21%
* $60,000–$114,999   16%
* $115,000–$575,000   25%
* Over $575,000   20%

Market Geography.   Region III entrepreneurs obtain Angel financing at greater distances than the U.S. average. Locally, only 6 in 10 transactions are within 50 miles of the entrepreneur, compared to the national average of almost three-quarters of all financings. The percentages of entrepreneurs by distance from investing Angels are:

* Under 10 miles   45%
* 11 to 50 miles   16%
* 51 to 150 miles   15%
* Other   24%

Region III Deal Structure

Higher risk of capital loss is anticipated by local Angels relative to the U.S. Composite. Angels believe that 40 percent of their deals will ultimately result in losing half or more of their original capital, compared to 30 percent nationwide. The percentages of risk anticipated by local Angels are:

* Under 10% risk   6%
* 11–20%   26%
* 21–30%   17%
* 31–40%   6%
* 41–50%   17%
* Over 50%   28%

Summary of Mid-Atlantic Markets

The informal risk capital market in Washington D.C., Philadelphia, Baltimore, and surrounding areas resembles the U.S. Composite on 30 out of 40 points. It diverges in that its Angels are better educated and form larger investor teams to finance a deal. Successful entrepreneurs obtain larger total amounts of risk capital at greater distances than their U.S. counterparts. The leading industry is retailing, followed by construction, with services in a distant fourth place. Comprehensive business plans are also more common than by U.S. standards. Deals between Angels and entrepreneurs carry a higher degree of risk as perceived by Angels, and the liquidation provisions are more likely to provide for selling back to insiders.

MIAMI, ATLANTA, MEMPHIS, AND
THE SOUTHEAST—REGION IV

These cities and their neighbors are shown on the map in Figure 10-1. The region includes the eight states of Alabama, Florida, Georgia, Kentucky, Mississippi, North Carolina, South Carolina and Tennessee. The markets in this economic area contain 15 percent of all U.S. business enterprises, numbering almost 759,000, as estimated by the U.S. Small Business Administration. Out of the total U.S. adult population about 18 percent lives in the markets of Region IV, earning 15 percent of U.S. personal income.

At present, Angels hold equity in 12 percent of the area's business enterprises, numbering about 89,000. The total number of local Angels runs to 127,000, and they make 75,000 deals a year financing 25,000 new successful entrepreneurs. Annually Angels invest total risk capital of $8.5 billion, of which 59 percent, or $5.0 billion, is equity and 41 percent ($3.5 billion) is in loan/guarantee form. A majority of local Angels would have invested 34 percent more dollars in entrepreneurs if given sufficient opportunity. This available but unused capital amounts to $2.9 billion per year. In total, the local Angel markets contained in Region IV can muster an annual risk capital pool of $11.4 billion.

Southeastern Markets

Angel capital markets in the Southeast are different. Their high-success probability characteristics can be seen in Market Profile 10-1, pages 158 and 159. Despite the fact that Region IV markets add up to one of the largest business areas of the U.S., they do not dominate or closely resemble the U.S. Composite. Half of all local profile items show important exceptions to U.S. patterns. Southern markets differ on many key features, including amounts invested, rejection reasons, target industries, voting control, and Angels' personal characteristics. These differences are not due to the proportionately larger rural sector in the South, because the market here as elsewhere is dominated by major metropolitan areas. It is rather that Southeastern cities are different from cities elsewhere.

Southern Angels

Personal Characteristics. The most notable differences about Southern Angels is that they are more entrepreneurial but have lower incomes and wealth than the U.S. standard. Virtually all local Angels (92 percent) are themselves entrepreneurs, compared to 83 percent nationwide. Angels in Southern cities have a lower annual income, with a median of $70,000, compared to the $90,000 U.S. Composite. There is a much higher concentration of local Angels in the under-$100,000 range than for the composite. The same general pattern is repeated when we look at local Angel wealth. The diversity of Southern Angel incomes is as wide as the composite's. The percentages of local Angels by income group are:

- Under $40,000   11%
- $40,000–$99,999   60%
- $100,000–$200,000   19%
- Over $200,000   10%

Nationwide 37 percent of Angels are millionaires but in Southern markets it's only 24 percent. The proportions of local Angels by net worth are:

- Under $500,000   58%
- $500,000–$999,999   18%
- $1,000,000 or more   24%

Market Activity.   Local Angels reject deals for their own special reasons, have larger informal portfolios, and are less satisfied with the performance of their investments. Southern Angels rank "insufficient time allowed for adequate appraisal" as their leading rejection reason. The top five reasons, in rank order, are:

1. Not enough time for adequate appraisal
2. Inadequate personal knowledge of entrepreneur/key personnel
3. Limited growth potential
4. Insufficient information
5. Overpriced equity

Local Angels invest at the same rate as the U.S. Composite (every 18 months), but they hold on to investments almost twice as long. This means that their total portfolio has five deals in it, compared to the nation's average of three and a half. Nevertheless, Southerners as a group are less satisfied with the performance of their portfolios than the U.S. Composite (61 percent versus 72 percent). The percentages of local Angels at each level of performance satisfaction are:

- Above expectation   32%
- About equal to expectations 29%
- Below expectations   39%

Investment Capacity.   In the area of investment capacity Southern Angels are very different. Their total informal portfolio investment is only half the U.S. average: $123,000 compared to $206,000. The major cause of this difference is a combination of smaller loans/guarantees and equity commitment. It is not unwillingness to lend but rather the small size of loans and guarantees made by local Angels. Their total of $35,500 in loans/guarantees is one-half the U.S. Composite's median of $75,000. An interesting contrast is that Southern Angels make over twice the number of large loans (over $500,000) and one-half the number of median-size

loans ($50,000 to $100,000) as the typical U.S. Angel. The percentages
of local Angels in each loan/guarantee size category are:

- None   11%
- Under $50,000   39%
- $50,000–$99,999   11%
- $100,000–$500,000   23%
- Over $500,000   16%

In the terms of committing equity dollars the typical Southern Angel
totals $88,000, compared to $131,000 for the U.S. Composite. Local Angels'
portfolio equity investment are:

- Under $50,000   30%
- $50,000–$124,999   31%
- $125,000–$249,999   13%
- $250,000–$499,999   6%
- $500,000–$1,000,000   12%
- Over $1,000,000   7%

Investment Objectives.   Angels in the South rate service industry firms
alone as their target of choice over the combination of service or FIRE
that is the U.S. Composite's first choice. The local Angel preference pattern for investments in major industry groups is:

- Natural resources/mining   6%
- Construction   25%
- Manufacturing—high-technology   16%
- Manufacturing—industrial products   17%
- Manufacturing—consumer products   20%
- Transportation, communications, and utilities   14%
- Wholesale trade   19%
- Retail trade   34%
- Finance, insurance, real estate   38%
- Services   47%

(The percentages do not add to 100% because Angels could express a
preference for more than one industry.)

Angels in Southern markets are the most aggressive in the nation
when the issue of voting control arises. The proportion who say that they
will seek 51 percent or more control is 28 percent, compared to the U.S.
Composite's 15 percent. This objective is overachieved—there are more
business Devils in Dixie (43 percent) than anywhere else.

Successful Entrepreneurs in the South

Total Investment Dollars.   Median Angel financing for Southern firms
is very small by contrast to the U.S. Composite. The typical successful
entrepreneur obtains only $73,800, compared to $176,700 nationwide.

This total financing is divided into 71 percent equity ($52,500) and 29 percent loans/guarantees ($21,300). The percentages of successful local entrepreneurs by size of equity investment are:

- Under $75,000   61%
- $75,000–$149,999   13%
- $150,000–$300,000   6%
- $300,000 or more   19%

Loans/Guarantees.   Southern entrepreneurs and their odds of receiving various sizes of Angel loans and guarantees are:

- Under $30,000   50%
- $30,000–$59,999   11%
- $60,000–$300,000   23%
- Over $300,000   16%

Firm Size.   Consistent with the smaller investment by local Angels, the proportion of firms with fewer than 10 employees at time of investment is much higher in the Southeast. These small firms obtained 90 percent of local Angel financing, compared to 74 percent nationwide.

Region IV Deal Structure

Dixie deals are different, especially in the key areas of equity and loans, voting control, and holding periods.

Equity per Angel.   Local Angels invest a median of only $17,500 per deal, compared to the U.S. Composite's $37,500. The deal odds by equity investment size are:

- Under $10,000   30%
- $10,000–$24,999   31%
- $25,000–$49,999   13%
- $50,000–$100,000   6%
- Over $100,000   20%

Loans/Guarantees per Deal.   Southern Angels make loans just as frequently as the U.S. Composite, but each is two-thirds smaller. The typical loan/guarantee is only $7,100 locally but $21,400 nationally. The percentages of local deals involving various size of loans are:

- None   11%
- Under $10,000   39%
- $10,000–$100,000   34%
- Over $100,000   16%

Voting Control.   Despite small equity and loan amounts, Region IV Angels get the highest percent of absolute voting control anywhere in the

United States. The median Angel obtains 40 percent voting share, and almost half the deals (43 percent) shift absolute majority control to the "Angel." The percentages of deals and resulting Angel voting power are:

- Under 25%   24%
- 25%–49%   14%
- 50%   19%
- Over 50%   43%

Investment Holding Period.   Southern Angels hang on to their investments almost twice as long as the U.S. Composite. Angel deals in the South anticipate a typical period of seven and a half years liquidation in contrast to four years for the U.S. Composite. The percentages of deals for expected Angel holding periods are:

- Under one year   0%
- 1–3 years   19%
- 4–5 years   19%
- 6–10 years   34%
- Over 10 years or unimportant   28%

Summary of Southeastern Markets

The market for Angel financing in Miami, Atlanta, Memphis, and surrounding areas is very unlike the U.S. Composite. Out of 40 items of comparison, Southeastern markets differ on half. The differences are distributed among some of the most important market characteristics. Dixie Angels are more frequently entrepreneurs themselves but have smaller incomes and wealth than the national norm. They reject deals mostly because of too little time to perform due diligence, but nevertheless they have larger informal portfolios with poorer performance records. The size of Angel investments in their informal portfolios is smaller when it comes to both equity and loans/guarantees. Dixie Angels are the most aggressive in their desire for voting control.

Entrepreneurs in the Southeast get fewer total, equity, and loan dollars than their U.S. Composite colleagues. Successful entrepreneurs in the South have smaller firms and more often supply Angels with a comprehensive business plan. In other respects they are similar to the national pattern.

Individual investment deals are small in Southern metropolitan markets but transfer absolute voting control to the Angel more often than anywhere else. Angels in the South stick with their deals for almost twice as long as the U.S. Composite. In sum, the South is one of the largest markets for informal capital in the U.S. and also one of the least likely to resemble national patterns.

CHICAGO, DETROIT, CLEVELAND, MINNEAPOLIS, AND THE INDUSTRIAL HEARTLAND—REGION V

The Heartland cities are shown as Region V in Figure 10-1 and include the metropolitan markets clustered throughout the states of Illinois, Indiana, Michigan, Minnesota, Ohio, and Wisconsin. Almost 20 percent of all U.S. business enterprises are in these markets, along with 20 percent of the U.S. adult population, earning 20 percent of total U.S. family income. The U.S. Small Business Administration estimates that the business community in this area numbers almost 950,000 business establishments. Among these businesses 8.4 percent, or 80,000 entrepreneurs, currently have Angel financing.

The total pool of local Angels includes 139,000 individuals who finance some 23,000 new entrepreneurs each year, with a total number of 93,000 annual deals (one Angel and one entrepreneur). The total of risk capital invested each year is $10.5 billion, divided into $6.2 billion (59 percent) equity dollars and $4.3 billion (41 percent) in loans/ guarantees. Unlike most other local markets only a minority of the local Angels (45 percent) want to invest more dollars than opportunity has permitted. Nevertheless that minority, if fully extended, would supply another $2.9 billion in risk capital for area economic growth. The annual pool of Angel risk capital, both invested and uninvested, equals $13.4 billion in the region's local markets.

The Region V Market

This area is aptly named "Heartland" since its local profile closely typifies the overall national patterns of informal capital markets. On the basis of over 40 points of comparison contained in Profile 10-1 (pages 158–159), only 10 differ from the U.S. Composite. And most of the differences are a matter of degree rather than of kind. We turn to those differences next.

Region V Angels

Personal Characteristics.   Local Angels are similar to their nationwide colleagues in personal characteristics.

Market Activity.   Heartland Angels have larger informal portfolios and decline deals more often for lack of entrepreneurial talent than does the U.S. Composite. The rank order of the top five deal rejection reasons is:

1. Firm's management lacked experience or talent necessary for success.
2. Proposed value of firm's equity was unrealistic.
3. Venture's chances for growth seemed limited.
4. Venture concept needed further development.
5. Not enough time for adequate appraisal.

Portfolio.   Local Angels accumulate larger informal capital portfolios not because they invest more frequently but because they hang on to their informal assets for longer periods of time. Their median time to liquidation is seven and a half years, versus four years for the U.S. Composite.

Investment Capacity and Objectives.   Local market Angels are similar to the national pattern in investment capacity and objectives.

Region V Entrepreneurs

Entrepreneurs in the industrial Heartland obtain larger amounts of total risk capital than the U.S. Composite Entrepreneur because Angels invest more equity dollars here than elsewhere. Consistent with this larger supply of equity is the fact that the firms of successful entrepreneurs are larger than usual in terms of employment when the investment is made.

Total Risk Capital.   Typically, total risk capital obtained by successful Region V entrepreneurs is $210,000, compared to $176,700 nationwide. This difference is due entirely to larger equity infusions by Angels and not to larger amounts of loan dollars. The percentages of entrepreneurs obtaining various sizes of Angels' equity cash are:

- Under $40,000   22%
- $40,000–$99,999   23%
- $100,000–$199,999   18%
- $200,000–$399,999   15%
- $400,000–$1,000,000   15%
- Over $1,000,000   7%

Firm Size.   Local Angels invest in entrepreneurs with larger firms in the following pattern:

- Under 10 employees   65%
- 10–19   22%
- 20–100   10%
- Over 100   4%

All other characteristics of successful Region V entrepreneurs are similar to the U.S. Composite.

Heartland Deals

Out of 10 points of comparison, Region V markets deviate from the U.S. Composite on 3: loan size, the length of the investment holding period, and liquidation method.

Local deals provide smaller amounts of Angel loans and loan guarantees. The local median is $15,000 in loans, versus $21,400 nation-

wide. The percentages of deals bringing various sizes of Angel loans/
guarantees are:

• Under $10,000	42%
• $10,000–$19,999	16%
• $20,000–$100,000	33%
• Over $100,000	9%

Provisions for liquidating the deal have a regional holding period of seven
and a half years in contrast to the U.S. Composite's four years. The percentages of local deals by expected holding period are:

• Under 3 years	17%
• 4–5	26%
• 6–10	35%
• Over 10 or not important	22%

Heartland deals specify their exit plan more frequently than usual
(85 percent versus 78 percent for composite) and with a disproportionate emphasis on combinations of liquidation methods. Only 18 percent of U.S. Composite deals use combinations, compared to 37 percent
in Region V. The percentages of deals and the use of various exit provisions are:

• None	15%
• Sell back to company	34%
• Sell to other inside investor	10%
• Sell/merge with another company	3%
• Sell to institutional investor	0%
• Public offering	1%
• Other and combinations	37%

Summary of Region V

The theme that runs through industrial Heartland markets is one that
is generally very similar to the U.S. pattern. Out of 40 comparisons, only
10 differ, and mostly it is a matter of degree rather than different direc-
tions. When local Angels depart from the U.S. pattern it is because they
reject proposals for lack of talent on the part of the proposing entrepreneur
and they have larger informal portfolios due to longer asset-holding
periods. The Region V market rewards successful entrepreneurs with
larger-than-usual total equity investments, and these investments go to
bigger-than-average firms. The deals put together involve smaller Angel
loans/guarantees, longer holding periods, and more frequent use of combinations of exit plans.

HOUSTON, DALLAS, NEW ORLEANS, AND THE MID-SOUTH—REGION VI

The mid-Southern area is defined as the five states of Texas, Arkansas, Louisiana, New Mexico, and Oklahoma. Over 575,000 business enterprises (12 percent of the U.S. total) are in this market, along with 11 percent of the total U.S. adult population and family income. Among local businesses some 67,000 (12 percent) have an Angel investor at any given time.

The area's total pool of active Angels includes 81,000 individuals who finance 14,000 new entrepreneurs each year via 57,000 deals (one Angel–one entrepreneur). Annually the total Angel capital invested is estimated at $6.5 billion, composed of $3.8 billion equity dollars and $2.7 billion more in Angel loans/guarantees. A 40-percent minority of local Angels would have invested another $1.8 billion each year if opportunity had permitted. The annual pool of Angel risk capital, both committed and potential, adds up to $8.3 billion available to simulate economic growth in the region's local markets.

The market profile for local Angel risk capital appears in Profile 10-2. Out of the 40 comparisons, 14 market characteristics differ importantly from national patterns, and many of these are key market elements. Over half the local differences involve Angels' market performance; the balance are found among successful entrepreneurs. Local deals closely resemble the U.S. Composite.

Region VI Angels

Personal Characteristics.   Personal differences center on Angel demographics, education, and wealth. Local Angels have the largest proportion of minority males and the fewest females of any region in the United States. Three out of 10 local Angels are minority males, which is double the U.S. Composite rate. The percentages of Region VI Angels by gender and ethnicity are:

- Females   0%
- Minority males   30%
- Nonminority males   70%

The absence of any females in the sample is not a sign that there are none in the local markets; rather, it indicates that there are probably not many, and it happened that none are represented in the local Angel sample.

Educationally, local Angels have the same amounts of education as the U.S. Composite, but their degree fields are substantially different. The mid-South has many more engineering-trained Angels and far fewer business-educated Angels than average. The percentages of local Angels by degree field are:

- Business   20%
- Engineering   32%
- Natural science   8%
- Medicine/law   16%
- Other   24%

Even though engineering-educated Angels are most numerous and engineering is a relatively high-income occupation, the level of local Angel income and wealth is well below the U.S. Composite. The fabled "oil patch" millionaires (and others) are underrepresented among local Angels and add up to far fewer (21 percent) than the 37 percent found nationwide. The percentages of local Angels by income and net worth are:

Income

- Under $40,000   12%
- $40,000–$59,000   32%
- $60,000–$99,000   42%
- $100,000–$200,000   7%
- Over $200,000   7%

Net Worth

- Under $500,000   51%
- $500,000–$1,000,000   28%
- Over $1,000,000   21%

Market Activity.   Region VI Angels fit the U.S. Composite quite well with the exceptions that they reject deals mostly because of overpriced equity and that more coinvestors are involved.

The leading deal killer in the U.S., inadequate growth potential, is not even in the local top five. Mid-South Angels rank the top five reasons for rejecting entrepreneurial proposals as:

1. Equity was overpriced.
2. Angel had inadequate personal knowledge of entrepreneur/key personnel.
3. Proposal didn't match Angel's long run investment objective.
4. Entrepreneurs lacked necessary talent.
5. Venture concept needed further development.

Investment Capacity.   Total informal portfolio investment is $156,000, compared to the U.S. Composite's $206,000. The shortfall is not because of fewer equity dollars but is due to the relatively small amounts lent by local Angels. Both locals and the U.S. Composite typically invest $131,000 equity dollars in their portfolios, but local Angels lend only

MARKET PROFILE 10-2. Regions VI-X

	U.S. Composite	Houston, Dallas, New Orleans, and Mid-South—Region VI	St. Louis, Kansas City, Omaha, and Plains States—Region VII	Denver, Salt Lake City, and Mountains—Region VIII	L.A., Phoenix, S.F., San Diego, and Southwest—Region IX	Seattle, Portland, and Pacific Northwest—Region X
ANGELS						
• Business owner/manager	69%	69%	73%	75%	71%	61% +
• Personal entrepreneurial experience	83%	83%	73% +	97% +	78%	88%
• Age*	47 years	47 years	43 years	39 years +	47 years	49 years
• White male	84%	69% +	90%	86%	85%	75% +
• College degree	72%	67%	67%	56% +	76%	47% +
• Annual family income*	$90,000	$70,000+	$90,000	$70,000 +	$150,000 +	$90,000
• Net worth*	$750,000	$400,000+	$750,000	$750,000	$1,000,000 +	$750,000
• Primary information channel	Friends and associates	Friends and associates	Friends +	Associates +	Friends and associates	Associates +
• Deal acceptance rate*	30%	30%	30%	30%	30%	30%
• Main deal rejection reason(s)	Growth	Price +	Price, growth +	Growth	Talent +	Growth
• Investment frequency/firms in portfolio	18 mos./3.5	18 mos./3.5	18 mos./3.5	18 mos./3.5	18 mos./3.5	36 mos./1.7 +
• Satisfied with past investments	72%	76%	70%	67%	72%	81% +
• Number of coinvestors*	Two	Three +	Three +	Two	Three +	Two
• Equity invested in informal portfolio*	$131,000	$131,000	$131,000	$131,000	$131,000	$63,700 +
• Loans/guarantees to portfolio firms*	$75,000	$25,000 +	$75,000	$25,000 +	$75,000	$75,000
• Preferred industry	Service/FIRE	FIRE	Service	Service	FIRE	Service
• Minimum ROI target*	35%	48% +	38%	34%	49% +	38%
• Active as consultant, board member, or employee	22%	22%	22%	22%	22%	22%
• Does not seek voting control	81%	75%	88%	88%	69% +	79%
• Dollars available for more investment than opportunity permitted	85%	82%	97% +	82%	80%	75% +
	35%	26% +	32%	31%	40%	28%

ENTREPRENEURS/FIRMS

Total Angel financing* (equity & loans)	$176,700	$178,400	$235,600+	$134,000+	$236,000+	$245,000+
Equity	$112,500	$150,000+	$150,000+	$112,500	$150,000+	$112,500
Loans/guarantees*	$64,200	$28,400+	$85,600+	$21,400+	$86,000+	$132,500+
Number of individuals providing funding	Three	Four+	Four+	Three	Four+	Three
Entrepreneur is white male, age 25–35	79%	73%	90%+	86%	81%	75%
Zero to nine employees	74%	86%+	75%	83%+	71%	78%
Start-up or infant stage firm	69%	66%	67%	78%+	72%	69+
Firms most frequently financed	Service	FIRE	Service	Service	Service	Retail
50 miles or less from investor's home or office	17%	23%+	25%	29%+	24%	16%+
Comprehensive business plan	72%	69%	68%	65%	67%	72%
	61%	74%+	68%	56%	58%	40%+

HIGH-PROBABILITY DEAL STRUCTURE

Equity per investor*	$37,500	$37,500	$37,500	$37,500	$37,500	$37,500
Angel loans/guarantees*	$21,400	$7,100+	$21,400	$7,100+	$21,400	$44,100+
Voting power transferred to investor	37%	31%	41%	33%	30%	40%
Majority control to Angel	27%	30%	23%	21%	22%	32%
Capital risk seen by Angel*	30%	30%	30%	20%+	30%	30%
Expected annual ROI* (average ROI)	25% (27%)	N/A (27%)	25% (18%)+	25% (32%)	25% (28%)	25% (31%)
Common stock or partner equity instrument	79%	75%	78%	80%	83%	86%
Liquidation horizon*	Four years	Four years	Four years	Four years	Four years	Seven and a half years+
Buyback by insiders planned	50%	55%	53%	44%	34%+	31%+
Investor is or becomes employee	39%	36%	42%	39%	33%	43%

* Median value—half higher, half lower.   + = Differs importantly from U.S. Composite.   N/A = Not available.

183

about $25,000 to portfolio entrepreneurs, compared to the $75,000 lent
by the U.S. Composite. The local loan gap does not reflect fewer loans
but rather smaller loans, as seen below. The percentages of local Angels
by the size of loans to their informal portfolios are:

- None   11%
- Under $50,000   39%
- $50,000–$99,999   11%
- $100,000–$500,000   26%
- Over $500,000   13%

Angel Investment Targets.   Local Angels differ from the national pattern in their industry preference and desire to invest more than they actually did. Almost half of all local Angels (48 percent) have a strong
preference for investing in the finance, insurance and real estate industry.
The target pattern by major industry groups is:

- Natural resources/mining   11%
- Construction   22%
- Manufacturing—high-technology   13%
- Manufacturing—industrial products   24%
- Manufacturing—consumer products   13%
- Transportation, communication, and utilities   4%
- Wholesale trade   15%
- Retail trade   13%
- Finance/insurance/real estate   48%
- Services   26%
- Other   2%

(The percentages do not add up to 100 percent because Angels could
have multiple targets.)

Mid-South Angels are the most satisfied with the amount of their
recent investments. Unlike the U.S. pattern, only a 40-percent minority
of local Angels wanted to invest more than their deal flow allowed. When
that desire is averaged over all local Angels, the result is that only 26
percent more would have been invested given the opportunity. This is
the lowest in the United States.

Region VI Entrepreneurs/Firms

Mid-South Angels puncture U.S. patterns for successful entrepreneurs/
firms by heavy local emphasis on equity dollars over loans, smaller-than-
usual firms, a strong commitment to FIRE investments, and frequent use
of comprehensive business plans.

The total amount invested in any single entrepreneur is similar to
the U.S. Composite but differs substantially in the relative size of the
equity and loan/guarantee components. Equity dollars per firm are

$150,000, versus $112,500 for the nation, while local loans per firm are $28,400, versus $64,200 for the U.S. Composite. The percentages of successful entrepreneurs by equity dollars received are:

- Under $40,000   31%
- $40,000–$99,999   17%
- $100,000–$199,999   20%
- $200,000–$400,000   7%
- Over $400,000   25%

The range of loans/guarantees and the percentages of successful entrepreneurs are:

- Under $60,000   44%
- $60,000–$119,999   12%
- $120,000–$575,000   29%
- Over $575,000   15%

Local Angels generally invest in groups of four coinvestors. The percentages of entrepreneurs by number of coinvestors providing funding are:

- 1 Angel   21%
- 2   15%
- 3   15%
- 4   12%
- 5–10   32%
- Over 10   6%

Successful entrepreneurs are found most often in the FIRE industry, in contrast to the national pattern of service industry firms. The percentages of entrepreneurs receiving Angel dollars by industry are:

- Natural resources/mining   8%
- Construction   12%
- Manufacturing—high-technology   4%
- Manufacturing—industrial products   11%
- Manufacturing—consumer products   5%
- Transportation, communication, and utilities   3%
- Wholesale trade   2%
- Retail trade   9%
- Finance/insurance/real estate   23%
- Service   20%
- Other   4%

Region VI Deal Structure

Investment deals in the mid-South are structured on the U.S. pattern, with the one exception of much smaller loans and guarantees. Nine out of 10 profile comparison characteristics are the same! The local exception involves only $7000 in loans from any one Angel to any one firm, compared to $21,400 nationwide. The percentages of local deals by loan sizes are:

- None   11%
- Under $15,000   39%
- $15,000–$29,999   11%
- $30,000–$150,000   26%
- Over $150,000   13%

Summary of Region VI

Angels, entrepreneurs, and their deals in Houston, Dallas, New Orleans, and other metropolitan areas of the mid-South have their own special brand of market compared to the U.S. Composite. Angels in the mid-South have more minority members, more engineering school graduates in their ranks, and lower incomes and wealth than their U.S. counterparts. They are more sensitive to equity price and reject deals most often for over-pricing. Local Angels make smaller but not fewer loans to their entrepreneurs. Their investment dollars strongly target finance, insurance and real estate deals over the national preference for both service and FIRE proposals. Moreover, by U.S. standards, mid-South Angels are remarkably less interested in increasing their rate of investment.

Locally successful entrepreneurs receive a larger proportion of their Angel risk capital in equity dollars and far less in loans than do composite entrepreneurs. They are more likely to be entrepreneurs of very small firms in finance, insurance, or real estate. Three-fourths of mid-South entrepreneurs provide up-front comprehensive business plans.

The structure of investment deals between local Angels and entrepreneurs follows the national pattern right down the line with the exception of smaller loans/guarantees.

ST. LOUIS, KANSAS CITY, OMAHA, AND
THE PLAINS STATES—REGION VII

Region VII, shown in Figure 10-1, encompasses the four-state area of Missouri, Iowa, Kansas, and Nebraska. Almost 290,000 business enterprises inhabit this series of local Angel markets, representing 5.8 percent of all U.S. business enterprises, as estimated by the U.S. Small Business Administration. In addition, local markets contain 5.1 percent of the U.S. adult population, earning 4.9 percent of U.S. personal family income.

Among local business enterprises about 6 percent have an Angel-investor at any one time, adding up to about 17,000 Angel-assisted enterprises. The area's pool of Angels numbers 37,000, and they conclude some 29,000 deals annually with around 7300 successful entrepreneurs/firms.

Angels each year invest $1.9 billion plus another $1.3 billion of Angel loans/guarantees, for a total risk capital flow of about $3.2 billion annually. A 57-percent majority of Angels wanted to invest more than their deal flow allowed. Averaged over all investors, the annual increase in risk capital funds is 32 percent, or $1.0 billion. In total, annual local Angel funding, including both committed and potential, amounts to about $4.2 billion dollars.

Region VII Markets

The markets dissected here exist in the geographic and informal capital center of the nation. Simply put, they are a good (though not perfect) mirror of the U.S. pattern. On 40 points of comparison (Market Profile 10-2, pages 182–183), real differences exist at only 11 points: Angels have less entrepreneurial experience, emphasize friends as information sources, and say they almost never seek absolute voting control; successful entrepreneurs receive more risk capital than usual and are predominantly white males; and Angel deals anticipate a lower average ROI than the U.S. Composite.

Region VII Angels

Local Angels are similar to Angels everywhere except that they are somewhat younger and fewer (73 percent) have personal entrepreneurial experience. Angel communication channels place a very heavy local emphasis on friends and not business associates. The percentages of Angels who describe various information sources as "frequently used" are:

- Friends   27%
- Business associates   8%
- Entrepreneurs   13%
- Investment bankers   12%
- Brokers   9%
- Others   0%

Local Angels are much less aggressive in seeking voting control than their national colleagues, with 97 percent saying they desire less than 51 percent of voting power.

Region VII Entrepreneurs/Firms

Entrepreneurs who succeed with local Angels are rewarded with higher levels of risk capital funding than their U.S. counterparts. However, the larger level of funding is due to the greater number of coinvestors per deal and not because of the dollars per Angel (which are quite average).

Entrepreneurs are more predominantly white males here than anywhere else, probably reflecting the area's population mix. The percentages of entrepreneurs by demographic class are:

- White male   90%
- Female   8%
- Minority   4%

Region VII Deals

Except for a low average expected ROI (only 18 percent), local deals are typical by U.S. standards. This expected return is so low by all comparisons that extreme caution is advised. It may be a statistical fluke, or it may reflect the high rate of inexperienced investors (regarding their entrepreneurship, not investing).

Summary of Region VII

The St. Louis, Kansas City, and Omaha areas are about as similar to the U.S. pattern as you can get. Local market profiles offer little variance from U.S. norms, and even the differences are not especially notable, except that the personal entrepreneurial experience among Angels is the lowest of anywhere in the U.S. and so is ROI. In terms of investor satisfaction the lack of experience does not seem to make much difference. It may, however, be reflected in the Angels' extraordinarily low ROI expectations.

DENVER, SALT LAKE CITY, AND THE MOUNTAINS— REGION VIII

The Region VIII market area, shown in Figure 10-1, is made up of North and South Dakota, Wyoming, Montana, Colorado, and Utah. These markets include only 3 percent (192,000) of all U.S. business enterprises, as estimated by the U.S. Small Business Administration. In terms of population, the area contains 3.4 percent of both the adult U.S. population and personal income. Business Angels at present have investments in about 11,000 (6 percent) local business enterprises. The pool of Angels numbers 20,000 individuals who each year make 17,000 deals to finance about 5700 entrepreneurs/firms. The value of the equity dollars totals $1.1 billion each year, with an additional $800 million in Angel loans/guarantees. Angels wanted to invest 31 percent more than they could, which would be $590 million more in uninvested risk capital. Thus local markets have about $2.5 billion of actual and potential risk capital yearly for business creation and expansion.

Local market conditions for the mountain region are presented in Profile 10-2 on pages 182–183. Special characteristics that mark this area as unique occur in 13 out of 40 comparisons of profile elements.

Angels in the Mountains

Region VIII investors have a practical streak—they have the nation's highest rate of personal entrepreneurial experience and the lowest number of college degree holders. They are younger by 10 years, they have lower family incomes, and they loan less money to their entrepreneurs than the U.S. Composite. The younger Angel age may help account for both their lower incomes and smaller entrepreneurial loans. The percentages of local Angels in each age class are:

- 34 years or less   16%
- 35–44   39%
- 45–54   29%
- 55–64   16%
- 65 or over   0%

The U.S. Composite shows that 72 percent of all Angels have a degree, compared to only 56 percent locally. The percentages of Denver–Salt Lake City Angels by education class are:

- High school or less   22%
- Some college   22%
- College graduate   44%
- Graduate   11%

Perhaps as a reflection of both younger age and shortened schooling the annual family income of local Angels is $70,000, versus $90,000 nationwide. The percentages of local Angels by income class are:

- Under $60,000   38%
- $60,000–$79,999   24%
- $80,000–$99,999   15%
- $100,000–$200,000   15%
- Over $200,000   9%

Lower income has apparently not hindered wealth accumulation—local Angels still reflect a level of net worth equal to the U.S. pattern of $750,000. Nevertheless, lower income levels do show up when it comes to Angels lending or guaranteeing loans. Local Angels typically lend/guarantee only $25,000 total to all portfolio firms, compared to the $75,000 U.S. pattern. The reduced level of lending is not because of fewer loans but rather because loans are smaller. The percent of local versus U.S. Angels who have made no loans is 17 percent and 14 percent, respectively. The percentages of local Angels reporting loans in various size classes are:

- None   17%
- Under $50,000   33%

- $50,000–$99,999   8%
- $100,000–$500,000   28%
- Over $500,000   14%

Region VIII Entrepreneurs/Firms

Local firms successful in obtaining Angel financing are young, like their Angels. Entrepreneurs in the Denver–Salt Lake City area received smaller total risk capital than usual, but that is a reflection of smaller loans and not of less equity capital. Successful entrepreneurs have smaller and younger firms than the U.S. Composite, which may also help explain the small risk capital invested by Angels. Eighty-three percent of local firms with Angel funding have fewer than 10 employees, compared to 74 percent nationwide. The percentages of local firms by employment size at the time of receiving Angel financing are:

- 0–4 employees   69%
- 5–9   14%
- 10–19   8%
- 20 or more   9%

These smaller firms are also younger. Start-up and infant growth stage firms (usually one year old or less) make up 78 percent of firms financed, compared to 69 percent nationwide. The local percentages of firms by growth stage when Angel funding arrives are:

- Start-up   66%
- Infant   12%
- Young   13%
- Established   9%

Region VIII Deal Structure

The most notable differences between mountain-area deals and those of the U.S. Composite are lower expected risk and higher ROI. Any given deal here is expected by the Angel to involve only a 20-percent chance of substantial capital loss, whereas the U.S. Composite expects 30 percent. One in five local deals is thought to be a sure winner! This is the nation's highest level of expected risklessness. (The U.S. pattern expects only 7 percent riskless deals.) The percentages of deals by anticipated risk of loss are:

- Zero risk   21%
- 1–19%   30%
- 20–29%   9%
- 30–39%   9%
- 40–50%   12%
- Over 50%   19%

Ordinarily, lower risk means that less is expected as a return on investment. Local markets turn this usual relationship on its head. Local deals result in Angels expecting a median and mean ROI of 25 percent and 32 percent, respectively. The percentages of local deals by anticipated ROI at deal time are:

- Under 20% ROI   37%
- 20–29%   32%
- 30–39%   7%
- 40–49%   6%
- 50–100%   13%
- Over 100%   6%

Summary of Region VIII

The market for informal risk capital in the Denver, Salt Lake City, and the Mountain areas has its own unique blend of investment characteristics. Local Angels have almost 100 percent personal experience as entrepreneurs, yet they are 10 years younger than the U.S. Composite Angel. Fewer local Angels have finished college, and they report lower-than-average family income levels. One outcome of this is that successful entrepreneurs usually receive less Angel capital, with the shortfall confined entirely to smaller but not fewer Angel loans. Consistent with this reduced capital level is the fact that locally successful entrepreneurs have smaller and younger firms when they achieve Angel financing. Local deals are structured in a mostly typical fashion, with the exception that these deals are viewed with a combination of the lowest risk perception and one of the highest ROI expectations anywhere in the United States. In all other respects the local market profile resembles the U.S. Composite.

LOS ANGELES, PHOENIX, SAN FRANCISCO, AND THE SOUTHWEST—REGION IX

Metropolitan markets encompassing the urban areas of Los Angeles, San Diego, Phoenix, and San Francisco are shown as Region IX on the map in Figure 10-1. Even though this is only a four-state area (California, Arizona, Nevada, and Hawaii), the local informal capital markets contain 14 percent (680,000) of all U.S. business enterprises, along with 13 percent of the U.S. adult population and 14 percent of its personal income.

Business firms with Angels are less common locally (5.8 percent) then the national average (9.0 percent). However, the absolute number of firms with Angel financing is large and totals 39,000 firms. Local markets add up to a pool of 94,000 Angels who make some 68,000 deals each year with 17,000 successful entrepreneurs. Deals between Angels and entrepreneurs are valued at about $7.7 billion per year, composed of

$4.5 billion equity and $3.2 billion personal loans/guarantees. Almost two out of three Angels (63 percent—the nation's highest) wanted to invest more than opportunity permitted, which means another $3.1 billion unused Angel risk capital is available. In sum, the local pool of Angel risk capital is about $10.8 billion per year.

California and the Southwest are generally viewed as "different" from the rest of the United States. The informal market characteristics shown for Region IX in Market Profile 10-2 (pages 182–183) reinforce that view, especially as it applies to the market characteristics of Angels themselves. Out of nine major differences, Angel characteristics account for five.

Region IX Angels

Local Angels differ from the U.S. Composite because of higher levels of income and wealth. West Coast Angels have median family income and net worth of $150,000 and $1,000,000, respectively, compared to the nationwide medians of $90,000 income and $750,000 net worth. Local Angels have the highest median income of any market in the United States. The percentages of local Angels by family income class are:

- Under $40,000   4%
- $40,000–$59,999   11%
- $60,000–$79,999   17%
- $80,000–$99,999   11%
- $100,000–$200,000   33%
- Over $200,000   24%

In terms of wealth, local Angels are the "millionaires" of financial mythology. Here we see an exception that proves the rule that Angels are not millionaires—but they are in Los Angeles. The percentages of Region IX Angels by net worth category are:

- Under $300,000   9%
- $300,000–$499,999   6%
- $500,000–$1,000,000   34%
- Over $1,000,000   51%

While the U.S. Composite Angel kills serious deals because of inadequate growth potential, local Angels do so mostly because they believe the entrepreneurs lack talent. The rank order of the top five local deal killers is:

1. Entrepreneurs or key personnel lack talent necessary for success.
2. Growth potential is too limited.
3. Angel has insufficient personal knowledge about entrepreneur/key personnel.
4. Proposal objectives do not fit Angel's long-term objectives.
5. Equity is overpriced.

Two other exceptions to the U.S. pattern are that Region IX Angels target FIRE investments very strongly and that they are relatively inactive in their firms' daily operations. Half of all Southwest Angels target FIRE as their preferred industry, compared to 39 percent nationwide. Conversely, local Angels are not fond of construction industry firms (20 percent interest), whereas the U.S. preference is 31 percent. The percentages of local Angels with strong interests in investing in particular industries are:

- Natural resources/mining   6%
- Construction   31%
- Manufacturing—high-technology   26%
- Manufacturing—industrial   18%
- Manufacturing—consumer   14%
- Transportation, communication, and utilities   8%
- Wholesale trade   20%
- Retail trade   28%
- Finance/insurance/real estate   49%
- Services   31%
- Other   10%

(The right-hand column does not add to 100 percent because of multiple interests.)

If we define an inactive Angel as one who only reviews periodic reports and attends stockholders meetings, then Region IX's inactive Angels outnumber the U.S. Composite's (17 percent inactive). The percentages of local Angels by type of participation in the firm are:

- None, other than reviewing periodic reports   27%
  and attending stockholders meetings
- Representation on the board of directors   11%
- Providing consulting help as needed   24%
- Working part time with the firm   21%
- Working full time with the firm   12%
- Other   4%

Region IX Entrepreneurs/Firms

Entrepreneurs who achieve success with Southwest Angels differ little from the U.S. Composite, aside from the larger amount of risk capital they obtain. Local entrepreneurs typically are funded at the $236,000 level, versus $176,700 nationwide. This higher total funding is derived from larger groups of coinvestors who individually invest only typical amounts. The percentages of entrepreneurs by equity dollars received are:

- Under $40,000   12%
- $40,000–$99,999   23%
- $100,000–$199,999   21%
- $200,000–$399,999   22%
- $400,000–$1,000,000   15%
- Over $1,000,000   7%

The percentages of entrepreneurs who obtain various sizes of total loans and loan guarantees from Angels are:

- Under $60,000   41%
- $60,000–$114,999   18%
- $115,000–$575,000   25%
- Over $575,000   16%

Region IX Deal Structure

West Coast deals, strangely enough, are pretty average. Out of 10 points of comparison to the U.S. Composite, only 1 characteristic stands out locally: the method of liquidation. Local investment agreements between Angels and entrepreneurs are more likely than the national pattern to anticipate either a merger or public stock offering. The percentages of local deals favoring various liquidation methods are:

- None   26%
- Sell back to company   11%
- Sell to another coinvestor   23%
- Sell or merge with another firm   13%
- Sell to institutional investor   0%
- Public stock offering   13%
- Other   15%

Summary of Region IX

The informal risk capital markets in Los Angeles, San Diego, Phoenix, San Francisco, and adjoining communities do not resemble the U.S. pattern. These markets stand out because their Angels have higher incomes and wealth, reject deals for lack of entrepreneurial management talent, form larger coinvestor groups, and are less actively involved in day-to-day firm operations than the national norm. Local entrepreneurs receive more total Angel dollars, including more of both equity and loans. Southwest deals diverge from the U.S. pattern by the clear tendency to more often plan investment liquidation by sale to outsiders.

SEATTLE, PORTLAND, AND THE PACIFIC NORTHWEST— REGION X

Seattle and Portland and their neighbors make up the Pacific Northwest area. The local markets in Region X have over 4 percent (208,000 firms) of all U.S. business enterprises, as estimated by the U.S. Small Business Administration. The area contains 3.4 percent of the U.S. adult population, earning 3.2 percent of total U.S. personal income.

Local Angels have an active interest in 6 percent of local enterprises at any one time, amounting to 12,000 businesses. The pool of local Angels is estimated to number 27,000 individuals who make 21,000 deals to finance 7000 entrepreneurs/firms each year. The annual equity value of these deals amounts to $1.4 billion, with another $1.0 billion in Angel loans/guarantees for a total of $2.4 billion in risk capital. One out of two Angels wanted to invest more than deal flow allowed, averaging 28 percent of all risk capital and equalling $700 million. Thus the actual and potential pool of risk capital in the Pacific Northwest totals $3.1 billion available each year for local business development and growth.

Region X Markets

The Region X data shown in Profile 10-2 (pages 182–183) encompasses a wide-ranging mixture of usual and unusual market characteristics.

Region X Angels

The investors in the Pacific Northwest are less often well-educated, white male business owners than the national pattern. More-than-usual numbers of "other professionals" make up for the shortfall in the owner/ manager group and the complete absence of any Angels with sales occupations. The percentages of Angels by principal occupation are:

- Business owner/manager   75%
- Sales   0%
- Science/engineering professionals   6%
- Other profesionals (doctors, lawyers, CPAs, etc.)   13%
- Other   6%

Demographically, Region X Angels include much larger numbers of people of Spanish origin than usual. The percentages of Angels by demographic group are:

- White male   75%
- White female   6%
- Minority male   19%
- Minority female   0%

The proportion of local Angels who have completed college is the lowest of anywhere in the United States: 47 percent versus 72 percent nationwide. The proportions of Angels by level of education completed are:

- High school or less   20%
- Some college   33%
- College degree   13%
- Graduate degree   34%

The above factors do not seem to hurt Angel investment success rates. If anything, it has helped raise them well above national standards. Eight out of 10 (81 percent) local Angels say their informal investments perform equal to or better than originally expected, compared to 72 percent nationwide. The percentages of Seattle–Portland-area Angels by investment performance are:

- Well above expected   13%
- Above   20%
- Equal to   48%
- Below   0%
- Well below expected   19%

Local Angels are not frequent investors, and they rely less on friends and more on business associates for information on investment opportunities. Less frequent investments result in local Angels having both smaller portfolios and less total risk capital commitment. The percentages of Angels and their frequency of investing are:

- 1 in 36 months   69%
- 2   25%
- 3   0%
- 4 or more   6%

In terms of investment goals, local Angels more often seek absolute control of their target firm than does the U.S. Composite. Over 25 percent of local Angels seek to gain over 51 percent control, compared to 15 percent of Angels nationwide. Note that when it comes to actually *gaining* control, locals match U.S. standards.

Region X Entrepreneurs/Firms

Seattle-Portland entrepreneurs who obtain Angel financing are commonly in retail trade and are rewarded with larger-than-usual amounts of risk capital. The local total per firm is $245,000, compared to $176,700 nationwide. The difference is entirely made up of Angel loans/guarantees, which are twice as large as usual. Local success for retail trade industry entrepreneurs stands in contrast to the national pattern of investing in service or FIRE firms. The percentages of successful entrepreneurs by industry for local investments are:

- Natural resources/mining   6%
- Construction   12%
- Manufacturing—high-technology   13%
- Manufacturing—industrial   13%
- Manufacturing—consumer   9%
- Transportation, communication, and utilities   0%
- Wholesale trade   3%

- Retail trade   16%
- Finance/insurance/real estate   13%
- Services   9%
- Other   6%

While the U.S. Composite Entrepreneur has a written comprehensive business plan in 6 out of 10 cases, the frequency is much lower for the Seattle–Portland area, with only 40 percent having such plans.

Region X Deal Structure

The deals made between Region X Angels and investors involve larger-than-usual Angel loans and anticipate a longer holding period with less planned resale of Angel equity back to insiders. Angels' personal loans/guarantees have a median per deal of $44,000, versus $21,400 nationwide. A partial reason for this greater amount of Angel loans is that only 6 percent of local Angels have *not* loaned to their entrepreneur, compared to the U.S. Composite's 14 percent. The size of equity invested per deal is quite normal, however. The percentages of local deals by size of Angel loans are:

- None   6%
- Under $25,000   38%
- $25,000–$49,999   25%
- $50,000–$249,999   19%
- $250,000 or more   12%

Anticipated investment holding periods are over seven years locally, versus four years by U.S. standards. The percentages of deals by expected holding periods in Seattle–Portland are:

- 3 years or less   20%
- 3–5   27%
- 6–10   7%
- 10 or over or not important   47%

Area deals contain specific buy-out plans in over two-thirds of the cases. However, the anticipated source of cash for the liquidation is an insider in only 31 percent of the deals, versus 50 percent nationwide. Local emphasis is on public offerings and combinations of exit methods. The percentages of deals by plans for equity liquidation are:

- None   31%
- Sell back to firm   25%
- Sell to existing coinvestor   6%
- Sell/merge with another firm   0%
- Public offering   13%
- Other   25%

Summary of the Pacific Northwest

The market for informal risk capital in Seattle, Portland, and the Pacific Northwest shows a unique blend of local characteristics. Quantitatively the region's profile and the U.S. Composite differ on 15 important points out of 40. Unlike the U.S. Composite, Angels locally are less often business owners/managers, white males, and college graduates. They are unusually well satisfied with the performance of their informal investments. Corporate control figures more often into their professed investment objectives, but in actuality they achieve control at about the same rate as elsewhere. Local entrepreneurs with Angel financing receive larger amounts of risk capital than their colleagues nationwide, but the extra is all in the form of more-frequent and larger-than-usual Angel loans. Retail entrepreneurs are unusually successful in the Pacific Northwest even though they have written comprehensive business plans much less often than the U.S. Composite. Investment holding periods here are almost twice as long as usual, and when plans to liquidate are made, more often than not Angels and entrepreneurs look to sell out to outsiders rather than sell equity back to the firm or to existing coinvestors.

11

DEVILS, DEAD ENDS, AND DEAL BREAKERS

Increasing the probability of successful deals means knowing when to be cautious and what situations to avoid. For example, some investors want to get control of the firm from the entrepreneur. I call these investors business "Devils" rather than Angels. Entrepreneurs should know how they operate and what to look for to increase their chances of avoiding them. Each of the preceding chapters has emphasized the positive or "what you should do or look for" aspects of successful Angel financing. I reverse that principle in this chapter by describing in detail a series of investment scenarios that may lead to trouble down the road. The cast of characters in these potentially troublesome scenarios include "Devils," "High Fliers," "Impatient Angels," "Green Angels," "Nickel and Dime Angels," and "Corporate Achievers." Each of these flawed Angel types is defined and profiled in one of the following sections. The concluding section, "The Kiss of Death," warns of ways to effectively kill an investment deal or to end up in a blind alley.

BUSINESS DEVILS

Angels who gain absolute majority voting control from entrepreneurs are defined as business "Devils." This often unpleasant result is more common than many believe. One in every five "Angels" (21 percent) is a Devil. These Devils win control from the entrepreneurs in 27 percent of all deals. The spiritual Devil has a reputation of affecting innocent disguises, and business Devils do the same. They are not easy to spot (if they were obvious they wouldn't be a problem). Superficially they resemble the U.S. Composite in most personal characteristics except education and income (they have less of both). The unlucky entrepreneurs who are most at risk present a clearer profile: They have very few employees, have firms physically close to the Devil's home or office, and provide a comprehensive business plan more often than usual. Devil deals are more risky than usual, and Devils are twice as likely to be or to become an employee of the firm. Business Devils are profiled in Market Profile 11-1.

Characteristic Differences of Devils

Out of 20 personal points of comparison, Devils and Angels differ on only 6. Devils are less educated, have lower incomes, rely on friends for information, are very sensitive to equity pricing, admit seeking voting control, and are very active in day-to-day operations.

The Devil has completed less education. The major difference occurs for the high school or less group, where Devils are found at twice the usual rate. One in three "Angels" with no college degree is a Devil. Graduate degree holders are the least likely to be devilish; only one in seven gains control. The odds of finding a Devil by education level are:

- High school or less   19%
- Some college   18%
- College graduate   42%
- Graduate degree   21%

Devils also have lower incomes than usual—$70,000, versus the composite $90,000. The income class between $40,000 and $80,000 is the worst, where almost one in every two investors becomes a Devil. The Devil probabilities by income group are:

- Under $40,000   13%
- $40,000–$59,999   23%
- $60,000–$79,999   24%
- $80,000–$99,999   13%
- $100,000–$200,000   17%
- Over $200,000   9%

Devils are exceptionally sensitive to equity pricing, citing it as the leading reason for rejecting a deal. Inadequate business growth potential is their second most common cause of rejection, while insufficient knowledge of the entrepreneur is third. Devils are very active in their firms' daily operations; virtually all of them participate in one form or another, but especially as employees—57 percent versus the composite's 39 percent. The percentages of Devils by level of firm involvement are:

- None   6%
- Board of directors   15%
- Consultant   18%
- Full-time employee   31%
- Part-time employee   26%
- Other   5%

MARKET PROFILE 11-1. Business Devils

DEVILS	U.S. Composite
• Business owner/manager is principal occupation (71%)	(69%)
• Has personal entrepreneurial experience (89%)	(83%)
• 49 years old*	(47 years)
• White male (77%)	(84%)
+ • College degree (63%)	(72%)
+ • $70,000 annual family income*	($90,000)
• $750,000 net worth*	($750,000)
+ • Friends are the primary information channel	(Friends and associates)
• Accepts 3 of 10 investment opportunities*	(3)
+ • Rejects deals mostly due to price, growth potential	(Growth potential)
• Invests about every 18 months and has 3.5 firms in portfolio*	(18) (3.5)
• Satisfied with past investment (73%)	(72%)
• Two other coinvestors*	(Two)
• $131,000 equity invested in informal portfolio*	($131,000)
• $75,000 more via loans/guarantees to portfolio firms*	($75,000)
• Prefers investing in service firms (44%)	(Service/FIRE)
• Minimum ROI target for informal portfolio (22%)*	(22%)
+ • Active as a consultant, board member, or employee (94%)	(81%)
+ • Does not seek voting control (55%)	(85%)
• Wants to invest 31% more than opportunity permitted	(35%)

SUCCESSFUL ENTREPRENEURS/FIRMS

• $176,700 total Angel financing* (equity and loans)	($176,700)
• $112,500 in equity and $64,200 more in loans/guarantees*	($112,500) ($64,200)
• Three private individuals supply funding*	(Three)
• Entrepreneur is white male, age 25–35 (72%)	(79%)
+ • Zero to nine employees at time of investment (83%)	(74%)
• Start-up or infant stage of firm growth (64%)	(69%)
• Service firms are most frequently financed (22%)	(17% in service)
+ • 50 miles or less from investor's home or office (81%)	(72%)
+ • Has a comprehensive business plan (71%)	(61%)
• Has detailed marketing and financing plans	

HIGH-PROBABILITY DEAL STRUCTURE

• $37,500 in equity per investor*	($37,500)
• $21,400 in loans/guarantees by Angel*	($21,400)
+ • Over 51% voting power transferred to investor	(37%)
+ • Majority control to Angel in 100% of investments	(27%)
+ • 40% capital risk seen by Angel*	(30%)
• 25% expected annual ROI (28% average)	(25%) (27%)
+ • Common stock or partner equity instrument (70%)	(79%)
• Liquidation horizon of four years*	(Four years)
• Liquidation buyback by insiders planned (45%)	(50%)
+ • Investor is or becomes an employee in 57% of investments	(39%)

*Median amount—half higher, half lower.   + = Differs importantly from U.S. Composite.

Many Devils readily admit seeking absolute majority control when asked by disinterested questioners. Almost one out of two Devils admit they are looking for control, compared to only one in seven for the composite Angel.

Firms that fall victim to Devil takeovers are typically smaller than usual, are in very close proximity to the Devil's home/office and supply comprehensive business plans ("blueprints?") more than usual. Entrepreneurs who lose control to a business Devil usually have fewer than five employees. The percentages of Devils by employment size of the victim firm are:

- 0–4 employees   59%
- 5–9   23%
- 10–19   10%
- 20 or more   8%

Firms targeted by Devils are physically close to where the business Devil lives or works. Half are almost within walking distance. The percentages of victim firms by distance from the Devil's home or office are:

- 10 miles or less   48%
- 11–50   33%
- 51–150   11%
- Other   9%

Devils are persistent in insisting that entrepreneurs supply them with a business "blueprint" prior to the investment. Comprehensive business plans are much more likely prior to a Devil investment than for the U.S. Composite. This is especially unusual considering the small firm size. The percentages of Devil-targeted firms with a comprehensive plan are:

- Zero   8%
- 20% or less   1%
- 21–40%   4%
- 41–60%   13%
- 61–80%   4%
- 81–100%   71%

The Devil's deal is not easily distinguishable from the normal, except for three special features. The Devil perceives greater risk than does the composite investor, there is greater use of exotic equity instruments, and Devils are or become employees in 6 of 10 deals, as previously discussed. The most interesting feature is the increased use of unusual debt-equity instruments. The most noteworthy differences are increased use of notes (loans) with warrants (to obtain more equity ownership) and combinations of equity instruments. In both these cases, one in three to four investors is a potential Devil. (See also the "Corporate Achievers" section for discussion regarding the use of notes with warrants.) The percentages of Devil deals by type of equity instrument are:

- Common stock   35%
- Convertible preferred stock   3%
- Notes with warrants   14%
- Convertible debentures   2%
- Partnership equity interest   35%
- Combinations and others   10%

Key Points about Devils

Business Devils are investors who gain absolute majority control from the entrepreneur. These Devils are not easy to detect. There is no dead giveaway that you're dealing with a potential business Devil, and no one characteristic definitively stands out, but a combination of the following items should signal "caution" to the entrepreneur:

- Low educational achievement, especially in the high school or less category
- Lower-than-usual income levels, especially in the range of $60,000 to $80,000
- Strong sensitivity to equity pricing
- Virtually 100-percent participation in the firm's operation, usually as employees (almost one in three of these Angel employees gains control)
- Fewer than five employees in Devil target firms
- Very close proximity of firm to the Devil's home or office
- Unusually high requirement for comprehensive business plans prior to investment
- More frequent use of notes with warrants and unusual combinations of equity instruments

HIGH FLIERS

Angels investing only for high annual rates of return are called "High Fliers." By "high" I mean that they make no investment at less than 40 percent ROI (mean average of 79 percent), compared to the composite average of 27 percent. They are not common, representing only about 1 Angel in 10. But they are potential trouble unless your equity pricing is low enough to suit their targets. Moreover, they usually end up as dissatisfied investors. As a group, High Fliers are easy to distinguish from the usual Angel pattern—they stand out on 21 of 40 profile element comparisons. Only the most important will he highlighted here.

High Fliers are almost always wealthy businesspeople who invest infrequently. They are very sensitive to equity price and usually end up
dissatisfied with the performance of their investments. They tend to be
inactive with their firms and are eager to invest more than they have been
able (who wouldn't be eager at 79 percent ROI?). The firms they invest
in differ in that they are larger and farther away than usual and are most
often manufacturing firms specializing in industrial products. High Fliers
rarely obtain voting control. They believe informal investments are very
risky, but they are patient when it comes to holding periods. Profile 11-2
contains their Market Profile.

Characteristic Differences of High Fliers

High Fliers are almost always business owners/managers. The only other
occupation group represented is doctors and lawyers. Their median family income is $150,000, compared to the composite's $90,000, and 53 percent of them are millionaires. The pattern of High Flier income is interesting in its concentration under $80,000 or over $100,000. The percentages
of High Fliers by income class are:

- Under $40,000   6%
- $40,000–$79,999   39%
- $80,000–$99,999   0%
- $100,000–$200,000   33%
- Over $200,000   22%

Deal rejection is mostly based on equity pricing issues or lack of growth
potential (imagine that!). Commensurate with their tough standards, High
Fliers make very few investments and hold small informal portfolios. The
percentages of High Flying Angels by the number of their deals in three
years are:

- 1   55%
- 2   35%
- 3   5%
- 4   5%
- 5 or more   0%

Not surprisingly, High Flying Angels are the most dissatisfied of all
Angels with the performance of their informal investments. Is this because
they expect too much? Do they see what they want to see at deal time,
ignoring the rest? Or do they just exercise poor judgment? I can't impute
motives, but whatever the case, half of all High Fliers believe that their
investments have performed below expectations. The percentages

---

MARKET PROFILE 11-2. High Fliers

ANGELS	U.S. Composite
+ • Business owner/manager is principal occupation (90%)	(69%)
• Has personal entrepreneurial experience (80%)	(83%)
• 49 years old*	(47 years)
• White male (85%)	(84%)
• College degree (75%)	(72%)
+ • $150,000 annual family income*	($90,000)
+ • $1,000,000 net worth*	($750,000)
+ • Friends are the primary information channel	(Friends and associates)
• Accepts 3 of 10 investment opportunities*	(3)
+ • Rejects deals mostly due to price, growth potential, and personal knowledge	(Growth potential)
+ • Invests about every 36 months and has 1.7 firms in portfolio	(18) (3.5)
+ • Satisfied with past investments (50%)	(72%)
• Two other coinvestors*	(Two)
+ • $63,800 equity invested in informal portfolio*	($131,000)
+ • $25,000 more via loans/guarantees to portfolio firms*	($75,000)
• Prefers investing in FIRE firms (40%)	(Service/FIRE)
• Minimum ROI target for informal portfolio (22%)*	(22%)
+ • Active as a consultant, board member, or employee (70%)	(81%)
+ • Does not seek voting control (63%)	(85%)
+ • Wants to invest 47% more than opportunity permitted	(35%)

SUCCESSFUL ENTREPRENEURS/FIRMS

• $156,600 total Angel financing* (equity and loans)	($176,700)
• $112,500 in equity and $44,100 more in loans/guarantees*	($112,500) ($64,200)
• Three private individuals supply funding*	(Three)
• Entrepreneur is a white male, age 25–35 (83%)	(79%)
+ • Zero to nine employees at time of investment (65%)	(74%)
• Start-up or infant stage of firm growth (72%)	(69%)
+ • Manufacturing—industrial product firms are most frequently financed (23%)	(17% in service)
+ • 50 miles or less from investor's home or office (60%)	(72%)
• Has a comprehensive business plan (59%)	(61%)
• Has detailed marketing and financing plans	

HIGH-PROBABILITY DEAL STRUCTURE

• $37,500 in equity per investor*	($37,500)
+ • $14,700 in loans/guarantees by Angel*	($21,400)
• 31% voting power transferred to investor	(37%)
+ • Majority control to Angel in 16% of investments	(27%)
+ • 50% capital risk seen by Angel*	(30%)
+ • 75% expected annual ROI (79% average)	(25%) (27%)
• Common stock or partner equity instrument (82%)	(79%)
+ • Liquidation horizon of seven and a half years*	(Four years)
• Liquidation buyback by insiders planned (47%)	(50%)
+ • Investor is or becomes an employee in 30% of investments	(39%)

---

*Median value—half higher, half lower.   + = Differs importantly from U.S. Composite.

of High-Fliers by level of satisfaction with investment performance are:

- Well above expectations   5%
- Above expectations   16%
- Equal to expectations   32%
- Below expectations   32%
- Well below expected   16%

Despite their high ROI targets, these Angels are relatively inactive when it comes to helping the firm's daily operations. The traditional stockholder role is the most common. The percentages of High Fliers by level of participation in the firm are:

- Stockholder only   31%
- Board of directors   12%
- Consultant   27%
- Employee full time   18%
- Employee part time   12%
- Other   0%

How do High Fliers reconcile their dissatisfaction with past investments with their strong desire to invest more? It is far from clear, but they somehow do. Their desire to invest more than they have been able shows the following pattern:

- Wanted to invest no more than they did   28%
- Wanted to invest up to 100% more   50%
- Over 100% more   22%

Entrepreneurs who attract High Fliers differ from others by having large firms (more employees), especially in the 10 to 19 employee range. High Flier firms are frequently in the manufacturing—industrial goods sector. The percentages of High Flier deals by industry group are:

- National resources/mining   3%
- Construction   7%
- Manufacturing—high-technology   3%
- Manufacturing—industrial   23%
- Manufacturing—consumer   13%
- Transportation, communication, and utilities   0%
- Wholesale trade   16%
- Retail trade   10%
- Finance/insurance /real estate   10%
- Services   10%
- Other   6%

High Flier deals rarely transfer majority control to the Angel; only 16 percent, compared to the composite's 27 percent. The percentages of High Flying Angels by size of their voting control per deal are:

- Under 25% control   38%
- 25–49%   41%
- 50%   6%
- Over 50%   16%

At least High Fliers are not in a hurry to get their 79 percent ROI. Their expected holding period is seven and a half years, compared to four years for other Angels.

Key Points about High Fliers

- High Flying Angels invest at 40 percent ROI or more, with an average of 79 percent.
- They are millionaire businesspeople with high incomes (with exceptions).
- They invest infrequently in larger industrial goods manufacturing firms and in return get relatively little equity share and are disappointed according to their investment peformance expectations.
- They tend to avoid involvement in daily operations of their financed firms more than other Angels, perhaps because more of them live farther away from their entrepreneurs.
- The High Flier sees a 50-50 chance of substantial capital loss.

IMPATIENT ANGELS

Angels who provide risk capital temporarily are a questionable asset to the entrepreneur. "In again–out again" investors disturb the growth process of new, small firms by diverting attention and effort away from production and sales. In some circumstances, of course, temporary risk financing may be desirable or may be all that is available. However, a longer and more stable capital base for economic development is preferable. Unfortunately, many Angels show a distinct pattern of investing for the *very short* run and making a quick exit in less than three years (median of 18 months). As most entrepreneurs know, three years is a very short time. It is expensive and time-consuming to structure and then restructure a firm's capital base so quickly.

Impatient or quick-exit Angels are those who anticipate liquidating their investment in less than three years. One in every five Angels is Impatient by this definition. The median holding period of all Angels (composite) is four years, with an average of five years. The actual holding period expectations of all Angels are:

- Under 1 year   2%
- 1–3 years   19%
- 4–5 years   31%

- 6–10 years   29%
- Over 10 or not important   19%

How can the entrepreneurs spot Impatient Angels ahead of time? The answer is relatively simple: Ask them. I suggest being "up-front" with the question early in the search process, because there is almost no way to distinguish quick-exit Angels based upon their market profile. Only three characteristics of Impatient Angels stand out from the composite: lower incomes, equity price sensitivity, and a preference for FIRE investments. These few symptoms are too general to be very useful.

If we can't tell the quick-exit Angels from the others, how about identifying very Patient Angels (holding periods of 10 years or more)? The answer is the same—they look like the composite Angel too. Going a step further, what differences appear if we directly compare Impatient with Patient Angels? Again, no important characteristic differences appear! The few differences that do show up have no pattern to provide a useful guideline, so no market profiles are shown here.

In summary, all evidence shows that the investment holding period has no important impact on the market profile. Neither Patient nor Impatient Angels look different from the composite or from each other. The conclusion must be that the length of the holding period is not an important preference for Angels. In other words, any given Angel may or may not be agreeable to any given investment holding period. When holding period length is important, ask the Angel early.

GREEN ANGELS

Entrepreneurs do not always welcome advice and guidance from their investors. Most, however, recognize that new entrepreneurs and their firms often need more from their Angels than just money. They need business experience and guidance too. Not all Angels have entrepreneurial experience—17 percent do not. This is not to say they don't have other valuable knowledge and experience. Nor am I suggesting that Angels without entrepreneurial experience ("Green Angels" for short) be avoided—just know what you're getting when you link up with one. Green Angel characteristics are outlined in Profile 11-3.

Characteristic Differences of Green Angels

For the most part Green Angels resemble the composite, except for far less business and management experience, lower incomes, fewer and smaller loans to entrepreneurs, and relative nonparticipation in firm operations. They claim almost no ambition of gaining majority ownership control. The firms they put their money into are relatively older and more developed companies.

MARKET PROFILE 11-3. Green Angels

ANGELS	U.S. Composite
+ • Business owner/manager is principal occupation (53%)	(69%)
+ • Has personal entrepreneurial experience (0%)	(83%)
• 49 years old*	(47 years)
• White male (89%)	(84%)
• College degree (74%)	(72%)
+ • $70,000 annual family income*	($90,000)
• $750,000 net worth*	($750,000)
• Friends and associates are primary information channel	(Friends and associates)
• Accepts 3 of 10 investment opportunities*	(3)
• Rejects deals mostly due to growth potential	(Growth potential)
• Invests about every 18 months and has 3.5 firms in portfolio*	(18) (3.5)
• Satisfied with past investments (71%)	(72%)
• Three other coinvestors*	(Two)
• $131,000 equity invested in informal portfolio*	($131,000)
+ • $25,000 more via loans/guarantees to portfolio firms*	($75,000)
• Prefers investing in service firms (32%)	(Service/FIRE)
• Minimum ROI target for informal portfolio (22%)*	(22%)
+ • Active as a consultant, board member, or employee (71%)	(81%)
+ • Does not seek voting control (99%)	(85%)
• Wants to invest 35% more than opportunity permitted	(35%)

SUCCESSFUL ENTREPRENEURS/FIRMS

• $178,600 total Angel financing* (equity and loans)	($176,700)
+ • $150,000 in equity and $28,600 more in loans/guarantees*	($112,500) ($64,200)
• Four private individuals supply funding*	(Three)
• Entrepreneur is a white male, age 25–35 (83%)	(79%)
• Zero to nine employees at time of investment (68%)	(74%)
+ • Start-up or infant stage of firm growth (56%)	(69%)
• Service firms are most frequently financed (23%)	(17% in service)
• 50 miles or less from investor's home or office (71%)	(72%)
• Has a comprehensive business plan (65%)	(61%)
• Has detailed marketing and financing plans	

HIGH-PROBABILITY DEAL STRUCTURE

• $37,500 in equity per investor*	($37,500)
+ • $7,100 in loans/guarantees by Angel*	($21,400)
+ • 26% voting power transferred to investor	(37%)
• Majority control to Angel in 20% of investments	(27%)
• 30% capital risk seen by Angel*	(30%)
• 25% expected annual ROI (30% average)	(25%) (27%)
• Common stock or partner equity instrument (78%)	(79%)
• Liquidation horizon of four years*	(Four years)
• Liquidation buyback by insiders planned (42%)	(50%)
• Investor is or becomes an employee in 33% of investments	(39%)

*Median value—half higher, half lower.   + = Differs importantly from U.S. Composite.

Having entrepreneurial experience and being a business owner/manager are clearly not the same thing. Despite having no entrepreneurial experience, half of Green Angels are business owners/managers. As might be expected, the big occupational difference is in "other professionals," who are almost three times as prevalent in the Green Angel group. The percentages of Green Angels by occupation are:

- Business owner/manager   53%
- Sales   3%
- Science/engineering professionals   7%
- Other professionals   19%
- Other   18%

Despite the abundance of professionals, the income level of Green Angels is well below the composite standard. They have a median family income of only $70,000, compared to $90,000 for all Angels. The percentages of Green Angels by income are:

- Under $40,000   15%
- $40,000–$59,999   19%
- $60,000–$79,999   17%
- $80,000–$99,999   12%
- $100,000–$200,000   25%
- Over $200,000   13%

Since Green Angels have the usual portfolio equity commitment coupled with a lower income, it suggests that they have stretched their risk dollars to make equity investments and frequently have little left over for the added flexibility of loans/guarantees. Inexperienced Angels are thus a little "short" as well as green. They apparently have sufficient capital to make the initial equity investment "down payment" but are less able to provide additional loans/guarantees that are often needed later. The percentages of Green Angels by size of loans/guarantees are:

- None   15%
- Under $50,000   39%
- $50,000–$99,999   10%
- $100,000–$500,000   22%
- Over $500,000   14%

Green Angels contribute to the firm's daily operations only half as frequently as experienced Angels. Inactive "stockholder type" Angels account for 29 percent of all Greens, but only 15 percent of those with entrepreneurial experience. Green Angels apparently do not contribute special nonentrepreneurial expertise to compensate for their lack of entrepreneurial input either. Their consulting activity with the firm is about the same as all Angels. The percentages of Green Angels by type of involvement in firm operations are:

- Inactive (reports only)   29%
- Board of directors   10%
- Consultant   25%
- Part-time employment   21%
- Full-time employment   12%
- Other   3%

Probably the best quality of Green Angels is their lack of ambition to "take over." Virtually all Green Angels say they have no majority control intentions, compared to 85 percent for all Angels.

Entrepreneurs with mature firms will find Green Angels more willing to listen to investment proposals. Only a little over half the firms financed by Green Angels are in their start-up or infant stage, compared to two out of three for all Angels. The big difference is the Green Angels' taste for "established" firms, which they invest in far more frequently than the composite's 18 percent. The percentages of firms receiving Green Angel financing by growth stages are:

- Start-up   42%
- Infant   15%
- Young   15%
- Established   29%

Green Angel deals resemble the U.S. Composite.

Key Points about Green Angels

- Green Angels have no entrepreneurial experience to contribute to the firm.
- Their low incomes are used to make equity dollar commitments, and little is left over for loans/guarantees.
- Green Angels invest in established firms at almost twice the frequency of other Angels.
- Green Angels are twice as likely to be passive or inactive investors. They do not consult with the firm any more than other Angels, which suggests it is only money and not any special expertise that entrepreneurs can anticipate from a deal with a Green Angel.

NICKEL AND DIME ANGELS

Capital starvation is the best-known route to business failure or stagnation. Small-time Angels who do not or cannot supply sufficient capital may well be more harmful than helpful. Angels who have made no equity investment larger than $10,000 I call "Nickel and Dime" Angels. This group is the extreme low end of the Small-Scale Angels profiled in Chapter 6. The Angels we see here have the shallowest pockets of all (while still having pockets). Even though this is an extreme group, they are frequent, accounting for over one in five (22 percent) of all Angels. However, these Angels collectively supply only 7 percent of all Angel capital. The impact of Nickel and Dime Angels on a given firm would not be so bad if the firms were unusually small or if these Angels formed large coinvestor groups. Unfortunately neither is true, and the result is that firms who accept Nickel and Dime Angels end up undercapitalized ($59,000 versus $177,000). Worse yet, the Angels very often end up dissatisfied as well.

Nickel and Dime Angels are easy to spot because of their large number of special characteristics. They stand out from the composite Angel on almost half of all comparisons. They are young, often not business owners/managers, are more frequently females and minority, have lower income and net worth, invest infrequently, and often are unhappy with the deals they've made. Entrepreneurs who deal with Nickel and Dime Angels are pretty typical, except for being seriously undercapitalized. Small-scale deals are matched with small Angel voting shares—majority control is rare. Deals are seen as riskier than average and with longer holding periods. The full market profile of Nickel and Dime Angels is shown in Profile 11-4. Only the most important differences are highlighted below.

Characteristic Differences of Nickel and Dime Angels

Nickel and Dime Angels are one of the few investor groups not dominated by business owners/managers. The odds of Nickel and Dime Angels by occupation group are:

- Business owner/manager   53%
- Sales   8%
- Science and engineering professional   7%
- Other professionals   11%
- Others   21%

They are younger than the composite Angel, with a relatively heavy concentration in the 35 to 44 age group and almost a total absence of those over 65 years old. The percentages of Nickel and Dime Angels by age are:

- Under 35 years old   12%
- 35–44   46%
- 45–54   22%
- 55–64   19%
- Over 65   2%

Female and minority Angels are found in this group more frequently than elsewhere. Females, especially, double their usual participation

---

MARKET PROFILE 11-4. Nickel and Dime Angels

ANGELS   U.S. Composite

+ • Business owner/manager is principal occupation (53%)   (69%)
  • Has personal entrepreneurial experience (79%)   (83%)
+ • 39 years old*   (47 years)
+ • White male (74%)   (84%)
  • College degree (71%)   (72%)
+ • $50,000 annual family income*   ($90,000)
+ • $150,000 net worth*   ($750,000)
+ • Friends are the primary information channel   (Friends and associates)
  • Accepts 3 of 10 investment opportunities*   (3)
+ • Rejects deals mostly due to personal knowledge   (Growth potential)
+ • Invests about every 36 months and has 1.7 firms   (18) (3.5)
     in portfolio*
+ • Satisfied with past investments (58%)   (72%)
  • Two other coinvestors   (Two)
+ • $8,500 equity invested in informal portfolio*   ($131,000)
+ • $25,000 more via loans/guarantees to portfolio firms*   ($75,000)
  • Prefers investing in service/FIRE firms (34%)   (Service/FIRE)
  • Minimum ROI target for informal portfolio (22%)*   (22%)
  • Active as a consultant, board member, or employee (77%)   (81%)
  • Does not seek voting control (82%)   (85%)
  • Wants to invest 41% more than opportunity permitted   (35%)

SUCCESSFUL ENTREPRENEURS/FIRMS

+ • $59,000 total Angel financing* (equity and loans)   ($176,700)
+ • $15,000 in equity and $44,000 more in loans/guarantees*   ($112,500) ($64,200)
  • Three private individuals supply funding*   (Three)
  • Entrepreneur is a white male, age 25–35 (71%)   (79%)
  • Zero to nine employees at time of investment (73%)   (74%)
  • Start-up or infant stage of firm growth (75%)   (69%)
  • Service firms are most frequently financed (22%)   (17% in service)
  • 50 miles or less from investor's home or office (76%)   (72%)
  • Has a comprehensive business plan (61%)   (61%)
  • Has detailed marketing and financing plans

HIGH-PROBABILITY DEAL STRUCTURE

+ • $5,000 in equity per investor*   ($37,500)
+ • $14,700 in loans/guarantees by Angel*   ($21,400)
+ • 28% voting power transferred to investor   (37%)
+ • Majority control to Angel in 16% of investments   (27%)
+ • 40% capital risk seen by Angel*   (30%)
  • 25% expected annual ROI (30% average)   (25%) (27%)
  • Common stock or partner equity instrument (77%)   (79%)
+ • Liquidation horizon of seven and a half years*   (Four years)
  • Liquidation buyback by insiders planned (47%)   (50%)
  • Investor is or becomes an employee in 40% of   (39%)
     investments

---

*Median value—half higher, half lower.   + = Differs importantly from U.S. Composite.

compared to the composite. The percentages of Angels by demographic characteristics are:

- White male　　　　　74%
- White female　　　　10%
- Minority male　　　　14%
- Minority female　　　 2%

Income, net worth, and the size of the informal portfolio are all smaller by half or more by composite standards. The percentages of Nickel and Dimers by net worth are:

- Under $300,000　　　　　54%
- $300,000–$499,999　　　13%
- $500,000–$999,999　　　21%
- $1,000,000 or more　　　13%

Entrepreneurs dealing with small-scale Angels end up seriously under-capitalized. Typically the entrepreneur receives only one-third the total risk capital of the composite firm ($59,000 and $177,000, respectively). A further difference is the top-heavy proportion of loans. In fact, loans are almost three times the size of equity invested. In other words, small-scale investors will more readily lend than invest equity capital. Nevertheless, one in three Nickel and Dime Angels makes no loans at all. Those Angels who do lend provide under $30,000 in 6 out of 10 cases. The percentages of deals by size of Angel loans/guarantees are:

- None　　　　　　　　　29%
- Under $30,000　　　　　59%
- $30,000–$59,999　　　　 8%
- $60,000–$300,000　　　　5%
- Over $300,000　　　　　 0%

The small amount of capital invested in the deal is reflected in the sharply reduced ownership share obtained by these Angels. The reduction is not proportionate to the decrease in total dollars invested, however—the Nickel and Dime Angel gets three-fourths of the typical voting share but puts up only one-third as much capital. The percentages of small deals by equity (voting) share are:

- Under 25% voting power　　52%
- 25–49%　　　　　　　　16%
- 50%　　　　　　　　　　16%
- Over 50%　　　　　　　　16%

Partially offsetting this disproportionate ownership share is the fact that Nickel and Dime Angels see informal deals as more risky than usual. The percentages of deals and the expected degree of risk of capital loss are:

- 20% or less   22%
- 21–30%   20%
- 31–40%   11%
- 41–50%   22%
- 51% or more   25%

Also partially offsetting excessive equity share is the longer-than-usual holding period. Small scale deals are not expected to mature for seven and a half years, compared to four years for the composite.

Key Points about Nickel and Dime Angels

- Nickel and Dime Angels invest less than $10,000 per deal, representing 7 percent of Angel capital but 22 percent of all Angels.

- They are young, infrequent investors with little income or wealth who see investing as more risky than others.

- They don't often get voting control, but their share of ownership is disproportionately large given the amount of money at risk.

- From the viewpoint of the firm, dealing with Nickel and Dime Angels results in serious undercapitalization and dissastisfied investors.

CORPORATE ACHIEVERS

Venture capital veterans describe an Angel who is said to be a "Corporate Achiever." These are Angels who have been partly successful in climbing the ladder of achievement in large corporations and who now want to become more entrepreneurial by investing in a small, growth firm *and* who want to occupy a key management position. In a figurative sense these Angels want to jump the large corporate ship and sign on near the top rank on a smaller vessel they think may be going somewhere more interesting. Definitively, the Corporate Achiever Angel:

- Is under 60 years old
- Seeks an employment position
- Is not a self-employed business owner or other professional

This operational definition is not a perfect match of the "war story" definition, but it is as close as possible given limited facts about Angels. This group of Angels is not very common, representing only 13 percent of Angels, or about one in eight. However, they do form a distinct Angel type.

Corporate Achievers, despite their occupational background, claim personal entrepreneurial experience more than usual! It is not clear where they got it, but they claim it. Relative to all Angels they have one of the lowest income and wealth levels. They invest less money than usual but *get majority control from the entrepreneurs in over half of their in-vestments!* Their leading reason for killing a serious investment proposal is that it doesn't match their long-term objectives. They are patient for their payoff when they do invest. As their definition suggests, they are very active in the invested firm's daily operations, especially as employees. Corporate Achievers target and invest most often in the FIRE industry. The complete set of their market characteristics and behavior is shown in Market Profile 11-5.

Characteristic Differences of Corporate Achievers

Lack of financial resources marks Corporate Achievers in their role as business Angels. They have the lowest income and net worth of any Angel group except Nickel and Dime Angels. Their annual family income is $50,000, compared to $90,000 for all Angels. They are twice as often in the under-$40,000 income class and one-third more frequently between $40,000 and $60,000 than is the composite Angel. The breakdown of Corporate Achievers by income is:

- Under $40,000   20%
- $40,000–$59,999   36%
- $60,000–$79,999   13%
- $80,000–$99,999   9%
- Over $100,000   22%

Their low income may be one of their investment motivations. Low income is also consistent with their low net worth level of $400,000, contrasted with $750,000 for all Angels. The big difference between Corporate Achievers and all Angels lies in the wealth class under $500,000, which accounts for 60 percent and 39 percent, respectively. Interestingly there is not much difference between Achievers and the Composite Angel when it comes to the percent of millionaires: 27 percent and 36 percent, respectively. The percentages of Corporate Achievers' net worth are:

- Under $300,000   31%
- $300,000–$499,999   29%
- $500,000–$1,000,000   13%
- Over $1,000,000   27%

Considering their incomes and net worth, we should not be surprised that Corporate Achievers cannot or do not put up as many dollars of equity capital as usual. Their average investment is $17,500, versus $37,500 for all Angels. The percentages of Corporate Achievers by equity dollars per deal are:

- Under $10,000   28%
- $10,000–$24,999   22%
- $25,000–$49,999   27%

MARKET PROFILE 11-5. Corporate Achievers

ANGELS   U.S. Composite

+ • Business owner/manager is principal occupation   (47%)   (69%)
  • Has personal entrepreneurial experience   (88%)   (83%)
  • 49 years old*   (47 years)
  • White male   (77%)   (84%)
  • College degree   (68%)   (72%)
+ • $50,000 annual family income*   ($90,000)
+ • $400,000 net worth*   ($750,000)
  • Friends and associates are the primary information   (Friends and associates)
    channel
  • Accepts 3 of 10 investment opportunities*   (3)
+ • Rejects deals mostly due to long-term objectives   (Growth potential)
  • Invests about every 18 months and has 3.5 firms   (18) (3.5)
    in portfolio*
  • Satisfied with past investments   (76%)   (72%)
  • Two other coinvestors*   (Two)
+ • $35,000 equity invested in informal portfolio*   ($131,000)
  • $75,000 more via loans/guarantees to portfolio firms*   ($75,000)
  • Prefers investing in FIRE firms   (43%)   (Service/FIRE)
  • Minimum ROI target for informal portfolio   (22%)*   (22%)
+ • Active as a consultant, board member, or employee
    (97%)   (81%)
+ • Does not seek voting control   (46%)   (85%)
  • Wants to invest 36% more than opportunity permitted   (35%)

SUCCESSFUL ENTREPRENEURS/FIRMS

+ • $116,700 total Angel financing* (equity and loans)   ($176,700)
+ • $52,500 in equity and $64,200 more in loans/guarantees*   ($112,500) ($64,200)
  • Three private individuals supply funding*   (Three)
  • Entrepreneur is a white male, age 25–35   (71%)   (79%)
  • Zero to nine employees at time of investment   (75%)   (74%)
  • Start-up or infant stage of firm growth   (65%)   (69%)
+ • FIRE firms are most frequently financed   (25%)   (17% in service)
  • 50 miles or less from investor's home or office   (72%)   (72%)
  • Has a comprehensive business plan   (65%)   (61%)
  • Has detailed marketing and financing plans

HIGH-PROBABILITY DEAL STRUCTURE

+ • $17,500 in equity per investor*   ($37,500)
  • $21,400 in loans/guarantees by Angel*   ($21,400)
  • 42% voting power transferred to investor   (37%)
+ • Majority control to Angel in 55% of investments   (27%)
  • 30% capital risk seen by Angel*   (30%)
  • 25% expected annual ROI   (26% average)   (25%) (27%)
+ • Common stock or partner equity instrument   (68%)   (79%)
+ • Liquidation horizon of seven and a half years   (Four years)
  • Liquidation buyback by insiders planned   (54%)   (50%)
+ • Investor is or becomes an employee in 68% of investments   (39%)

*Median value—half higher, half lower.   + = Differs importantly from U.S. Composite.

- $50,000–$99,999   7%
- $100,000–$250,000   9%
- Over $250,000   6%

What is surprising is that even with this low average dollar investment they get majority control from the entrepreneurs 55 percent of the time (27 percent for the U.S. Composite Angel)! Corporate Achievers' voting shares are:

- Under 25% voting share   18%
- 25–49%   9%
- 50%   18%
- Over 50%   55%

It is apparent the Corporate Achievers want majority control, and they do not hesitate to say so (to me, anyway).

The large proportion of Corporate Achievers who gain majority control helps explain why their leading deal killer is "doesn't match long-term objectives." The frequency of this killer is not surprising when most entrepreneurs have the same (conflicting) objective: majority ownership. The top four deal killers for Corporate Achievers are:

1. Failure to coincide with long-term objectives
2. Overpriced equity
3. Not enough time for due diligence
4. Inadequate personal knowledge about entrepreneur/key personnel

Corporate Achievers both prefer and make investments in firms in the FIRE industry. The percentage of Achievers expressing interest in the construction industry is also high in comparison to the composite. The percentages of their actual investments by industry group are:

- Natural resources/mining   2%
- Construction   15%
- Manufacturing—high-technology   6%
- Manufacturing—industrial   8%
- Manufacturing—consumer   5%
- Transportation, communication, and utilities   2%
- Wholesale trade   4%
- Retail trade   14%
- Finance/insurance/real estate   25%
- Services   18%
- Other   2%

A very unusual characteristic of Corporate Achievers is their frequent use of notes with warrants and combinations of equity instruments. By contrast, all Angels use common stock in 39 percent of their deals, notes with warrants in 9 percent, and combinations in 7 percent. The percentages of Corporate Achievers by type of equity instrument used are:

- Common stock   25%
- Convertible preferred stock   0%
- Notes with warrants   14%
- Convertible debentures   2%
- Partnership equity interest   43%
- Other and combinations   17%

Perhaps it is by combining debt and equity instruments with loans that Corporate Achievers can parlay unusually small equity investments into extraordinarily frequent majority control. The reduced use of equity dollars relative to loans when combined with notes with warrants means Corporate Achievers can often increase their original equity share by converting the notes into equity. Since majority control is an admitted objective, this use of stocks and notes with warrants may be a technique to achieve the control objective with maximum equity leverage. The control-seeking business Devils profiled earlier do not generally use this combination of equity and debt and do not starve the entrepreneur for initial equity. Corporate Achievers may use this special approach to offset their own general lack of wealth. Perhaps they ought to be renamed "Junior Corporate Raiders." That Corporate Achievers are willing to wait longer than usual to liquidate their investment must be cold comfort to many of their entrepreneurs.

Key Points about Corporate Achievers

- Corporate Achievers are a small but distinct set of Angels who are not self-employed and usually seek a key employment position along with their investment—often the entrepreneur's job, as it turns out.

- These "Angels" have little money to begin with, put up relatively little equity compared to loans, and parlay that combination into majority control in over half their deals.

- Deal rejection occurs most often because the Angel and entrepreneur have conflicting objectives, probably regarding company control.

- The control takeover technique seemingly involves the unusually frequent use of very small equity coupled with loans supported by notes with warrants or combinations of equity instruments.

- Victims are mostly small firms in the finance, insurance, and real estate industry, but construction firms are also an unusually frequent target.

KISS OF DEATH

Failure to gain financing is the entrepreneurs' Kiss of Death. Because almost any sound business proposal can find an Angel somewhere, there are no market profile characteristics that are absolutely and always fatal.

But there are some characteristics that are connected with very low odds of success. Here the focus is on these low-win market probabilities. The "most unlikely to succeed" profile elements are summarized in the following "10 Most Unwanted" list. Each characteristic on that list has less than a 1 in 10 chance of success, and some have less than 1 in 200. Chance of success is measured by how often the characteristic occurs in actual deals. This is not the best of all possible measures because it mixes investment preferences with investment opportunities. In other words, frequency of occurrence does not explain causation. It tells us only that the characteristic is not in the market's main stream. For example, few investments are made when the deal's liquidation horizon is 10 years or more. This fact does not tell us whether it is because Angels avoid such deals or because few deals take that long to ripen. Regardless of the reason, such low-win probabilities should be known in advance. The descriptions of the "most unwanted" items include mention of their high-win probability counterparts. The list is presented in no special order.

10 MOST UNWANTED LIST

No. 1: Deals in Transportation/Utilities or Natural Resources/Mining Industry

Of almost 1000 deals reported, very few involved firms in transportation/utilities or natural resources/mining. Their success probabilities (or lack of it) are 2 percent and 5 percent, respectively. Bear in mind the earlier caution that we can't say whether there were few such deals available or Angels are just not interested. The most likely deals are made in either the service and FIRE industries (17 percent each), followed by retail trade (14 percent).

No. 2: Exotic Investment Instruments

One of the key points in Chapter 3 and here in Chapter 11 is the importance of avoiding complex, multipart equity instruments or combinations, especially those that are semi-debt instruments. Specifically, the likelihood of successfully using convertible debentures, convertible preferred stock, or notes with warrants is 2 percent, 2 percent, and 9 percent, respectively. Unless circumstances demand such instruments, stay away from them. The high-win probability alternative is either simple common stock or partnership equity interest.

No. 3: Deal Liquidation Via Outsiders

Angel deals rarely make provisions to liquidate Angel equity by selling to persons outside the firm. Planned liquidation sale to an institutional type investor occurs once in 200 deals. Sale or merger with another firm and public stock offerings are also uncommon, appearing in only 7 percent of all deals. High-win "insider" approaches to exit planning focus on resale of equity to the firm (entrepreneurs) or to coinvestors.

No. 4: Non–Business Owners/Managers and Distant Investors

This caution about non–business owners/managers seems to exclude a large portion of the potential market, but in fact two out of three Angels are business owner/managers. By implication, each other occupational group is a low-win source. Even the second-most-common Angel occupation, professionals, qualifies as "unlikely" since they participate in only 1 out of 11 deals (9 percent). Be especially wary of sales occupations (0.5 percent) and science/engineering professionals (4 percent).

Angels at a distance of more than three or four hours' driving time (150 miles or more) are also unlikely candidates, participating in only 1 in 10 deals. Those within 50 miles are the best bet and make 71 percent of all deals. Better still, those within 10 miles account for 4 out of 10 deals.

No. 5: Coinvesting with Government Economic Development Agencies

For whatever reason, Angels and large organizations as coinvestors mix about as well as oil and water. The most unlikely Angel combination is with a government economic development agency, which occurs in only 3 deals per 100. Private individuals as coinvestors are the high-win probability match.

No. 6: No Comprehensive Business Plan and Large Firms

Most deal making is preceded by a comprehensive business plan. I suspect that when a deal is made and no plan is available the Angel is likely to be a family member, personal friend, or other very closely associated person. The rest of us better have a plan.

Equally unlikely is a deal when a firm has 20 or more employees. Firms this large account for only 1 in 10 deals, while their high-win counterpart is a firm with 4 employees or fewer (57 percent of all deals).

No. 7: Angels with Four or More Investments Already

Targeting Angels with four or more active informal investments in their portfolios is not a likely success tactic. Only 9 percent of the deals reported involved such an Angel. Conversely, the most likely situation is an Angel who has only one investment—and yours is next.

No. 8: Angels as Full-Time Employees

Active Angel participation in the firm is common, but very active participation as a full-time employee is not a frequent occurrence. While 17 percent of all Angels participate at one time or another at this high level, multiple investments per Angel mean that it happens in only 9 percent of the deals. Angel-employee deals are not only infrequent but also dangerous, since one in three full-time employee Angels gains control from the entrepreneur. The most frequent Angel participation is as a consultant (27 percent).

No. 9: Special Angel Types

Special types of investors like Corporate Achievers, High-Fliers, Nickel and Dimers, and Green Angels are not only low-success candidates but also bring with them numerous special disadvantages as well. The more the potential Angel resembles the U.S. Composite, the more likely you are to succeed.

No. 10: Old/Young Angels and Using Brokers

Age is one of the easiest Angel characteristics to detect. Poor success probabilities exist for finding Angels over the traditional retirement age of 65 (6 percent) and under the age of 35 (10 percent). The most promising Angel age lies between 45 and 55 years old and centers on 47. While age itself probably has little to do with informal deals, it is an indicator for many collateral characteristics that do influence chances of success. Age can be an effective preliminary screening device. Target the active investor age groups, but don't reject a good Angel candidate just because of age.

Choices regarding information channels also effectively screen out some deals. Those entrepreneurs or Angels who use investment or business brokers as a main source of information are seldom involved in successful deals, compared to the large majority of deals funneled through Angels' personal friends and associates or directly from entrepreneurs.

APPLYING PROFILES TO SPECIFIC CASES

The cautions in this chapter have highlighted some flawed Angel types and market strategies. Although the dangers are real, the warnings are one-dimensional—that is, they do not match the specifics of individual cases. This one-dimensional aspect is true whether we are viewing market "down sides" as in this chapter or the positive market opportunities of earlier chapters. The next chapter will take us one giant step closer to realism by showing how market profiles can be combined and assembled to more closely match your unique financing situation.

12

CUSTOMIZED MARKET PROFILES

Each set of Angel market circumstances is unique; consequently none of the market profiles thus far presented will exactly match your specific case. This chapter will show you how to assemble a customized profile to better fit your own investment requirements. Maximizing the probability of success requires using all relevant information available. A customized market profile (CMP) consolidates the representative experience of hundreds of thousands of real market transactions and keys them to a specific set of market facts. A CMP gives you the best available look into the future, providing a basis for rational capital search planning and revealing likely pitfalls. A CMP will help you go from analysis of your risk capital needs to successful market results, saving you time, effort, and money in the process.

There are two ways to obtain a customized profile for any specific set of risk capital needs. The first way, explained here in detail, is to assemble your own CMP from the basic profiles provided in this book. The second method is to contact the author for a computer match through the Applied Economics Group, Inc.* The assembly of a CMP from data in this book is necessarily mechanical in nature. The step-by-step guide to integrating data into a CMP is no substitute for thinking. Although the CMP is carefully produced according to specific rules, it is not magic and is not meant to be followed slavishly. The CMP you assemble is only a guide to what the market has to offer—it is not a blueprint. It is a basis for your own strategic thinking and planning, and for that there is no mechanical substitute.

In this chapter I will show the four steps required to customize a market profile. Each step is applied to examples of five hypothetical financing scenarios. The four steps are:

*The Applied Economics Group can be reached at (615) 693-2092.

224

1. Selecting relevant profiles from case parameters
2. Using the industry for a base
3. Modifying the industry base
4. Consolidating the CMP

Each of these steps will be thoroughly explained, with specific examples drawn from the following case descriptions:

Case I: Start-up manufacturing firm in Los Angeles requires $225,000 in risk capital. The entrepreneurs must retain an absolute majority control of the firm but can offer an ROI of over 40 percent. (See Custom Market Profile 12-1.)

Case II: Established retail firm in New York needs $60,000 new equity financing to open an additional location. The firm will allow any one Angel up to 33 percent control. Anticipated ROI is 12 percent. (See Custom Market Profile 12-2.)

Case III: Young service industry company in Houston is expanding faster than retained earnings can finance. The firm requires $500,000 risk capital with a solid ROI potential of 19 percent. The entrepreneur will sell up to 50 percent of the stock if necessary. (See Custom Market Profile 12-3.)

Case IV: Infant firm in the finance, insurance, and real estate industry in Atlanta is searching for investors for a total of $750,000 in risk capital. Angels will be allowed up to 25 percent control each, and equity is priced to yield 35 percent. (See Custom Market Profile 12-4.)

Case V: Young construction firm in Chicago wants to develop a major site and needs $100,000 external risk capital. Projected ROI is 29 percent, and the entrepreneurs insist on retaining 70 percent majority control. (See Custom Market Profile 12-5.)

CASE I: LOS ANGELES MANUFACTURING FIRM

The case of the Los Angeles manufacturing firm will be our model as we work through each of the steps needed to produce a CMP. The Case I CMP is shown in Profile 12-1. Case I is a start-up manufacturing firm in Los Angeles needing $225,000 with a maximum ROI of over 40 percent and Angels' minority share.

Step 1: Selecting Relevant Profiles from Case Parameters

We begin by taking known facts to guide our selection of additional relevant information. The facts that we take as "known" include the following from the description of the L.A. manufacturing start-up:

CUSTOM MARKET PROFILE 12-1.
Los Angeles Manufacturing Firm (Case I)

TARGET ANGELS	Column 1— Industry Profile	Column 2— Modifier Profile	Column 3— Custom Profile
• Business owner/manager is principal occupation	76%	72%	74%
• Has entrepreneurial experience	81%	78%	80%
• Angel age	49 years	49 years	49 years
• White male	88%	85%	87%
• College degree	79%	73%	76%
• Angel annual income	$90,000	$70,000	$80,000
• Angel net worth	$750,000	$750,000	$750,000
• Primary information channel	Friends and associates	Friends and associates	Friends and associates
• Acceptance rate	30%	30%	30%
• Main deal rejection reason	Growth potential	Growth potential	Growth potential
• Investment frequency	18 months	36 months	27 months
• Satisfied with investments	68%	69%	68%
• Number of other coinvestors	Three	Three	Three
• Zero to nine employees of firm at investment time	70%	71%	70%
• Start-up or infant growth stage	62%	72%	67%
• Active as a consultant, board member, or employee	85%	70%	78%
• Does not seek control	88%	86%	87%
• Wants to invest more than opportunity permitted	38%	34%	36%

TARGET DEAL

• Number of Angels needed to complete funding	Four	Four	Four
• Equity dollars per investor	$37,500	$37,500	$37,500
• Dollars of loans/guarantees by Angel	$21,400	$21,400	$21,400
• Voting power transferred to investor	27%	30%	28%
• Majority control to Angel (% of investments)	21%	24%	22%
• Capital risk seen by Angel (% failure)	30%	30%	30%
• Expected annual ROI	25%	26%	25%
• Common stock or partnership equity instrument used	80%	82%	81%
• Years to liquidation	7.5	4	6
• Liquidation buyback by insiders planned	35%	47%	41%
• Investor is or becomes an employee (% of investments)	35%	33%	34%

CMP Foundations	*Case Parameters*
• Industry	Manufacturing (all)
• Location	Los Angeles
• Growth stage	Start-up
• Likely number of Angels needed	Four
• Dollars needed per Angel	$56,000
• Voting share maximum per Angel	12–13%
• ROI class	40% or more

Where do the case parameters come from? Some are obvious from the case description: industry, growth stage, location, and total amount of risk capital needed. Other facts must be estimated. Here's how.

Likely Number of Investors.   The number of Angels needed is assumed to be the composite number of coinvestors typical of Case I's industry, all manufacturing firms. This number was found in Market Profile 9-1 in Chapter 9.

Dollars Needed per Angel.   The $56,000 amount needed per Angel is simply the total risk capital needed by the firm divided by the likely number of Angels ($225,000 divided by 4 equals $56,000).

Voting Share Maximum per Angel.   The entrepreneur says he must retain an absolute majority control (51 percent or more), so the maximum voting share he can sell is 49 percent. We assume it is divided equally among the likely four Angels, which comes out to be 12 to 13 percent each.

ROI Class.   The ROI class for the firm is more complicated. Estimating it requires three pieces of information: (1) average annual profit (including capital gains) during the Angel's holding period (P), (2) voting control or equity share percent per Angel (S), and (3) Angel's total equity commitment (D). These three factors relate to each other in the following formula:

$$ROI = \frac{P \times S}{D}$$

or more specifically for the case at hand,

$$ROI = 40\% = \frac{\$125,000 \times .12}{\$37,500}$$

The average annual profit comes from the growth projections contained in the firm's comprehensive business plans over the expected Angel holding period of seven and a half years (using the manufacturing industry's composite in Market Profile 9-1). Equity share per Angel was taken from the preceding section. The equity price must be your own estimate or the composite industry equity per deal as used here.

Relevant Market Profiles.   Now that the case parameters have been determined, select the corresponding market profiles presented in chapters 1 through 11. From these profiles you can obtain the facts necessary to fill in columns 1 and 2 on a blank CMP (Appendix). After these two columns are completed, we can then assemble Column 3, which is, in fact, the CMP modified to your specific case requirements.

Looking ahead to where this section is leading for the Los Angeles manufacturing case, the table below shows the case parameters and the corresponding relevant chapter profiles:

Case Items	Parameters	Relevant Chapter Profiles
Industry	Manufacturing	9–1
Location	Los Angeles	10–2
Growth stage	Start-up	8–1
Dollars per Angel	$56,000	9–1
Voting share max. per Angel	12%	6–3 (Low)
ROI class	Over 40%	6–4 (High)

The identification of relevant market profiles is easy in the case of industry, location, and growth stage, but dollars and equity share per Angel and ROI class may need further explanation.

Equity Dollars Needed per Angel.   Continuing to use four as the typical number of Angels and assuming that the total risk capital will be more or less equally contributed by each Angel, any one Angel on average is required to invest a total of $56,000. All of this is not equity dollars, however. The share of total risk capital represented by equity dollars is 64 percent for all industries except FIRE, where the equity share is 30 percent. Thus the expected amount of equity dollars per Angel is $35,800 (or $56,000 × .64).

The profile corresponding to the above equity size per Angel ($35,800) is defined in Chapter 6 as Mid-Size Angels. Since they resemble the U.S. Composite, we can use the composite column in Market Profile 9-1 for convenience. If the equity per Angel is below $25,000, then Market Profile 6-1 (Low) would be correctly selected. If it falls below $10,000, Profile 11-4 for Nickel and Dime Angels would be the correct one. Similar steps are taken in selecting the correct market profiles for voting control and ROI.

In this case example the voting control per Angel averages 12 to 13%. Market Profile 6-3 in Chapter 6 shows the characteristics for both high (larger than 50 percent) and low (less than 25 percent) voting control for Angels. The ''Low'' column is correctly used in this case. If voting control had been between 25 and 50 percent, then the U.S. Composite would be used since it represents this voting control class, as stated in Chapter 6. Selection of the proper ROI class (also from Chapter 6) is done according to the same rules for selecting the correct equity (voting) share profile.

Once all six relevant market profiles have been identified, it is time to fill in Column 1 on a blank CMP.

Step 2: The Industry Profile

The first item is to establish the basic industry profile in Column 1. This is easily accomplished by using the relevant industry profile (Manufacturing—All) from Chapter 9 and filling in the line items for that industry in our customized profile.

Step 3: Creating the Modifier Profile

The "modifier profile," Column 2 of CMP 12-1, represents the consolidated characteristics contained in the relevant market profiles for location, growth stage, equity size, equity share level, and ROI class. The consolidation of the line items from each profile into a single line item entry for the modifier profile follows definite rules. These rules vary depending on whether the line item is a numerical entry (e.g., 82%) or a qualitative item such as "friends and associates."

Numerical Consolidation Rule.   When numbers differ, find the median and use it for Column 2. For example, when consolidating Angel income levels for entry in Column 2, we see the following five income levels reported:

Case Parameters	Market Profile No.	Angel Income
Los Angeles	10-2	$150,000
Start-up	8-1	$ 70,000
Equity dollars	9-1	$ 70,000
ROI class	6-4 (High)	$ 90,000
Equity share class	6-3 (Low)	$ 70,000

The median value for Angel income is the number that exactly divides all rank-ordered incomes into two equal-size groups. First, income is ranked (low to high or reverse) to get the following:

$ 70,000
$ 70,000
$ 70,000 ◄— Median
$ 90,000
$150,000

The median is $70,000 since half the number of reported incomes are
lower and half are higher. Consequently, $70,000 is entered in Column 2
of CMP 12-1 for Angel income. Take another example, expected annual
ROI. The rank order (from high to low) of the five ROI values from the
relevant market profiles is:

$$
\begin{array}{l}
28\% \\
28\% \\
26\% \leftarrow \text{Median} \\
26\% \\
16\%
\end{array}
$$

The median is again the middle or third value in rank order, or 26 percent. This becomes the expected ROI entry in Column 2 of CMP 12-1.

You will not always have a convenient (odd-numbered) set of five
numbers to use for finding the median value, especially if additional profiles can be used. Assume we have another ROI value (29 percent) to add
to the above series. When we add it in, the new rank order of ROI values
looks like this:

$$
\begin{array}{l}
29\% \\
28\% \\
28\% \\
26\% \leftarrow \text{Median} \\
26\% \\
16\%
\end{array}
$$

The median now falls between the third and fourth ranked values—that
is, between 28 percent and 26 percent. The median value is 27 percent
because it divides the range of ROI values into two equal groups of three
values each. In the above example, if the median had fallen between two
numbers without a clear "middle," such as between 29 percent and
26 percent, then we would choose either 27 percent or 28 percent as the
median (technically, it's 27.5 percent). The median for any even-numbered
set of values can be found with this method.

Consolidation of Nonnumerical Characteristics.   Some market profile
characteristics are qualitative or nonnumerical including primary information channel, rejection reason, and others. To consolidate these entries from the relevant chapter profiles select the mode—the entry that
appears *most frequently*. Take, for example, the main deal rejection
reason. The responses from the five relevant profiles are:

Case Parameters	Market Profile No.	Rejection Reason
Los Angeles	10-2	Lack of talent
Start-up	8-1	Personal knowledge
Equity dollars	9-1	Growth potential
ROI class	6-4 (High)	Growth potential
Equity share class	6-3 (Low)	Growth potential

The mode, or most frequent reason, is clear: inadequate growth potential. This becomes the Column 2 entry in CMP 12-1.

Fall-Back Rule.   If by chance all five responses had been different (no mode existed), then we would use the industry line item entry from Column 1, since it remains the single best description. In fact, this "fall back to industry profile" rule can be used to resolve any conflict or ambiguity. In other words, when in doubt, repeat the Column 1 entry in Column 2. By following this rule and the others explained above, all of Column 2 can be filled in. The results are shown in CMP 12-1.

Additional Market Facts.   Sometimes a specific financing case will have other known facts that you want to incorporate into the customized profile. These can and should be added to the case parameters in exactly the same way as the others, if a relevant market profile is available. For example, assume that you have already had discussions with a potential Angel who is a practicing lawyer. This useful fact can be incorporated by consolidating Market Profile 4-5 (Dr. Kildare) into the five others to determine the Column 2 entries. Use any and all information you can. Don't stop with just the five foundation parameters if others are also known and relevant. At this point the industry profile and modifier profiles are completed for Case I.

Step 4: Assemble the Custom Profile

The final customized profile is contained in Column 3 of Custom Market Profile 12-1. It is derived by taking Column 1 and modifying it by Column 2. The modification follows the numerical (median) and nonnumerical (mode) rules previously explained. For example, in Profile 12-1, Angel income is $90,000 in Column 1 and $70,000 in Column 2. The correct entry for Column 3 is exactly halfway between the two, or $80,000. When nonnumerical column entries differ, fall back on the industry entry (Column 1) as the best representative. Using these rules, Column 3 is built out of Column 1, modified as necessary by Column 2.

The result in this case is that Column 3 is a custom market profile for a manufacturing firm that has been tailored to reflect important investment factors such as location in Los Angeles, its start-up growth stage, its need for $225,000 in total risk capital, retention of majority control, priced to offer an annual ROI over 40 percent.

CASE II: NEW YORK RETAILING
Step 1: Case Parameters and Relevant Profiles

Case II is an established retail firm in New York that needs $60,000 risk capital. Up to 33 percent control per Angel can be given, and anticipated ROI is 12 percent. Case parameters are determined in this example in the same way as before. Industry, location, and growth stage are self-evident, but equity dollars, equity share, and ROI need to be worked out. The firm wants a total of $60,000 in risk capital. In retailing the equity dollar percentage of total risk capital is 64 percent. Consequently this example firm can anticipate about $38,400 in equity and the balance ($21,600) in loans/guarantees. The retailing industry (Market Profile 9-1) typically has three Angels per firm, so the expected equity dollar estimate per Angel is $12,800 ($38,400 divided by 3). This equity-size Angel is profiled in Chapter 6 as a "Low" or "not so deep pockets" Angel in Market Profile 6-1. Equity share per Angel is the maximum total the firm is willing to consider selling, which is given as 33 percent. We know from Chapter 6 that Angels who get equity share in the 25% to 49% range have similar characteristics to the U.S. Composite. The U.S. Composite elements are given in almost all the market profiles; Market Profile 9-1 is a convenient one that shows both the composite and the industry characteristics. Lastly, the Angels' ROI of 12 percent is classed as "Low" in Profile 6-4. The case parameters and the relevant market profiles are summarized below:

Case Parameters		Relevant Chapter Profiles
Industry	Retail	9-1
Location	New York	10-1
Growth stage	Established	8-3
Dollars per Angel	$12,800	6-1 (Low)
Equity (voting) share per Angel	25–49%	9-1 (Composite)
ROI class	12%	6-4 (Low)

Step 2: The Industry Base Profile

Using the same method we used for the Los Angeles manufacturing firm, we fill out Column 1 of Custom Market Profile 12-2 from the retail industry profile in Market Profile 9-1.

Step 3: Creating the Modifier Profile

Following the rules explained in Case I, we assemble the entries for Column 2 by consolidating the line items from each of the relevant profiles. (Special attention is directed to the "Fall-Back Rule" to resolve any uncertainties, ties, or ambiguities.) Results of consolidating the five market profiles are entered in the Modifier Profile column of CMP 12-2. It would be a useful exercise to replicate the results yourself to reinforce your familiarity with the use of the consolidation rules.

Step 4: Assembling the Custom Profile

Once Columns 1 and 2 are complete it is a short step to modify them to produce Column 3 using the procedure detailed for Case I. With the

---

CUSTOM MARKET PROFILE 12-2.
New York Retailing Firm (Case II)

TARGET ANGELS	Column 1— Industry Profile	Column 2— Modifier Profile	Column 3— Custom Profile
• Business owner/manager is principal occupation	69%	69%	69%
• Has entrepreneurial experience	83%	82%	83%
• Angel age	49 years	49 years	49 years
• White male	87%	87%	87%
• College degree	59%	69%	64%
• Angel annual income	$70,000	$90,000	$80,000
• Angel net worth	$750,000	$750,000	$750,000
• Primary information channel	Friends and associates	Friends and associates	Friends and associates
• Acceptance rate	30%	30%	30%
• Main deal rejection reason	Growth potential	Growth potential	Growth potential
• Investment frequency	18 months	18 months	18 months
• Satisfied with investments	71%	75%	73%
• Number of other coinvestors	Two	Two	Two
• Zero to nine employees of firm at investment time	81%	76%	79%
• Start-up or infant growth stage	74%	77%	75%
• Active as a consultant, board member, or employee	88%	83%	86%
• Does not seek control	81%	85%	83%
• Wants to invest more than opportunity permitted	33%	35%	34%

TARGET DEAL

• Number of Angels needed to complete funding	Three	Three	Three
• Equity dollars per investor	$37,500	$37,500	$37,500
• Dollars of loans/guarantees by Angel	$21,400	$21,400	$21,400
• Voting power transferred to investor	37%	34%	36%
• Majority control to Angel (% of investments)	35%	27%	31%
• Capital risk seen by Angel (% failure)	30%	30%	30%
• Expected annual ROI	23%	24%	23%
• Common stock or partnership equity instrument used	82%	79%	81%
• Years to liquidation	Four	Four	Four
• Liquidation buyback by insiders planned	46%	46%	46%
• Investor is or becomes an employee (% of investments)	43%	40%	42%

completion of Column 3 a custom market profile now exists that better reflects the Angel capital market for the example retail firm modified by its New York location, established growth status, total $60,000 risk capital need, maximum ownership share for sale, and the equity pricing reflected in the 12 percent ROI.

CASE III: HOUSTON AREA SERVICE INDUSTRY FIRM

Step 1: Case Parameters and Relevant Profiles

Case III involves a young service company in Houston, Texas that requires $500,000 risk capital and will sell up to 50 percent equity share for an ROI of 19 percent. Case parameters are determined in this example in the same way as before. Industry, location, and growth stage are self-evident, but equity dollars, ownership share, and ROI require calculation. The firm needs a total of $500,000 in risk capital. Using the service industry equity dollar percentage, it can be calculated that this example firm can anticipate about $320,000 in equity and the balance ($180,000) in loans/guarantees. The industry typically has three Angels per firm, so the expected equity dollar estimate per Angel is $107,000 ($320,000 divided by 3). This equity-size Angel is profiled in Chapter 6 as a "High" or "Deep Pockets" Angel in Market Profile 6-1. Equity share per Angel is the maximum total the firm is willing to consider selling, which is stated in the case description as up to 50 percent and which divided among three Angels comes to 17 percent each. Chapter 6 describes Angels with equity share under 25 percent as "Low" in Market Profile 6-3. Finally, Angels within the ROI class of 13% to 39% are the same as the U.S. Composite and we use the U.S. Composite from the industry Market Profile 9-1 for convenience. The case parameters and related Market Profiles are summarized below:

Case Parameters		Relevant Market Profiles
Industry	Service	9-1
Location	Houston	10-2
Growth stage	Young	8-2
Dollars per Angel	$107,000	6-1 (High)
Equity (voting) share per Angel	17%	6-3 (Low)
ROI class	19%	9-1 (Composite)

Step 2: The Industry Base Profile

Proceeding as before, we fill out Column 1 of Custom Market Profile 12-3 from the service industry profile given in Market Profile 9-1.

CUSTOM MARKET PROFILE 12-3. Houston Service Firm (Case III)

TARGET ANGELS	Column 1— Industry Profile	Column 2— Modifier Profile	Column 3— Custom Profile
• Business owner/manager is principal occupation	74%	72%	73%
• Has entrepreneurial experience	81%	83%	82%
• Angel age	49 years	49 years	49 years
• White male	75%	84%	79%
• College degree	76%	71%	74%
• Angel annual income	$90,000	$90,000	$90,000
• Angel net worth	$750,000	$750,000	$750,000
• Primary information channel	Friends and associates	Friends and associates	Friends and associates
• Acceptance rate	30%	30%	30%
• Main deal rejection reason	Talent, personal knowledge	Growth potential	Talent, personal knowledge
• Investment frequency	18 months	18 months	18 months
• Satisfied with investments	74%	75%	74%
• Number of other coinvestors	Two	Three	Two
• Zero to nine employees of firm at investment time	78%	70%	74%
• Start-up or infant growth stage	68%	67%	68%
• Active as a consultant, board member, or employee	82%	81%	82%
• Does not seek control	86%	85%	86%
• Wants to invest more than opportunity permitted	38%	31%	35%

TARGET DEAL

• Number of Angels needed to complete funding	Three	Four	Three
• Equity dollars per investor	$37,500	$37,500	$37,500
• Dollars of loans/guarantees by Angel	$21,400	$21,400	$21,400
• Voting power transferred to investor	32%	32%	32%
• Majority control to Angel (% of investments)	31%	30%	31%
• Capital risk seen by Angel (% failure)	30%	30%	30%
• Expected annual ROI	27%	29%	28%
• Common stock or partnership equity instrument used	76%	76%	76%
• Years to liquidation	Four	Four	Four
• Liquidation buyback by insiders planned	52%	50%	51%
• Investor is or becomes an employee (% of investments)	40%	36%	38%

Step 3: Creating the Modifier Profile

Following the rules explained in Case I, we assemble the entries for Column 2 by consolidating the line items on each relevant profile. Resolve any uncertainties, ties, or ambiguities with the Fall-Back Rule. This consolidation of the five Market Profiles is shown in the Modifier Profile column of CMP 12-3.

Step 4: Assembling the Custom Profile

Once columns 1 and 2 are filled in, the next step is to modify them to produce Column 3, by following the consolidation rules as we did for the previous two examples. The custom market profile shown in Column 3 now reflects the Angel market for service industry firms modified by its Houston location, young growth stage, total risk capital needed, maximum control for sale, and ROI class reflecting equity pricing.

CASE IV: ATLANTA FIRM IN THE FIRE INDUSTRY

Step 1: Case Parameters and Relevant Profiles

Case IV is an infant firm in the FIRE industry in Atlanta that needs $750,000 risk capital and will sell up to 20 percent of equity per Angel priced to yield 35 percent ROI. Case parameters are determined in this example just as before. The firm needs a total of $750,000 in risk capital. In FIRE industry firms the equity dollar percentage of total risk capital is a low 0.30. This is calculated from the industry composite total risk capital (Market Profile 9-1):

$$\frac{\text{Equity}}{\text{Total Risk Capital}} = \frac{\text{Equity per Angel}}{\text{Loans \& Equity per Angel}}$$

or

$$\frac{\$37,500}{\$86,000 + \$37,500} = .30$$

Consequently this firm can anticipate about $228,000 in Angel equity and the balance ($522,000) in Angel loans/guarantees. The industry typically has three Angels per firm, so the expected equity dollar estimate per Angel is $76,000 ($228,000 divided by 3). This equity-size Angel is profiled in Chapter 6 as a "medium-size" Angel and is equal to the U.S. Composite, so we use Market Profile 9-1 (U.S. Composite column) for convenience. Equity share per Angel is the maximum total the firm is willing to consider selling, which is stated in the case description as up to 20 percent. Angels with equity share usually under 25 percent are categorized as "Low," and their characteristics are given in Market Profile 6-3.

Finally, Angels within the ROI class of 13% to 39% are the same as the U.S. Composite, whose profile we take from Market Profile 9-1. Thus the foundation parameters and related market profiles are:

Case Parameters		Relevant Market Profiles
Industry	FIRE	9-1
Location	Atlanta	10-4
Growth stage	Infant	8-1
Dollars per Angel	$75,000	9-1 (Composite)
Equity (voting)	20%	6-3 (Low)
share per Angel		
ROI class	30%	9-1 (Composite)

Step 2: The Industry Base Profile

Proceeding as before, we fill out Column 1 of CMP 12-4 directly from the FIRE industry column of Market Profile 9-1.

Step 3: Creating the Modifier Profile

Following the Numerical Consolidation Rule and the Fall-Back Rule, we assemble the entries for Column 2, "averaging" the line items from the relevant market profiles listed above. The results of this consolidation become the Modifier Profile of this customized profile.

Step 4: Assembling the Custom Profile

The custom market profile for Case IV is produced by consolidating Columns 1 and 2 on CMP 12-4, following the standard rules. The results are entered in Column 3. The CMP reflects the Angel market for FIRE industry firms modified by an Atlanta location, infant growth stage, $750,000 risk capital need, 20 percent per Angel maximum equity sale, and 30 percent projected ROI.

CASE V: CHICAGO CONSTRUCTION FIRM

Step 1: Case Parameters and Relevant Profiles

Case V is a young construction firm in Chicago that needs $100,000 risk capital. Equity share sold must not exceed 30 percent and is priced to produce a 29 percent ROI. Case parameters are determined in this example as before. The firm needs $100,000 in risk capital. In the construction industry the equity dollar proportion of total risk capital is 64 percent. Thus this firm can expect about $64,000 in equity and the balance ($36,000) in loans/guarantees. The industry typically has three Angels per firm, so the expected equity dollar range per Angel is $21,000 ($64,000 divided by 3). This equity size is characteristic of a "not so

CUSTOM MARKET PROFILE 12-4.
Atlanta FIRE Firm (Case IV)

TARGET ANGELS	Column 1— Industry Profile	Column 2— Modifier Profile	Column 3— Custom Profile
• Business owner/manager is principal occupation	60%	72%	66%
• Has entrepreneurial experience	91%	83%	87%
• Angel age	49 years	49 years	49 years
• White male	89%	84%	87%
• College degree	73%	73%	73%
• Angel annual income	$90,000	$70,000	$80,000
• Angel net worth	$750,000	$750,000	$750,000
• Primary information channel	Friends and associates	Friends and associates	Friends and associates
• Acceptance rate	30%	30%	30%
• Main deal rejection reason	Personal knowledge	Growth potential	Personal knowledge
• Investment frequency	18 months	18 months	18 months
• Satisfied with investments	78%	69%	74%
• Number of other coinvestors	Two	Two	Two
• Zero to nine employees of firm at investment time	71%	78%	74%
• Start-up or infant growth stage	73%	69%	71%
• Active as a consultant, board member, or employee	80%	84%	82%
• Does not seek control	80%	85%	82%
• Wants to invest more than opportunity permitted	31%	34%	32%

TARGET DEAL

• Number of Angels needed to complete funding	Three	Three	Three
• Equity dollars per investor	$37,500	$37,500	$37,500
• Dollars of loans/guarantees by Angel	$86,000	$14,700	$50,000
• Voting power transferred to investor	34%	34%	34%
• Majority control to Angel (% of investments)	27%	27%	27%
• Capital risk seen by Angel (% failure)	30%	30%	30%
• Expected annual ROI	27%	27%	27%
• Common stock or partnership equity instrument used	86%	79%	83%
• Years to liquidation	Four	Four	Four
• Liquidation buyback by insiders planned	42%	50%	46%
• Investor is or becomes an employee (% of investments)	36%	39%	37%

deep pockets'' Angel, profiled in Market Profile 6-1. Equity share per Angel is the maximum total the firm is willing to consider selling, which in this case is up to 30 percent, or a maximum of about 10 percent each. Angels with equity share under 25 percent are categorized as "Low" and profiled in Market Profile 6-3. Lastly, Angels within the ROI class of 13 percent to 39 percent are the same as the U.S. Composite; we will use the U.S. Composite column from Market Profile 9-1 for convenience. The case parameters and relevant market profiles are summarized below:

Case Parameters		Relevant Market Profiles
Industry	Construction	9-1
Location	Chicago	10-1
Growth stage	Young	8-2
Dollars per Angel	$21,000	6-1 (Low)
Equity (voting)	10%	6-3 (Low)
share per Angel		
ROI class	29%	9-1 (Composite)

Step 2: The Industry Base Profile

Column 1 of Custom Market Profile 12-5 is filled in using the characteristics of the construction industry column in Market Profile 9-1.

Step 3: Creating the Modifier Profile

Next we assemble the entries for Column 2 by consolidating the line items from each of the relevant profiles. Consolidate using median and modal values and the Fall-Back Rule to resolve any uncertainties. Results are entered as the Modifier Profile in Column 2.

Step 4: Assembling the Custom Profile

Once columns 1 and 2 are complete, it is an easy step to consolidate them to produce Column 3. Now we have a custom market profile that reflects the Angel market for construction industry firms modified by a Chicago location, young growth stage, $100,000 risk capital need, 10 percent per Angel maximum equity share, and sale priced to yield 29 percent ROI.

SUMMARY OF KEY POINTS

A custom market profile (CMP) is a tailor-made market profile that more closely fits the facts of any given financing situation than any of the generic profiles. The assembly of a CMP brings the collective experience of thousands of actual market deals to bear on a particular case. You can assemble your own customized profile and use it as a key tool for

CUSTOM MARKET PROFILE 12-5.
Chicago Construction Firm (Case V)

TARGET ANGELS	Column 1— Industry Profile	Column 2— Modifier Profile	Column 3— Custom Profile
• Business owner/manager is principal occupation	61%	70%	65%
• Has entrepreneurial experience	91%	78%	85%
• Angel age	39 years	47 years	43 years
• White male	84%	84%	84%
• College degree	72%	72%	72%
• Angel annual income	$70,000	$90,000	$80,000
• Angel net worth	$750,000	$750,000	$750,000
• Primary information channel*	Friends	Friends and associates	Friends
• Acceptance rate	30%	30%	30%
• Main deal rejection reason	Insufficient time	Growth potential	Insufficient time
• Investment frequency	18 months	18 months	18 months
• Satisfied with investments	76%	72%	74%
• Number of other coinvestors	Two	Three	Two
• Zero to nine employees of firm at investment time	88%	70%	79%
• Start-up or infant growth stage	80%	71%	76%
• Active as a consultant, board member, or employee	87%	81%	84%
• Does not seek control	78%	90%	84%
• Wants to invest more than opportunity permitted	30%	34%	32%

TARGET DEAL

• Number of Angels needed to complete funding	Three	Four	Three
• Equity dollars per investor	$37,500	$37,500	$37,500
• Dollars of loans/guarantees by Angel	$21,400	$15,000	$18,000
• Voting power transferred to investor	39%	32%	36%
• Majority control to Angel (% of investments)	35%	27%	31%
• Capital risk seen by Angel (% failure)	30%	30%	30%
• Expected annual ROI	34%	28%	31%
• Common stock or partnership equity instrument used	87%	76%	82%
• Years to liquidation	Four	Four	Four
• Liquidation buyback by insiders planned	57%	50%	54%
• Investor is or becomes an employee (% of investments)	38%	40%	39%

capital planning that allows a better match between risk capital needs and results, producing savings of time and money.

The foundation of the CMP is the industry profile, which represents the single best description of market characteristics. The foundation is modified (as necessary) by facts related to geographic location, size of risk capital investment, the firm's stage of growth, the maximum equity share at stake, and equity pricing as reflected in the projected ROI. Numerically clear and conservative consolidation procedures are employed to customize the basic industry profile. That means the CMP is sensitive only to large and important market influences.

Blank CMP forms are provided in the Appendix for your use. A custom market profile is not magic. It is only a mechanically produced tool to help you prepare better risk capital investment plans. It is not a substitute for on-the-spot knowledge, experience, or thinking.

At the beginning of the book I said that finding Angel capital is not easy. Until now the search was a blind, hit-or-miss effort with only your own experience to guide you. Throughout the ensuing pages I have shared with you the details of what other entrepreneurs and investors have learned the hard way from their own market experiences. The accumulation of experience presented in these pages and tailored to your specific business circumstances is now embodied in your custom market profile. This unique planning device is a "state-of-the-art" tool compared to what entrepreneurs and investors had before. You are no longer alone, nor must you learn the hard way anymore.

Your custom market profile arms you with the information you need for guidance down the most likely avenues while avoiding pitfalls and dead ends. Compare your capital financing plans against the experience of others in cases similar to your own. Use the custom market profile to plan or revise your strategy and tactics in accord with what is now known to work. The experience of hundreds of representative investors and entrepreneurs gives you solid information about how Angels think and act, what they want from entrepreneurs, and what they have to offer in return. Use your information to foresee and plan your own success in the informal risk capital market. Advance knowledge of how successful deals are structured aids in bargaining and puts you at an advantage by being able to recognize the difference between realistic and foolish proposals.

Buttressed by the successful experience of others as you now are, you still face a do-it-yourself search, but you are no longer blind, because now the most important things you don't know are the names and telephone numbers—that much remains for you to do.

GLOSSARY

Angel. (Also known as business Angel.) See Informal Investors.

Balkanized. A whole divided into parts that are small, isolated, and noninteracting.

Business Angel. See Informal Investors.

CMP (Custom Market Profile). Profile tailored to specific case parameters such as industry, location, stage of growth, equity dollar amount, ROI, and equity share.

Common stock. The ordinary ownership shares in a corporation.

Convertible debentures. Unsecured bonds that can be exchanged for ownership shares (stock) in the firm that issued the bonds. Exchange is usually at the bondholder's option.

Convertible preferred stock. Ownership shares that enjoy special privileges usually regarding dividend payments and that can be exchanged for common stock usually at the holder's option.

Corporate Achievers. A term used here for Angels who have been successful in a large corporate organization but now want to be more entrepreneurial in a smaller firm and in a top management role. They try to achieve this objective by becoming Angels.

Cousin Randy. A term used here to refer to investors who limit their investments to businesses owned by members of their own family.

Daddy Warbucks. A cartoon character symbolizing wealthy, benevolent businessmen. A term used here to describe the investment characteristics of the minority of Angels who are millionaires (Angels with a personal net worth of $1,000,000 or more).

Dead ends. See Kiss of Death.

Deal breakers. See Kiss of Death.

Debt instrument. A note, bill, bond, or other document that specifies the existence and details of a creditor–debtor relationship between its issuer (debtor) and its holder (creditor).

Deep pockets. A term used here to refer to any Angel who has made at least one investment of $100,000 or more in equity dollars.

De gustibus. . . . De gustibus non est disputandum, the Latin phrase that translates as "There is no accounting for taste."

Diversity. The frequency distribution ("odds") of actual market experience reported by Angels and grouped into convenient classes for summarization.

Due diligence. The fact-finding research process that knowledgeable investors perform prior to investment.

Entrepreneur. The principal owner of a new or growing small business. The entrepreneur is the principal bearer of the risks that often result from introducing change or innovation. Anyone who controls the direction and operation of a business.

Equity. Money or property investment in exchange for partial ownership in a business. The investor's financial return comes from dividend payments and from growth in the net worth of a business.

Established firm. Profitable firms that are growing too fast to finance their growth from retained earnings.

External risk capital. Ownership dollars invested by someone outside the current circle of investors/owners and their immediate families.

Fall-back rule. Rule used to resolve ties, uncertainties, and ambiguities arising from assembly of a CMP. Rule says resolve by using the "industry" profile entry.

Godfather. A term used here to describe the type of Angels who have been successful businesspeople but are now semiretired and want to stay active in business by being consultants or mentors to young entrepreneurs. They do so by becoming Angels.

Green Angels. A term used to describe Angels who have no personal entrepreneurial experience.

Growth stages. Four stages of a growing firm's life cycle or progress. They are: start-up, infant, young, and established. See each term for detailed definitions.

High-Fliers. Angels who invest only when the expected rate of return (ROI) at investment time is 40 percent or more per year.

High-Tech Angel. A term used here to describe Angels who invest only in firms manufacturing high-technology products.

Holding period. Length of time (measured in years) that an Angel expects to hold or own an informal investment. Also called liquidation horizon.

Hot button. The nonmonetary payoff that motivates some Angels. Examples include: humanitarian goals; personal recognition; a vested interest in a product, market, or entrepreneur; and satisfaction of aiding community's job and income growth, mentoring young entrepreneurs, or achieving success.

Impatient Angel. A term used here to describe an Angel who accepts an investment proposal only if it promises a quick exit or liquidation horizon of three years or less.

Infant firms.   Firms that may be losing money but have the potential for attractive profits in one to three years. Often they are about a year old.

Informal investors.   Any persons providing risk capital directly to a business. They do not invest through professionally managed venture capital funds, equity-oriented Small Business Investment Companies (SBICs), other institutional investors, or the public stock markets. Also known as business Angels, Angels.

Informal risk capital.   The equity and loan dollars invested by informal investors. No paid middlemen are involved in the capital investment process. Equity and debt capital for new and growing small firms. Typically these investments (1) have higher risk than investments in large, established firms, (2) have potential returns in proportion to the higher risks, and (3) have no ready market for resale.

Intermediary.   As used here the term refers to someone who acts as a paid go-between, or broker, in an investment transaction. Their brokerage activities are called intermediation.

Investment instrument.   The documentation signifying and detailing an investor's ownership status in the firm.

Investor.   As used here the term means an informal investor unless specifically defined otherwise.

Dr. Kildare.   A term used here to describe Angels who are professionally trained people such as physicians, lawyers, CPAs, and others. Excludes those trained in science or engineering.

Kiss of Death.   A collective term that refers to very low-probability (less than 10 percent likelihood) characteristics of Angels, entrepreneurs, or deals. Also known as dead ends and deal breakers.

Liquidation.   Sale or conversion of the value of an asset into monetary form.

Liquidation horizon.   Also known as "cash-out." See Holding period.

Loans/Guarantees.   A term used here to mean personal loans from Angels to the firms they have invested in or loans to those firms by third-party lenders whose repayment is personally guaranteed by the Angels.

Lone Wolf.   A term used here for an Angel who is unwilling to invest with any coinvestors.

Mean value.   The ordinary or common average. It is the sum of all numbers in a group of numbers divided by how many numbers are in the group.

Median value.   In a group of numbers it is the one that equally divides the group into higher and lower numbers. For example, when 25 numbers are ranked from lowest to highest it is the 13th number. Half of all numbers are larger than the median and half are smaller.

Mixed Couples.   A term used here to describe individual Angels who coinvest with a professional venture capital firm.

Mode.   A single value used to measure the central tendency of a group of numbers. Defined as the single number that appears most frequently in the group. Used as an alternative to averages and medians.

Near equity.   A term used here to refer to Angels' loan/guarantee dollars that are subject to much the same business risks as equity dollars.

Nickel and Dime Angels.   A term used here to describe an informal investor whose investments are all under $10,000.

Notes with warrants.   A note is a short-term debt instrument that usually comes due in less than five years. It carries provisions (warrants) allowing conversion of the debt into common equity stock under predetermined conditions and usually at the option of the note holder (creditor).

Odd Couple.   The term used here to describe a combination of Angels and entrepreneurs that results in very unsuccessful investments.

Partnership equity interest.   An ownership interest used in place of issuing common stock, usually when only a very small number of working owners are involved.

Patient and friendly.   The characteristics of most loans from Angels to their companies compared to the practices and attitude of outside lenders. It is this less pressing and more tolerant attitude of many Angels that puts their loans into the same risk category as equity dollars.

Peers.   Angels who are active business owners and entrepreneurs of prime age and who invest in the plans of fellow entrepreneurs.

Portfolio.   A collective term used to describe the total number of investments of specific type, such as a portfolio of informal investments, bond portfolio, blue chip stock portfolio, and so forth.

Professional venture capital(ist)/company.   Provides risk capital to a business in its formation stage, or in its first or second stage of expansion. A venture capital firm obtains funding through public issues or private commitments from individuals, pension funds, and industrial or financial companies interested in venture investment. Rarely interested in deals of under $1 million.

Risk.   As used here the term refers to the percentage or number of any 10 informal capital investments that turn out to be losers. A loser occurs when half or more of an original investment is eventually lost.

ROI.   Annual return on investment. It is the ratio of yearly investment earnings (including capital gains) to the dollar size of the original investment made, calculated over the holding period of the investment.

SBIC.   Small Business Investment Company, a privately owned company licensed and funded through the U.S. Small Business Administration and private sector sources to provide equity or debt capital to small businesses.

Start-up firms.   Business ventures in the idea stage or in the process of being organized. No formal financing may exist at this point. Equity funds may be provided to individuals or to inventors/innovators developing a new product, process, or other marketable concept.

Stockholder (The).   A term used here to describe an Angel who does not participate in day-to-day firm operations.

Successful entrepreneur.   Any entrepreneur who has obtained Angel financing.

Super Combos.   Angels and entrepreneurs who report that their informal investments have produced results that greatly exceeded original expectations.

Very Hungry Angels.   Term used here for the type of Angels who would have invested 100% more than they did if the flow of informal investment opportunities had been sufficient.

Voting control.   A majority of voting power is owned or controlled by a single ownership interest.

Voting power.   The percentage of voting stock owned or controlled by a single ownership interest.

Young firm.   Firm still establishing a track record, expecting to enter a period of rapid and profitable growth, and generally less than five years old.

APPENDIX

Blank Form for Custom Market Profile

CUSTOM MARKET PROFILE

	Column 1— Industry Profile	Column 2— Modifier Profile	Column 3— Custom Profile
TARGET ANGELS			

- Business owner/manager is principal occupation
- Has entrepreneurial experience
- Angel age (years)
- White male
- College degree
- Angel annual income
- Angel net worth
- Primary information channel
- Acceptance rate
- Main deal rejection reason
- Investment frequency (months)
- Satisfied with investments
- Number of other coinvestors
- Zero to nine employees of firm at investment time
- Start-up or infant growth stage
- Active as a consultant, board member, or employee
- Does not seek control
- Wants to invest more than opportunity permitted

TARGET DEAL

- Number of Angels needed to complete funding
- Equity dollars per investor
- Dollars of loans/guarantees by Angel
- Voting power transferred to investor
- Majority control to Angel (% of investments)
- Capital risk seen by Angel (% failure)
- Expected annual ROI
- Common stock or partnership equity instrument used
- Years to liquidation
- Liquidation buyback by insiders planned
- Investor is or becomes an employee (% of investments)

INDEX